Object-Oriented Methods
for
Software Development

Object-Oriented Methods for Software Development

Jag Sodhi

Prince Sodhi

McGraw-Hill

New York   San Francisco   Washington, D.C.   Auckland   Bogotá
Caracas   Lisbon   London   Madrid   Mexico City   Milan
Montreal   New Delhi   San Juan   Singapore
Sydney   Tokyo   Toronto

Library of Congress Cataloging-in-Publication Data

Sodhi, Jag.
    Object-oriented methods for software development / Jag Sodhi, Prince Sodhi.
        p.   cm.
    Includes bibliographical references and index.
    ISBN 0-07-059574-7
        1. Object-oriented programming (Computer science)   2. Computer software—
Development.   I. Sodhi, Prince.   II. Title.
    QA76.64.S65   1996
    005.1′1—dc20
                                                                                    96-15421
                                                                                    CIP

McGraw-Hill

A Division of The **McGraw·Hill** Companies

1 2 3 4 5 6 7 8 9 0   DOC/DOC   9 0 1 0 9 8 7 6

ISBN 0-07-059574-7

*The sponsoring editor for this book was John Wyzalek, the editing
supervisor was Penny Linskey, and the production supervisor was
Pamela Pelton. It was set in Century Schoolbook by Priscilla Beer of
McGraw-Hill's Professional Book Group composition unit.*

Printed and bound by Donnelley / Crawfordsville.

McGraw-Hill books are available at special quantity discounts to use
as premiums and sales promotions, or for use in corporate training programs. For more information, please write to the Director of Special
Sales, McGraw-Hill, 11 West 19th Street, New York, NY 10011. Or
contact your local bookstore.

This book is printed on acid-free paper.

Contents

Part 3   Object-Oriented Software Implementation

Preface

This book consists of three parts. Part 1 reviews object-oriented paradigm, evolution, and concepts. Object-oriented standards, reusability, and database have also been discussed in this part.

Chapter 1 defines objects, principles, the importance of the object-oriented approach, and evolution of object-oriented software engineering. With this approach, software is defined in terms of objects that compose a system and the behavior of those objects. The object-oriented approach is receiving wide acceptance as a standard technology within the software industry. This chapter includes examples to supplement the process.

Chapter 2 deals with the object-oriented concept. This chapter covers object-oriented characteristics, goals, and principles and a comparison between object-oriented and conventional methods.

Chapter 3 presents object-oriented standards. Most of the software developers create their own standards and follow them in their organizations. Suggested object-oriented standard guidelines are discussed. Standards for object-oriented design method notations are suggested. This chapter also covers tailoring standards techniques.

Chapter 4 discusses the object-oriented database (OODB) which promises that applications will be made faster to develop, more flexible, more reliable, and easier to modify and extend as requirements change. OODB stores objects of any size, which expands the type of data that can be used. Each object is stored as a complete and self-contained entity that has distinct characteristics and behaviors. The basic functional capabilities of an object-oriented database include query capabilities, smooth recovery in case of system failure, secondary storage management for high performance, concurrency control, and persistence. The main features of Objectivity/DB are discussed.

Chapter 5 focuses on the object-oriented database management system (OODBMS), OODBMS manages OODB systems by storing, sorting, retrieving, modifying, adding, and deleting volumes of database records in a well-organized manner. Structured Query Language (SQL) database management system operates within a client-server architecture. Selection criteria of a good OODBMS have been discussed. This chapter also covers ObjectStore.

Chapter 6 discusses the reusability and portability strategy. Reusability finds ways that existing software can be reused in new software development. The object-oriented approach provides convenient ways that pretested software can be reused. Software reusability results in increased achievement of object-oriented software engineering goals and reduces cost and schedules of new software development during the maintenance life cycle.

Part 2 describes object-oriented software architecture, system engineering, identifying domain, system requirements analysis, requirements traceability, software life-cycle models, software requirements analysis methods, and design methods.

Chapter 7 presents a system perspective of the object-oriented software architecture. A computer system consists of both hardware and software requirements. These requirements are originated by a customer/user. The software developer properly analyzes and understands the customer's requirements before starting system design and other object-oriented software development phases. This chapter covers building a system, allocating requirements, multiple views of the software requirements model, requirements traceability, and preparing an object-oriented software development plan. A comparison study of various object-oriented methods is discussed.

Chapter 8 explains object-oriented software life-cycle issues. This chapter presents concepts and approaches for object-oriented software architecture activities over the life of system software. This chapter also covers domain engineering, domain analysis for software reuse, and object-oriented software life-cycle models. Many models such as the waterfall, incremental, prototyping/simulation, assembling reusable components, spiral, operational, and transformational are discussed in this chapter. The basics of the IDEFO model are also discussed.

Chapter 9 covers the object-oriented software requirements analysis method. The object-oriented method (OOM) concept is the understanding of the customer's requirements and then graphically shows the customer requirements logically as stated by the customer. Then OOM determines objects and establishes relationships between objects. The instantiation criteria for objects and their relationships are determined, and functional processes are developed. The OOM covers all phases of the software development life cycle. Many object models such as analysis, information, and process models, including examples, are discussed.

Chapter 10 covers object-oriented software development methods that include ObjectOry and OOSD. Many examples and case studies are discussed to supplement the process. ObjectOry includes system development, system analysis, use cases, entities, interface objects, services, and system design.

Chapter 11 covers object-oriented design (OOD) methods and CASE tools. The OOD method focuses on the design and implementation aspects of the software process. OOD addresses these activities—preliminary design, simulation, prototyping, detailed design, coding, testing, and software maintenance. Palladio software and OOD by Palladio cover Booch OOD models, class diagrams, object diagrams, state diagrams, templates, and process diagrams. ObjectTeam by Cadre and ObjectMaker by Mark $\vee$ Systems are discussed to support the process. These CASE tools describe methods of Rumbaugh, Shlaer and Mellor, Bailin, Berard and Coad and Yourdon.

Part 3 presents object-oriented software implementation languages—Ada and C++.

Chapter 12 covers an overview of object-oriented programming (OOP) languages. The object-oriented software development method is receiving wide acceptance as a standard technology within the software industry. The new technology changes the nature of software analysis and design as an industrial process. Software products can be developed as an industrial process. Software products can be developed in a way similar to hardware products. OOP changes from writing instructions to interconnecting reusable software components. In the future, a system engineer or domain engineer will be equipped with a components catalog. The components with which he or she interconnects can be used for higher-level products, application products, or other more specialized components. This process will result in high productivity, low software development cost, short schedule, and quality products. The object-oriented developed software will be easier to maintain. This chapter also presents an overview of Simula, SmallTalk, Object COBOL, and Ada 95.

Chapter 13 covers an overview of Ada. Ada is an object-oriented language with the limitation that it supports objects and classes but limited inheritance. Ada 95 has made Ada a complete object-oriented programming language. Ada includes specific features to discipline the guidance of software engineering. The Ada language provides many important features that are used to develop reliable, long-lasting systems software. This chapter covers Ada construct, data typing, data type classes, packages, conditional statements, exception handling, generics, and tasks. This chapter includes many examples and a case study.

Chapter 14 presents an overview of C++, which is an evolutionary object-oriented language. This chapter describes major features of C++, which include objects, classes, inheritance, polymorphism, and reuse. A sample program is included.

The text in square brackets throughout the book refers to the references listed in App. B. All abbreviations and acronyms in the book are also defined at the end of the book in App. A. And a list of vendors is found in App. C.

This book presents state-of-the-art material; you can be assured it reflects what is currently happening in the object-oriented field. Use of the book's appendices is encouraged. You can consult respective vendors for further information.

The information and data contained here have been compiled from various sources and are intended to be used for reference purposes. Neither the publisher nor the authors guarantee the accuracy of the information and data.

Jag Sodhi

Prince Sodhi

Acknowledgments

We thank the McGraw-Hill editors, staff, and friends who convinced us of the need for this book. They also supported us in its development.

We owe a great debt to our friends who have contributed to the development of this book: Greg Neal, Ascent Logic Corporation, San Jose, CA; Diana Bitten, Applied Business Technology Corp., New York; William Sautter, Business Objects, Inc., Menlo Park, CA; Harold Duncan, CACI, La Jolla, CA; Harry Merkin, CADRE Technologies, Providence, RI; Laura Peterson, Evergreen CASE Tools, Inc., Redmond, WA; Herman Fischer and Greg Free, Mark V, Encino, CA; Linda Souza, Meridian/Verdix Company, Irvine, CA; Craig Woods, Objectivity Inc., Menlo Park, CA; John Treadway, Object Design, Burlington, MA; Valerie Schmidt, Palladio Software Corp., Brookfield, WI; Sarah Bell, Stepstone Corp., Sandy Hook, CT; Ted Lewis, Verilog Inc., Dallas, TX; Craig Priess, Pamela Bythrow, and Lisa Stewart, Westinghouse Electric Corporation, Baltimore, MD; and Christopher West, Venue, San Carlos, CA.

We express our appreciation to our friends who contributed in different ways toward the completion of this book: Aion Corp., Palo Alto, CA; Shakil Kidwai, EDS, Herndon, VA; Software Engineering Institute, Carnegie-Mellon University, Pittsburgh, PA; Edward Colbert, Absolute Software Co., Los Angeles, CA; Tucker Taft, Intermetrics, Cambridge, MA; Jane Raditz, Logicon, San Diego, CA; Lewis Gray, Ada Pros Inc., Fairfax, VA; Edward Berard, Berard Software Engineering, Gaithersburg, MD; Ralph Crafts, Ada Software Alliance, WV; Feridoon Moinian, Cameron University, OK; Dr. Charles Engle and William Woodward, Florida Institute of Technology, Melbourne; Ashim Kohli, University of Minnesota; Dr. Charles McKay, University of Houston, TX; Dr. Joyce Tokar, Tartan, Monroeville, PA; Dr. K. M. George, Oklahoma State University; Capt. David Cook, U.S. Air Force Academy, CO; and Chris Anderson, PM Ada 9X, Kirtland AFB, NM.

We thank wholeheartedly all our friends, students, and colleagues who contributed in different ways toward the completion of this book. To list them all is not easy. We thank all the people at the publishing company who were involved in the editing and production of the text.

Finally, we commend members of our families, who diligently supported us so that this project could be finished successfully. Without their love and support, we would not have completed such a project.

Object-Oriented Methods
for
Software Development

Object-Oriented Paradigm

*"Imagination is more important than
knowledge."*
ALBERT EINSTEIN

1

Object-Oriented Evolution

The object-oriented approach is an evolving software development in the computer industry. With this approach, software is defined in terms of objects that compose a system and the objects' behavior. The object-oriented approach is receiving wide acceptance within the software industry; software products can be developed in a manner similar to the development of hardware products. The object-oriented approach involves conveniently interconnecting reusable software components. It makes the software applications faster to develop, more flexible, and more reliable. It can be easily modified and extended as requirements change. This chapter presents the definition of an object, object-oriented principles, the importance of an object-oriented approach, and the evolution of object-oriented software engineering.

Why Objects?

Why use objects, when there are so many other methods and methodologies available in the computer industry that can be used to develop software? A few of these methods are as follows:

- Structured analysis and design
  - Functional decomposition
  - Hierarchy charts
  - Data flow diagrams
  - State transition diagrams
- Data-oriented analysis and design
- Events-oriented analysis and design

In each of these categories there are many variations of these methods. Why is the computer industry looking for another paradigm shift in software development when it is already saturated with methods?

Software development applications are suffering from high costs and schedule overruns, even with the existence of many methods and methodologies. Software development applications are growing more complex and large. Reduction of the cost and time for software development and maintenance is pertinent, so a standard method such as the object-oriented approach can be adhered to. Primary goals of the object-oriented method are to improve software quality and productivity; the cost and the risk that is associated with software development are reduced. The introduction of object-oriented technology brings simplification and better understanding of requirements analysis. This leads to easy, logical design, and logical design maps directly into object-oriented coding.

Quest for Objects

Objects provide a way of structuring data and software. An object represents a real-world entity, such as your checkbook, car, television, or house, which needs a computer system to store information. Some of the real-world entities represented as objects are shown in Fig. 1.1. Each object operates in a well-defined way. Each object is complete and self-contained with distinct characteristics and behaviors. A human being is a perfect example of such an object. The human brain, with its many billions of cells, is the most complex object in the known universe.

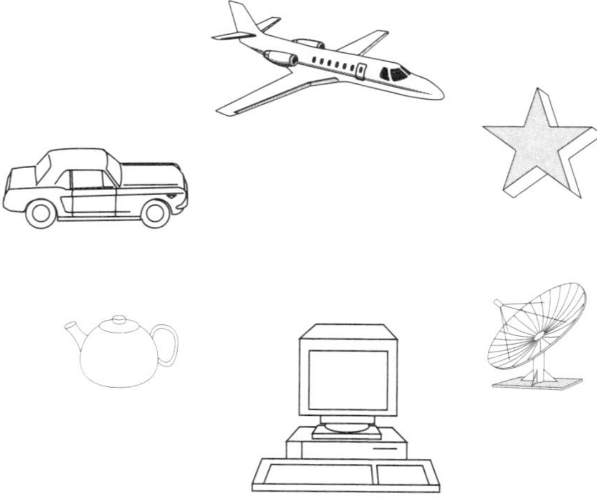

Figure 1.1 Objects.

An object also contains software that can perform processing tasks that relate to the real world. Objects can represent structures within a computer such as a file system, protocol, or a collection of other objects. The objects can be transferred and reused in other processes.

In traditional software development approaches, operations and data are regarded as distinct and loosely coupled. Operations determine the structure of the system. Data are of secondary importance. In object-oriented software development, operations and data combine to form objects. A system decomposition is based on objects, and data primarily determine the structure of the software. An object-oriented system is regarded as a network of cooperating objects which interact by sending each other messages, maintaining their own state, and having an individual identity.

Defining Objects

Objects are defined in terms of what they do, not by how they do it. The object-oriented process identifies independent objects in the software requirements. These objects interact and operate on their components. Actions are done to objects, and actions are taken by objects that communicate by messages. Actions that are taken within objects are hidden from the user. The only interface that is seen is the resulting message from the object.

The object-oriented approach requires a change in mind-set. It considers the world as an object that can act. My son, Thomas, was very fond of playing with balls when he was young. When he started talking, he would look at the sky during the day, point out the moon, and say, "Ball, ball." A child speaks the truth. He saw an object that looked like his ball. Each round object has certain properties and attributes that make its characteristics unique.

Objects, from a very high-level view, are entities that exist uniquely in time and space. In other words, objects have a state and are characterized by the actions which they perform and by the actions that are performed on them. The objects must communicate. The communication requirement helps with data hiding and makes object-oriented languages such as C++, SmallTalk, and Ada 95 possible.

Functionality and data are not separated into programs and database, but are encapsulated in a single unit called *objects*. A set of similar objects is called a *class*. The attributes of one class may be inherited by any object or class, which includes any method that is defined as part of the class. The actual objects are instances of an object class.

Inheritance provides the most recently defined class with all the attributes of the previous classes. A class is also defined as a type with various attributes that are used so that other classes and objects can be defined. Thus, a class is a general category of similar objects. An object that is created within a class also inherits the basic attributes that are common to that class. A class is the passive defining construct. An object is the active instantiation of a class. Classes are used to relate objects and their attributes. The existence of a class allows for the inheritance of attributes and actions, which in turn allows for new objects so they can inherit attributes from older objects. A software system can be thought of as a collection of objects that forms some entity, which is an abstract machine that has specific attributes and exhibits a particular behavior.

Understanding an Object-Oriented Approach

An object-oriented system is designed around objects that exist in the model of reality. An *object* is defined as an entity that

- Has state
- Is characterized by the actions that it suffers and that it requires of other objects
- Is a unique instance of some (possibly anonymous) class
- Is denoted by a name
- Has restricted visibility of and by other objects
- Can be viewed by either its specification or its implementation

The first two points show that an object is something that exists uniquely in time and space and can be affected by the activity of other objects. The *state* of an object denotes its value, and the objects are denoted by this value. For any well-structured object-oriented system, each object encapsulates some state, and all states within the system are encapsulated in some object.

The concept of a method emerges from SmallTalk. A method denotes the response by an object to a message from another object. The activity of one method may pass messages that invoke the methods of other objects. Abstract data types deal with operations in a related way. Liskov and Zilles* suggest that operations can be divided into two groups:

1. Groups that do not cause a change of state, but do allow observation of some aspect of the state
2. Groups that cause a change of state

---

*See App. B for a list of references.

One other kind of operation is iteration, which permits visiting of all subcomponents of an object.

An object exhibits both static as well as dynamic semantics. Static semantics are expressed by the existence of the operations that the object suffers or requires of other objects. Dynamic semantics are expressed by the effect that each operation has on the object. Dynamic semantics can include concurrency among objects.

If the state of an object is a function of time, then the object is implemented by using some multiprocessing construct, which is provided by an underlying language such as tasks in Ada. Another important characteristic of an object is that each object is a unique case of some class. Alternately, a class denotes a set of similar but unique objects.

The rule is as follows: Objects are unique cases of a class, and names only serve to denote objects. Every object has two parts and can be viewed in two different ways—outside and inside. The outside view of an object serves for capturing abstract behavior. One object can interact with another object only by viewing the outside. It does not know how the other object is represented or implemented. The outside view of an object or class of objects is its *specification*. The specification captures all the static and dynamic semantics of the object. In the specification of a class of objects, several resources are exported to the rest of the system by including the name of the class. Operations are defined for objects of the class.

The inside view indicates how the behavior is implemented and is not visible from the outside. In the body of an object or class, you choose one of many possible representations that implement the behavior of the specification. The benefits of separation interface and implementation should be clear. Not only does this separation enforce the abstractions and help manage the complexity of the problem space, but also by localizing the design, decisions are made about an object and the scope of change in the system may be reduced.

Object-Oriented Principles

The object-oriented method devises a model of a system that is based on real entities. A problem space is always rooted somewhere in the real world, and the solution space is implemented by a combination of software and hardware. H. Ledgard developed a model that describes a typical programming task. An example of this task is shown in Fig. 1.2.

In the problem space, there are some real-world objects, each of which has a set of appropriate operations. These objects can be as simple as a checkbook ledger or as complex as an interplanetary spacecraft. In the problem space, there are some real-world algo-

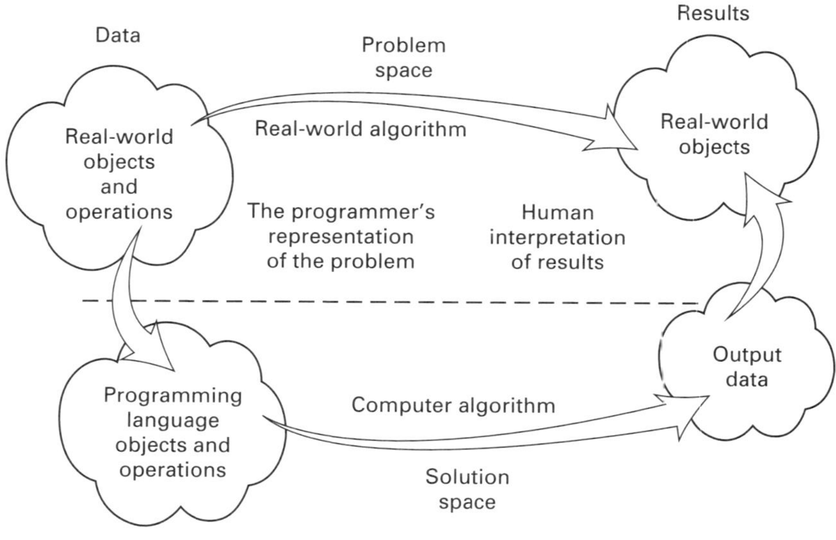

Figure 1.2   Typical programming task model.

rithms that operate on objects and provide transformed objects as results. For example, a real-world result might be a balanced checkbook.

Almost all human languages consist of two primary components: noun phrases and verb phrases. A parallel structure exists in programming languages because they provide constructs for implementing objects (noun phrases) and operations (verb phrases). Object-oriented programming concentrates on defining

- Abstractions from the problem space as objects

- Collections of abstractions as classes

- Relationships among objects and classes as inheritance

(Abstraction and inheritance will be discussed in detail in subsequent chapters.) However, most languages other than object-oriented ones are primarily imperative, which means they provide a rich set of constructs for implementing operations but are generally weak when abstracting real-world objects. Thus these conventional languages create a wider gap than the object-oriented languages between the problem space and the solution space. Similarly, most design methods avoid a reasonable implementation of the real-world object abstraction where the notion of an object plays the central role. MacLennan suggests, "Programming is object-oriented mathematics." Dijkstra was perhaps the first person who identified the importance of composing systems in levels of abstraction. The real world is neither flat nor sequential, but is multidimensional and often highly parallel. These methods are forced into a sequential way of thinking and do not provide any tools for identifying parallelism that is inherent in the problem space. A mental transformation from the solution space to the problem space is necessary.

Importance of an Object-Oriented Approach

The importance of an object-oriented approach lies in the development of software which follows the building blocks pattern. The object-oriented approach creates models that attempt to build complex systems by using classes and objects as building blocks. The object-oriented approach attempts to model the real world via abstraction. The conventional structured methodologies tried to build complex systems by using algorithms as the fundamental building blocks. The algorithmic decomposition highlights the ordering of events in a system. The object-oriented approach simplifies the system modeling techniques and smoothes the transition from one phase to another of software development. The object-oriented approach promises the application of reusability that saves cost and time in software development and maintenance.

The object-oriented approach also facilitates the addition of new requirements in the software life cycle without disturbing the existing structure. For example, customer requirements are to fill up automobiles with gasoline and wash them. The object "automobiles" can be of any class—a passenger car, van, or truck. Initially, let us suppose that the requirements are only to wash passenger cars and vans and fill them with gasoline. There are literally two functions:

1. Wash cars and vans

2. Fill up cars and vans with gasoline

Let us follow the conventional functional concept and construct the system on these two functionalities—one for washing and one for fueling. Here the delegation of authority is by the service provided (verb). Both cars and vans must go to the job site but not necessarily at the same time. A collection of subprograms exists. All transactions are processed by the entire collection. Each program performs a function and transaction.

A new requirement is received from the customer. It is the addition of trucks to the existing structure. To do so, the existing structure must be modified. This new requirement can be implemented, and all areas of the system must be modified.

Now let us build the same system with an object-oriented approach. Here, the delegation of authority is by the entity (noun). Only one car or van must go to the job site. A collection of subprograms exists. Subprograms are grouped by entity: Each subprogram within a group addresses an event. Here, you are looking at objects with data and behavior. The "data" are gasoline and water that can be stored. The object's behavior can use the data and will act upon the passenger cars and vans. The important point is that the subprograms can do both of these functions with the data they carry.

When the new requirements were received from the customer, the trucks were included in the existing structure. Thus the existing structure did not need any changes. A new object can be added without any modification to the existing object.

Object-Oriented Software Engineering Evolution

Computer professionals have been striving since its inception to engineer quality software that is cost-effective, within budget, and in time. *Software engineering* is a systematic approach to the development, operation, maintenance, and retirement of software; *software development* is the process by which user needs are translated to software requirements. These requirements are transformed to design; design is implemented in code; and code is tested, documented, and certified for use.*

Software engineering was first defined by Fritz Bauer in 1968 at a conference sponsored by the Science Committee of the North Atlantic Treaty Organization (NATO). Bauer used the term to mean the application of systems engineering principles to software development and maintenance. The conference was convened so that the state and prospects of software production could be assessed. By the capture of software developers' imagination, software engineering achieved popularity during the 1970s. It now refers to a collection of management processes, software tooling, and design activities for software development. *Software engineering* can be defined as the disciplined application of engineering along with scientific and mathematical principles and methods in the economical production of quality software. Software engineering and software development have a long history of evolution, as shown in Table 1.1.

The importance of software engineering lies in its systematic approach to software development, implementation, and maintenance

---

*IEEE Software, November 1990.

TABLE 1.1 Object-Oriented Software Development Evolution

Before 1970	Software development was out of control because of cost overruns and failures, especially in operating systems development. The term *software engineering* was coined as the theme of the NATO-sponsored meetings in 1968 and 1969. Object-oriented thinking started with Simula 67 efforts in the 1960s.
1970–1971	First principles were established through research into "good" programming practices. Advantages of top-down design, stepwise refinement, and modularity were recognized. New languages that included Pascal and new group techniques that included chief programmer teams were introduced. Object-oriented programming was first discussed in Norway in the early 1970s in connection with the Simula language.
1972–1973	Structured programming and notions of programming style emerged. The "go to" controversy subsided. Awareness of total software life cycle grew, and management and development aids were proposed. The C language was introduced. SmallTalk was developed in 1972.
1974–1975	Reliability and quality assurance concerns gave rise to systematic testing procedures, notions of formal program correctness, and models of fault tolerance and total system reliability. Early analysis of actual allocation of development effort and expense appeared.
1976–1977	Requirements, specification, and design were the focus. Renewed attention was paid to early development phases before coding. Abstraction and modular decomposition were viewed as design techniques; structure charts and metacode were viewed as design representations. There were increasing efforts made to integrate and validate successive development phases of the life cycle.
1978–1980	The use of automated development tools increased. Many software-engineering courses were developed. The first principles of the 1969–1971 era found widespread use in software industry. The birth of object-oriented programming took place.
1981–1982	This era marked the rise of *computer-aided software engineering* (CASE) and the software-engineering workstation. Automated tools that corresponded to each phase of the life cycle appeared on stand-alone workstations.
1983–1985	The U.S. Department of Defense standardized Ada language (MIL-STD-1815A). Object-oriented design methods appeared. Grady Booch published his first book on an object-oriented method.
1986–1990	Object-oriented analysis methods appeared. Many object-oriented CASE tools and workstations cropped up. Software reusability, maintainability, manageability, quality, and modularity that were related to object-oriented design appeared. Revision of ANSI/MIL-STD-1815A was initiated, and it was called Ada 9X. Also C++ was developed.
1991–1995	This period saw the application of expert techniques and object-oriented methods to software engineering. Wirfs-Brock et al. published *Designing Object-Oriented Software*. Coad Yourdon published *Object-Oriented Analysis*. The combination of software-engineering workstations, expert systems, and object-oriented and automated techniques for development found widespread use in the software industry. Rumbaugh et al. published *Object-Oriented Modelling and Design*. Software standards were revised and included the object-oriented concept. Shlaer and Mellor published *Object-Lifecycles: Modelling the World in Data*. Many international conferences and journals have been formed in response to the evolution of object-oriented approaches. Martin and Odell published *Principles of Object-Oriented Analysis and Design*. Ada 95 has been accepted as an international object-oriented language.

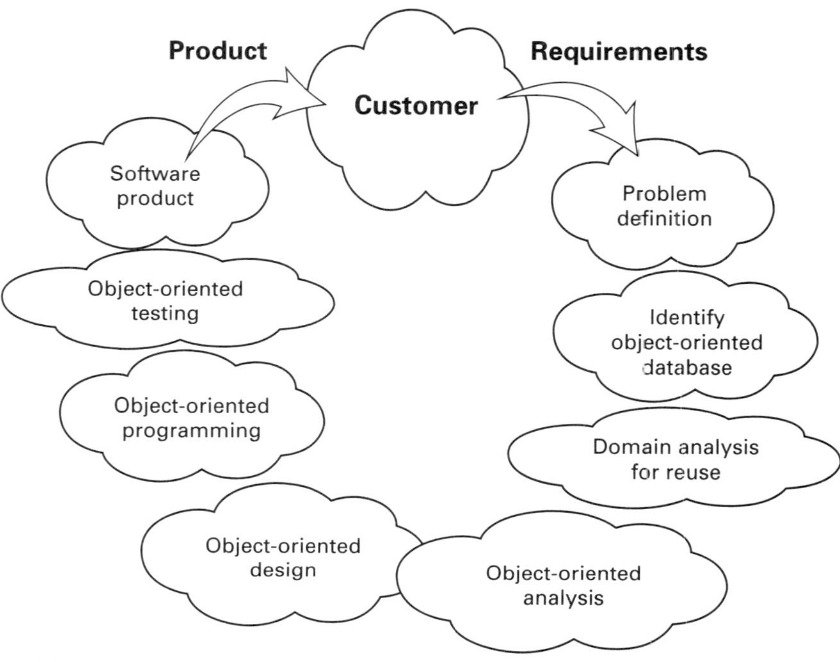

Figure 1.3   Object-oriented software development life cycle.

throughout the life cycle of the computer system. Software engineering consists of a set of structured object-oriented methods—requirements analysis, design, programming, testing, procedures, and tools, as shown in Fig. 1.3—that are used to engineer quality, cost-effective software. Object-oriented analysis is a technique which examines the requirements and essence of the system, uses the perspective of classes and objects, and employs the vocabulary of the problem domain. In object-oriented analysis, we model a system in terms of classes and objects from the problem domain.

Object-oriented design (OOD) is a method of software designing that captures the logical and physical (plus the static and dynamic) properties of the system that uses object-oriented decomposition. In object-oriented design, the object-oriented analysis is being partitioned or decomposed into object models. Loose coupling and tight cohesion properties are thoroughly followed during the design. Dependency diagrams are constructed so the objects' interrelationship can be understood. The analysis models are enhanced and refined. We will discuss these topics in detail later in this book. Like many other software development methods and methodologies, the object-oriented technique also started with object-oriented programming.

Object-oriented programming (OOP) is a method of implementation in which programs are represented as instances of classes and classes may be arranged in a hierarchy. The programming implements objects in an object-oriented language. Object-oriented programming is defined as structured and designed around objects. OOP includes encapsulation (the class concept), extensibility (inheritance by prefixing), and reusability (specialization and dynamic binding). In OOP, the class serves as the abstraction mechanism whereby concepts are formalized. Classes resemble abstract data types in that they contain both data and the code that manipulates the data. Also the classes can be multiple instantiations of objects that can be used to build data structures. Furthermore, an existing class can be extended or specialized with the help of a prefixing mechanism, whereby a subclass inherits attributes from its parent class. This facilitates the development of reusable software.

OOP is an ideal design for next-generation programming techniques. This is why the American National Standard Institute's (ANSI's) Object-Oriented COBOL Task Group is working to remodel COBOL as an OOP language, and it will be called COBOL Object-Oriented Language (COOL). Over time, legacy application code could be retooled into objects, probably with assistance from artificial-intelligence-based conversion products [Datamation].

The basic concepts of OOP are encapsulation, inheritance, polymorphism, dynamic programming, constructors, and destructors. These terms will be explained in detail in this book. Briefly, *encapsulation* is the combining of data and the operations which manipulate into a single package. *Inheritance* is the medium that creates a hierarchy of types derived from a base type. *Polymorphism* is used in the creation of extensible programs. *Constructors* and *destructors* are employed and handle initialization and cleanup of user-defined types. OOP allows for the creation of a "computer" representation of the problem such that there is a one-to-one relationship between the computer world and the real world. This abstraction can accurately capture the constraints of real-world objects as well as model the operations that occur in the real world. The solution space is a replica of the problem space. Objects are created that represent their real-world counterparts. The process of solving the problem shows what the objects should be and what they should look like.

OOP includes identification of objects, classes, and inheritance. OOP supports polymorphism during the runtime environment. Polymorphism covers binding that also includes dynamic binding. (Polymorphism and binding will be explained in greater detail in subsequent chapters.) OOP defines a new type of object in terms of an existing one, called *inheritance.* Adding new components by adding new properties to an object, as well as adding or redefining the operations allowed on the object, is called *type extension.*

OOP explicitly identifies common characteristics of the kinds of objects represented. The objects contain hierarchies of categories which group common characteristics. OOP defines objects by the use of categories and performs interactions between the main program and objects. Also OOP performs interactions between different objects via operations of the objects. This hierarchical categorization establishes a set of relationships where all the entities represent kinds of objects throughout the software model.

The code reuse is performed from the beginning of the OOP coding process, as all similar characteristics of a set of objects are factored into the uppermost level of the hierarchy that contains them. Software reuse will not happen automatically in OOP. The power of OOP languages is that they allow easy reuse of code. The fact is that most of OOP has built-in class libraries, programs can be pieced together with minimal coding. If you program a class that implements a "patient" object for one system, you can use that same code when another system needs a "patient" object. In fact, the more systems you implement in OOP languages, the better you will be able to reuse code, as it becomes more likely that you have already coded an object in a past system. Polymorphism combines with dynamic binding and helps move OOP closer to the ideal of a truly generic code. This helps when code is being written which specifies only generic instructions and delegates implementation details to particular involved objects. So to make reuse possible, programmers will write code in the form of independent segments called *objects.* Thus the same code can be reused on several different types of objects. This implies that we need not care how a task is handled inside an object, only that the object does what we want when we send the correct message. So a program could include an entire set of objects. All objects are derived from different object classes that respond to the same messages, even though their methods are different.

The major characteristics of OOP are understandability and maintainability. *Understandability* applies when the software written in OOP is easily understandable. Comments are sometimes necessary so difficult logical operations on objects can be explained. But a high percentage of comments (more than 100 percent) in OOP code can clearly verify that the problem has not been designed properly in the object-oriented design.

The objects that exist in the problem space are also present in the solution space with analogous characteristics and behavior. Object-oriented system development models the problem as a set of types or classes from which objects are created. This set is partitioned into hierarchical categorization that emphasizes reuse by relegating common characteristics and behaviors to the highest possible level. Once the modeling structure is completed, coding is easy, for it consists of merely creating the necessary objects from the defined classes and invoking the behavioral operations of the objects.

Maintainability of a system throughout the life-cycle evolution is costly if not properly documented during the software development. Proper documentation means that the customer's requirements are analyzed, logical design is present, coding has been properly commented, and all these are fully documented. Maintainability of a system can last 5 to 7 times longer than the duration of the software development time. Due to the enforcement of abstraction and encapsulation, the object-oriented systems accommodate system evolution.

Maintainability of an object-oriented system is easy because the characteristics and behaviors are localized. When a local behavior is modified, it will not necessarily affect external entities via logical interfaces. Such systems are easily adaptable to new and changing requirements because of high reusability inherent in an object-oriented environment.

OOP is a method that addresses difficult programming problems. OOP considers systems as independent objects. They interact and have operations that are performed on their components. *Object* will be defined properly in OOD. Actions are done to objects, and actions are taken by objects that communicate by messages. The only interface that is seen is the resulting message back from an object. This is the change of mind-set needed and it begins with thinking about the world as objects that can act.

Existing data structures are inherently part of an object. The attributes of a class may be inherited by any object or class and defined with the previously defined class. This includes any methods that are defined as part of the class. Inheritance can form a change where the most recently defined class will have all the attributes of the classes used in defining it and its ancestors. A class can be defined as a type with various attributes that are used in defining other classes and objects. Thus a class is a general category of similar objects. An object created within a class by definition also inherits the basic attributes of that class. The method defined for processing messages and data is also part of the class. The class is a passive defining construct. An object is the active instantiation of a class. Classes are used in relation to objects and the attributes that objects can take on. The existence of classes also enables inheritance of attributes and actions, which in turn allows new objects to inherit "things" from older objects. Functions and procedures exist in OOP but are part of an object and are hidden from any user of the object.

OOP's strength of the approach is the way in which a complex system can be expressed in terms of its components and their relations, rather than a system that is addressed as one large process. OOP language has the potential of moving application software development away from coding altogether. This will enable nontechnical people to create their own software without sacrificing either performance or functionality.

OOP also includes multiple inheritance, which is another capability of an object that lets characteristics be inherited from more than one parent.

OOP is not a panacea that solves all the software development problems. OOP's weakness lies in the learning of an object-oriented language. Depending on the degree of expertise, coding time will be comparatively longer. It will be necessary for management to change the process and the culture to accept the objects. It requires a change in expectations and attitude for OOP. Once management and software developers understand and experience OOP in developing systems, perceptions about OOP will change.

Object-Oriented Concept

This chapter establishes the object-oriented concept. It covers the object-oriented characteristics, object-oriented software engineering goals and principles, and comparison between object-oriented and conventional methods.

Object-Oriented Characteristics

The characteristics of the object-oriented concepts are abstraction, classification, encapsulation, inheritance, and polymorphism. Abstraction concentrates on important essentials while the unimportant details are temporarily ignored. Good software engineering is hierarchical by an abstraction level. The hierarchy is based on functionality, process, data, and/or object considerations. This is the main technique and is used in the management of the complexity of software engineering. In object-oriented software, the software engineers first concentrate on a design which promotes good modularity of major entities. With fewer implementation details to worry about, they can focus on the "what" modules in a system. These upper level modules can be designed first. They then become less and less abstract with more implementation detailing as they get to lower level modules.

Abstraction

Abstraction aids software design so the software engineers can disregard nonessential details and concentrate on the problem space. Abstraction is closely related to the goal of modifiability and promotes good modularity. For example, when you point to a personal computer (PC) on your desk, you think of the abstract word *computer* for this object, not a box that consists of memory chips, integrated electronic circuits, capacitors, resistors, inductors, or power supplies. The essential details of the object *computer* to some of you are visual display and keyboard, while to others they may be the modem, printer, disk drive, etc. Inessential details are integrated circuits, memory chips, capacitors, and resistors. As another example, suppose that this year you will get your taxes done by an accountant. You give her your total income, bills, deductions, etc., and you get a completed tax return back. To you, the abstraction "I will have my taxes done this week" is complete. How the accountant does your taxes is unimportant.

Information hiding and *abstraction* are practically synonyms except information hiding is the ability to access data. Here, only the operations on an object are visible to an application program; the data and the way the operations are implemented are hidden. Therefore, no operations can be performed other than those specified in the interface. Information hiding (and encapsulation) makes applications more flexible and extensible and provides more reusable code. Both are mechanisms that hide code and data from application programs and protect them from implementation changes in a system's lower layers. Information hiding and encapsulation allow the software developer to create a clean interface between the specification and implementation of an operation. As a result, an object-oriented application program is effectively independent of the implementation of the operations it uses.

Classification

Classification is the grouping of objects with similar behavior (methods or operations) and characteristics (data). An object's data and methods are determined by its class. A class is similar to a type declaration in conventional structured programming. Here an object is an instance of a class, just as a variable is an instance of a type in structured programming. Because all objects of a specific class share the same internal structure and external behavior, they will respond to a method call in the same way.

The class of objects should define "the object, the whole object, and nothing but the object." An object can be classified as an actor, server, or agent. Classification depends on how the object relates to surrounding objects. An *actor* object suffers no operations, but operates only on other objects. Thus, actors tend to be fairly autonomous entities. A *server,* however, only suffers operations and cannot operate on other objects. An *agent* is an object that performs an operation on behalf of another object. A class is characterized by a set of values and a set of operations that are applicable to objects of the class. Thus, constructors, selectors, and iterators apply here as a way of categorizing the operations of a class. For example, your car is a class of items with applicable operations, such as

- Starting
- Turning
- Stopping

For all instances of this class, such as your car, my car, his car, etc., these same principles apply. Thus, the car class serves as a factor for all common car operations. In some cases, the class of an object might be anonymous. A special kind of class is the abstract class. This class is one for which objects (instances) cannot be created. Abstract classes are primarily used as templates for other classes through the use of inheritance.

Encapsulation

Encapsulation means that an object contains both a state and an operation that can be performed on that state. The bundling of procedures and data, called *encapsulation,* is the foundation of the object-oriented concept. Actions on an object's state are called *methods* and are initiated by messages that are sent to the object. The encapsulated data in an object are not freely accessible from outside the object. Only an object's own methods can directly manipulate its data. Methods are invoked either by another method of the object or by a procedure call from another object (message) within the application program. With encapsulation, the user does not worry about how an object performs its function; the user simply knows what the object can and cannot do. Users can be confident that when an object is added to the existing code, unpredictable things will not happen to other parts of the program.

Encapsulation is the opposite of abstraction. Abstraction focuses upon the observable behavior of an object, and encapsulation focuses upon the implementation of the behavior. Encapsulation hides the implementation details whereas the user of the abstraction knows only the essence of behavior. Here is an example of encapsulation in Ada:

```
package Light_Switch is
type Switch is limited private
procedure Turn_on(The _Switch : in out Switch);
procedure Turn_off(The_Switch : in out Switch);
function Switch_on(The_Switch : Switch) return Boolean;
private
...
end Light_Switch;
```

Inheritance

Inheritance is the ability to associate characteristics that are common to all members of a class (type) of objects. In object-oriented methods, a subclass of objects can inherit characteristics of the class (type) to which it belongs. When a new type of object is defined, a similar object already exists. In these cases you can simply define the new object type in terms of the existing object type; then new properties can be added, or existing ones can be modified. When the new object type is defined in terms of an old object type, the new object type inherits properties from the old object type.

The new object type can then supplement these with its own new properties. For example, when a square or a triangle is drawn, it uses methods that are inherited from the method of drawing a polygon. Different types of triangles in turn inherit characteristics from the general class of triangles.

A new type can be defined in terms of an existing object type (base type). The newly derived type is then termed a *derived type* of the base type. The derived type normally includes new fields and methods that are not present in the base type. It redefines or overrides the implementation of a method that is defined in an underlying object type, after the override has been explicitly declared. Any method not overridden by the derived type is automatically inherited from the nearest underlying object type. Similarly, the derived type inherits all properties (attributes, operations) of its underlying object types. Although a derived type can redefine inherited methods, it cannot redefine inherited properties. It can, however, add new properties of its own. For example, objects in a simulation often need the capability that will contain a queue of other objects.

```
VehicleObj = OBJECT(QueueObj)
...
END OBJECT;
```

The object type VehicleObj inherits the properties of QueueObj. Here QueueObj is a base type of VehicleObj, and VehicleObj is termed a derived type of QueueObj. Any number of new object types can be derived from a single base type.

New object types can also be defined in terms of other derived types. A hierarchy of object types occupying multiple layers is shown in Fig. 2.1. The hierarchy is modeled after the structure of an actual combat model [MODSIM II]. Any object type that is either a base type of SomeObject or a type many levels below SomeObject is referred to as an *underlying type* of SomeObject; and SomeObject includes all the properties of the underlying types. Here VehicleObj is a base type of

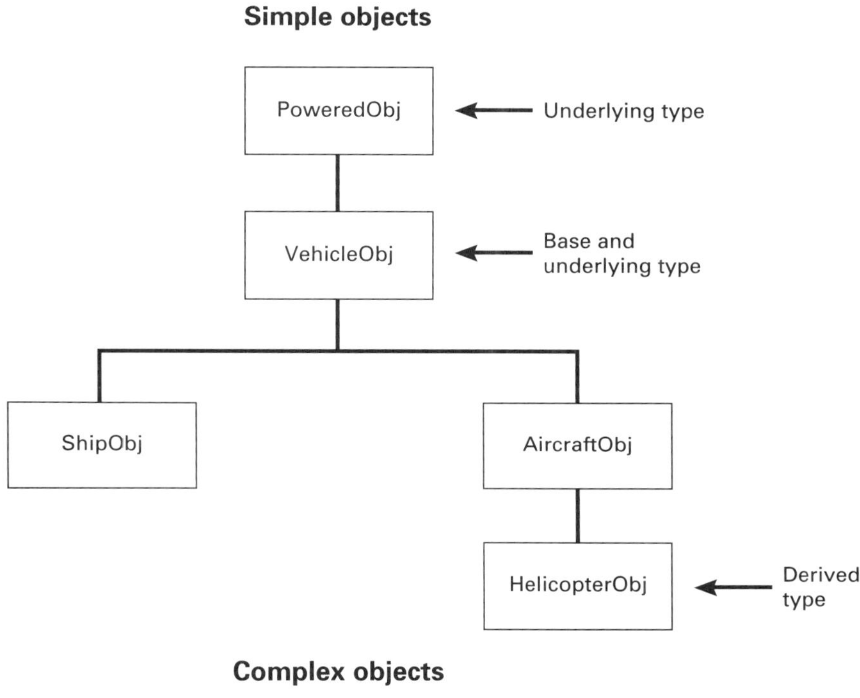

Figure 2.1   Sample inheritance tree (*Courtesy of MODSIM*).

AircraftObj as well as the underlying type of HelicopterObj and ShipObj. HelicopterObj is a derived type of AircraftObj.

A derived type can have more than one base type by means of multiple-path inheritance. This capability is called *multiple inheritance*. Figure 2.2 illustrates the multiple-inheritance concept.

```
MissileObj = OBJECT(AircraftObj, WeaponObj)
...
END OBJECT;
```

When a new object type is defined in this way, it has a copy of each field and each method of its base types. If the base types from which the new object type has been derived have used the same names for any of their fields or methods, then an ambiguous situation can arise. This particular situation can be avoided if the fields with matching names have been derived from two base object types and are referenced. This is done by assigning the reference value of the type derived and then multiplying the inherited object by a reference variable of one of the base types. The desired field can then be referenced.

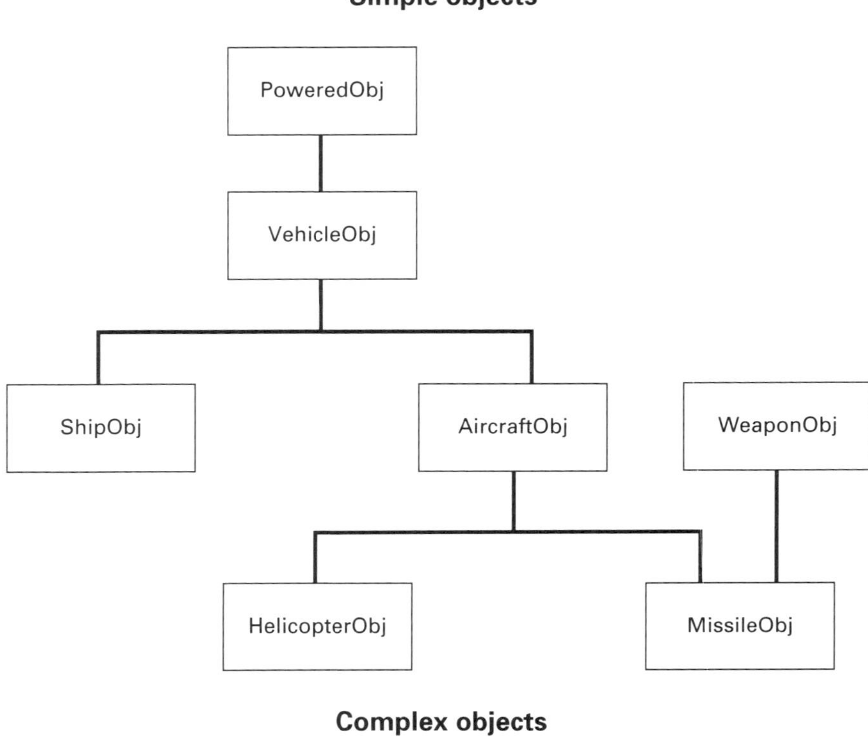

Figure 2.2   Multiple-path inheritance (*Courtesy of MODSIM*).

Inheritance allows one class to adopt the attributes (behavior and characteristics) of another class. The class that adopts the attributes is called the *subclass,* while the class whose attributes are adopted is called the *superclass,* as shown in Fig. 2.3. The relationship between all subclasses and their superclasses is called the *class hierarchy.*

Systems that allow a class to inherit the attributes of only one other class are said to support *single inheritance,* while systems that allow inheritance from more than one superclass support *multiple inheritance.* The use of inheritance can easily add new classes without redefining what is common to all of them. Inheritance is a powerful modeling tool because the software developer can describe an application and its components precisely and without redundancy.

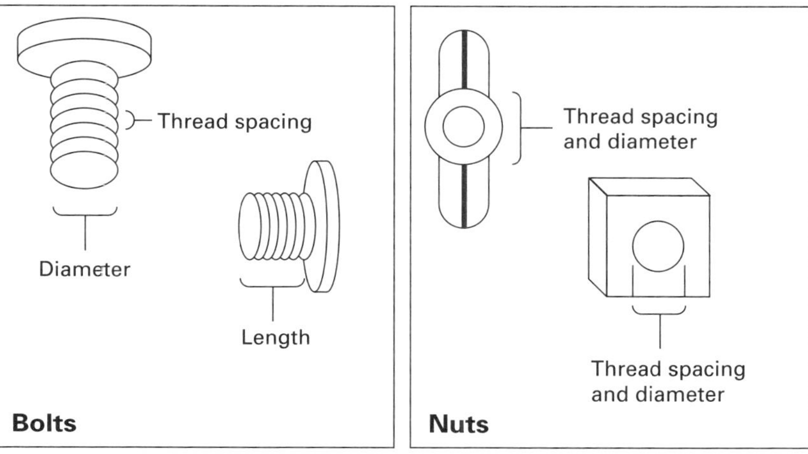

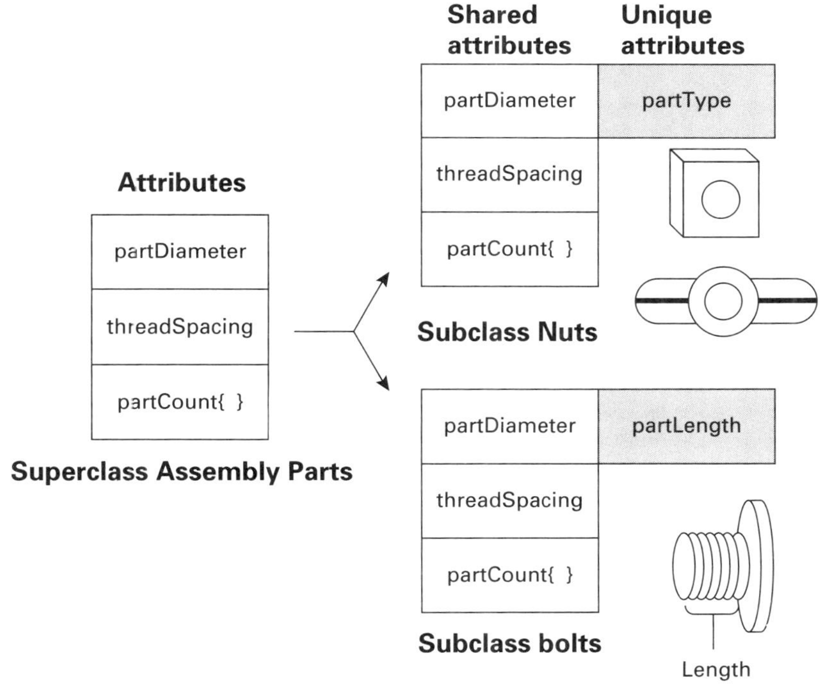

Figure 2.3 Inheritance (*Courtesy of Objectivity*).

Polymorphism

Polymorphism derives from a Greek word that means "many forms." So when an operation is performed on an object, it is determined by the type of object the operation addresses. The same command that will "edit" the text for this chapter, for example, acts differently when applied to the text of a generic letter, because the characteristics of the two objects are different as are the internal methods that act on them. But the software developer and the user need only deal with the concept of "edit."

With polymorphism a subclass can modify or add to the attributes that it inherits. A method call can cause different results. It depends on the type (class) of object that is receiving the call. A procedure call name is overloaded when it invokes different operations to objects of different classes. For example, in Fig. 2.4, the object of class Circle, Rectangle, and Square understands and responds to the method call

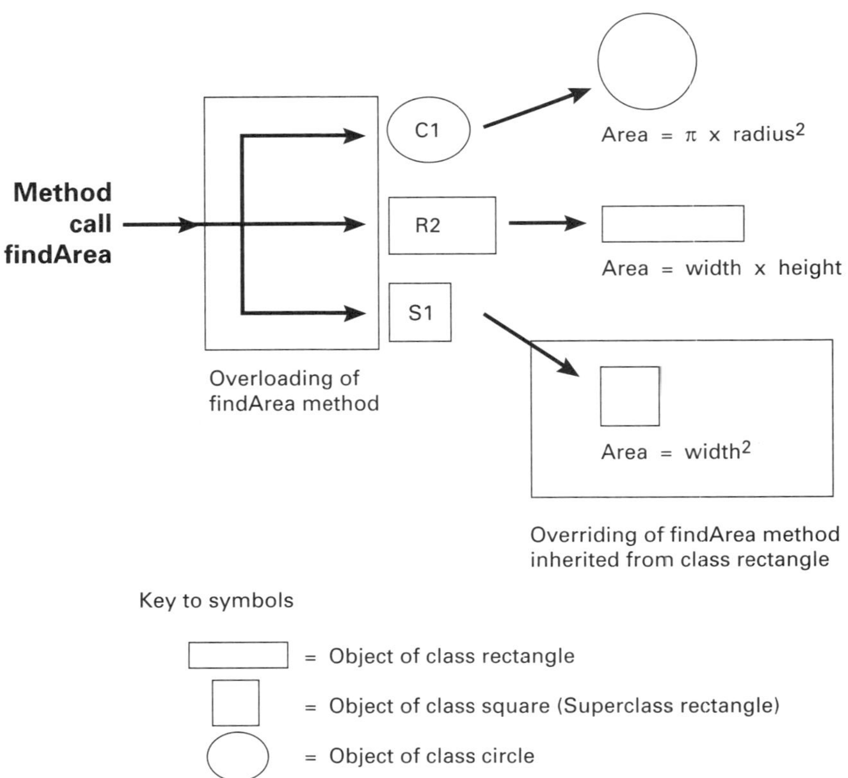

Figure 2.4 Overloading and overriding (*Courtesy of Objectivity*).

findArea, but the algorithms that perform the calculations are different for each class. Thus, the call findArea is said to be overloaded.

A class overrides the implementation of a particular method when the operation inherited from its superclass is inappropriate. In Fig. 2.4, class Square inherited the findArea method from Square's superclass Rectangle. The findArea method of class Rectangle calculates the area by using the height-times-width algorithm. However, since width-squared is a more efficient algorithm for calculating a square's area, class Square overrides the findArea method it inherited from Rectangle.

Figure 2.5 depicts a hypothetical graphics environment which allows various geometric shapes to be created by calling methods of specific objects. Here, C1, S1, T1, and R2 respond to the same method call drawObject. The method call drawObject allows this one call to draw circles, squares, triangles, or rectangles. The actual implementation of the method call drawObject is redefined for each type of object. The ability to generalize behavior over many types of objects

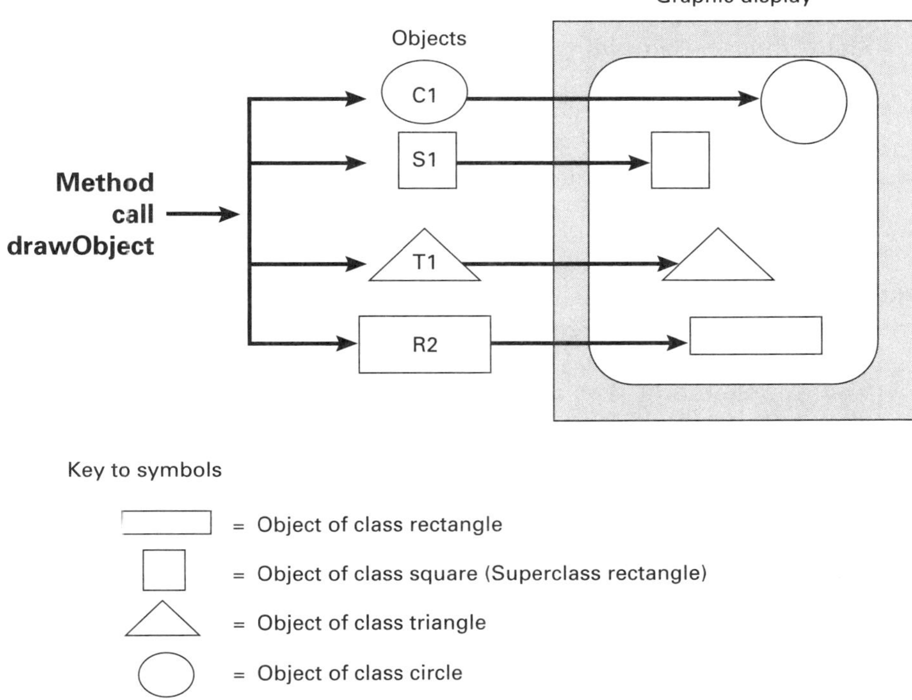

Figure 2.5 Runtime polymorphism (*Courtesy of Objectivity*).

allows a higher degree of abstraction in software development, since the software developer thinks about specific actions rather than the details of how they will be implemented.

Object-Oriented Software Engineering Goals

One object-oriented software engineering goal is to engineer quality software which is reliable and meets the requirements specifications. The other object-oriented software engineering goals are reliability, modifiability, maintainability, understandability, adaptability, reusability, and efficiency.

Reliability is a system's ability to operate correctly under all conditions. Metrics are established so that the correctness of a system can be measured. Mathematical formulas and statistical graphics are available for monitoring a system's reliability. The object-oriented approach has several features that protect data integrity and enhance reliability. With the use of exception handlers, you can validate input data and, if necessary, reprompt the user for the correct data. Software engineers can hide implementation details from users and let them see only the part of a program unit which specifies the name of the object and the form of data to the input or received from the data. Information hiding enhances reliability by protection of implementation details.

Modification allows changes to be made without alteration of the original structure of a system. Requirements will change during the life cycle of a system. New versions will be created with new modifications and changes of requirements. The changes must be cost-effective. Modifiability is achieved in a system by the design of small meaningful modules, use of localized data in these modules, and very little use of global data or numeric literals.

The object-oriented concept includes data values and range constraints for a given type of data in one place—the type declaration. A change made in a type declaration is all that is necessary for these data to be modified throughout the object-oriented software.

Maintainability keeps the system effectively live and useful in the life cycle. Requirements will change or be modified during postdeployment of the system software. These changes will modify the system. Modifiability and maintainability are directly related. The design of a system must be robust for these changes.

Maintenance of object-oriented software is eased by the fact that characteristics and behaviors are localized. When a local behavior is modified, it cannot unduly affect external entities. When a local characteristic is modified, it cannot unduly affect external entities if all accesses to it are through logical interfaces.

Understandability helps software engineers with the management of a complex system. Remember, software design and code are only written once, but they must be read by others many, many times. In object-oriented software, uniformity, readability, and modularity enhance understandability. The data operations that are involved are understandable. An understandable system has enhanced maintainability. A system is understandable when it directly reflects how the problem will be solved and provides its readable solution. The real-world problem and the computer problem must be parallel at every point in the process. A well-designed object-oriented software models the problem space in an intuitive manner. Objects that exist in the problem space also exist in the solution space along with analogous characteristics and behavior.

Adaptability in a system is easily accomplished in a diversified environment. Object-oriented software can be easily adapted to new changing requirements because of the high reusability that is inherent in an object-oriented environment.

Reusability is a big issue these days. Pretested software should be used to save both costs and time. The development of an object-oriented software means modeling the problem as a set of types or classes from which the objects are created. This set is partitioned into a hierarchical categorization that emphasizes reuse by relegating common characteristics and behaviors to the highest possible level. Once this modeling has been done, coding (translation of algorithms to program) is easier since it consists of mere creation of necessary objects from the defined classes and invokes the behavioral operations of objects. Coding can be anthropomorphized since the objects and behaviors are isomorphic with the real world.

Efficiency is achieved by the use of available resources in an optimal manner. The factors that involve efficiency are execution speed, user time, computer memory, and computer storage. The object-oriented concept has a large selection of efficiency-related features. They are low-level I/O, parallel programming, and error handling.

Principles of Object-Oriented Software Engineering

Object-oriented software engineering principles are applied to achieve the established goals. These principles are abstraction, information hiding, completeness, confirmability, modularity, localization, and uniformity.

Information hiding is the protection of implementation details in an object-oriented software. Information hiding is the deliberate hiding of information from those who might misuse it. This differentiates the "what" from the "how." The "what" is essential information that should be available to everyone. This information includes specifications and interface information. The "how" information should be available only to a limited group and includes implementation details such as data structure.

Information hiding supports and enforces abstraction by the suppression of details. It increases quality and supports reusability, portability, and maintainability. It avoids confusion for the user, promotes correct data input, and enhances reliability. Information hiding enhances localization and usually includes cohesive data. Hence good modularity is achieved, and the goal of modifiability is more easily approached.

For example, for your PC, it is not a requirement that you know much about the electronic engineering of your computer's functions. This is information hiding for you. You learn about the keyboard, how to enter your data, and how to get your desired result. Sometimes you must learn about the software so you can achieve the desired results. Another example is the person who drives a car. It is not essential that the person know how the car's engine functions. It is information hiding. The person's main knowledge concerns how the car can be used effectively.

Completeness ensures that all requirements are included in the system. Completeness is the assurance that every possible aspect of the problem has been considered. Software engineers must consider and plan for all possible problem and solution facets which may include future requirements changes. Application of the principle of completeness helps achieve the goals of reliability, efficiency, and modifiability.

Confirmability states that a module, a group of modules, or a complete system software is readily testable. A testable system implies a verifiable design. The testing of a system will confirm whether it has been correctly designed. The system confirms the inclusion of the customer's requirements. Module independence is an important factor for a verifiable system. Thus, for good confirmability, modules are loosely coupled and contain cohesive data.

Modularity is defined as the breaking down of a program into small manageable units. Modularizing an object-oriented system software breaks the solution space into smaller units. The modules are grouped around a data type and objects of that type. Only subprograms which contain operations for objects of a certain type are grouped together. For example, an array type may be in a package along with subprograms for calculating the average of array elements, which find elements with the maximum positive value and elements with the most negative value.

In a well-modularized system software, the top modules are generally the "what" of the process, while lower-level modules constitute the "how" of the process. This implies that the lower the module is in the module group, the more implementation details it contains. In other words, upper-level modules are the most abstract modules in the group, while lower-level modules are the most detailed.

Good modularity also implies loose coupling between modules. Coupling is a measure of dependence between modules. Global data shared by modules also increase this intermodular dependence. The passing of only required data via parameters or the localizing of data within a module decreases coupling. Loose coupling guarantees confirmability (independent module testing) and enhances the principle of modularity. Loose coupling also implies that if there are two modules, say, module A and module B, and if module A gets modified, then module B will not be affected by the changes made in A. Thus in addition to enhancing the modularity principle, loose coupling brings closer the goal of modifiability.

Besides loose coupling, there is another factor required for good modularity. This factor is called *data localization*. By localizing data in only those modules which require them, three principles are applied: modularity, confirmability, and localization. Together these three principles facilitate easier modifiability. Only very highly related or cohesive data are localized in a module. Thus, for good modularity, loosely coupled modules must contain localized and cohesive data that are highly related.

Localization consists of placing highly related cohesive data only in modules which operate on these data. Only necessary data are passed from module to module, and then they are passed only through parameters. This guarantees data integrity. Data localization implies independent modules and loose coupling. These are factors which must be present for good modularity.

In sum, important factors for good modularity are as follows:

- Data localization
- Loose coupling
- No data passing except via parameters
- Information hiding

The presence of these factors enhances reliability, efficiency, and modifiability. If the data range is increased due to a requirements change, then only that data type statement in a particular module needs changing.

Uniformity includes the use of good, consistent, standardized features in all phases of object-oriented software development. Uniformity can begin at requirements analysis and apply throughout the implementation stages. This includes testing and maintenance. This also implies that meaningful data and program names must be established. All the team players must follow the established standards throughout the software's life cycle. The result of this agreement is a uniform, easily readable, and understandable software.

Object-Oriented versus Conventional Methods

Object-oriented methods basically differ from conventional methods for software development. Object-oriented concept models of entities are constructed as self-contained components. Data and procedures are combined into entities and are called objects, as shown in Fig. 2.6. This system is defined by the interactions and behavior of the components. An important aspect of the design process patterns the behavior of the models so that it is visible only when interactions are expected with other entities. A model inherits or extends the characteristics of other models. Furthermore, program entities can refer to objects of more than one class. The strength of the object-oriented approach lies in the way in which a complex system can be expressed in terms of its components and their relations, not the addressing of a system as one large process.

Object-oriented programming helps with the writing of code that specifies only generic instructions and delegates implementation details to particular involved objects. The code can be reused on several different types of objects. This implies that the object will do what you want when you send the correct message, but how the task is handled by the object is not very important to the software engineer. A program can include an entire set of objects that are all derived from different classes but respond to the same message, even though their methods are different.

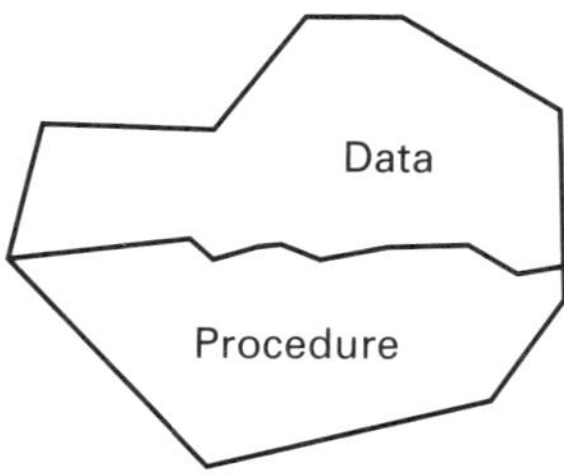

Figure 2.6 An object.

It is worth mentioning here that there is no one standard of notation available in object-oriented methods. For example, *type* is called *class* by Booch and by Rumbaugh et al., *class and object* by Coad and Yourdon, *object* by Shlaer and Mellor and by Jacobson et al., and *object type* by Martin and Odell. Similarly, the term *association* is called *uses* by Booch, *instance connection* by Coad and Yourdon, *relationship* by Shlaer and Mellor, *association* by Rumbaugh et al. and by Martin and Odell, and *acquaintance association* by Jacobson. The term *subtype* is called *inherits* by Booch, *gen-type* by Coad and Yourdon, *subtype* by Shlaer and Mellor and by Martin and Odell, and *generalization* by Rumbaugh et al. The term *aggregation* is called *containing* by Booch, *part-whole* by Coad and Yourdon, *aggregation* by Rumbaugh et al., and *composition* by Martin and Odell. All these methods may differ in notations and symbols, but they do discuss the object-oriented approach for developing software.

The object-oriented approach is most suitable for problem requirements which lack predictability. If all aspects of a problem are well understood and require control logic, then a more conventional approach is probably needed. Conversely, if you are sure what action should be performed next, then express the problem requirements in terms of its constituents, states, and desired behaviors. The major advantages of this approach are that the software is more modular, robust, extensible, portable, reusable, and easy to use.

There are a few conventional methods available in the computer industry besides the object-oriented approach. Some of these methods are listed for comparison:

- Structured functional approach

- Entity-related approach

- Event-oriented approach

The *structured functional* is the top-down approach for the software development life cycle. It concentrates on functionality and data. The focal points are procedures; data are static entities that are applied to procedures as needed. In the analysis phase, hierarchical and functional relationships between objects and activities are identified. At each level in the decomposition, components of the system are characterized in terms of the parent component, input, output, control, activity, and mechanism that support the component. The strengths of this approach are that it is graphical and easy to understand. The requirements analysis data flow diagrams provide input to the design. It is well documented at each phase of the software's development life cycle. It is supported by a number of automated tools. It follows the waterfall model. This approach has certain disadvantages.

The decomposition follows the heuristic approach. Its emphasis is on data flow instead of the encapsulation of data structure. The steps involve stronger transform analysis and transaction analysis rather than location of the central transform. It lacks data abstractions and information hiding.

The *entity-related approach* uses the *entity relationship* (ER) model and categorizes the information from the real-world problem domain. It recognizes that the database, as well as the code, needs consideration at logical and physical levels. This information is conveyed when the entities are defined in the domain and when the interrelationships of those entities and attributes are possessed by the entities. These concepts must ultimately be mapped into a plan that can be implemented on a database management system. The advantages of the approach are that it is prescriptive and uses abstraction. It concentrates on information and identifies entities and their relationships. The disadvantage is that it is too complex for larger systems.

The *event-oriented approach* is characterized by the concept of a stimulus response, where events are the stimuli to the system and responses are composed of actions taken by the system and the resultant outputs. Events orientation builds the system on the basis of the kinds of events the system is likely to encounter. This approach is widely used in real-time interactive systems. The advantages are that it identifies external events and establishes a system boundary early in the analysis. The response constraints are highly visible. Acceptance tests are easily constructed. The disadvantages are that there are always time constraints which are needed in the forefront of other methods for requirements analysis.

Object-Oriented Standards

There is no single object-oriented standard available in the industry. Some of the de facto object-oriented standards are by Booch, Coad and Yourdon, Rumbaugh et al., Shlaer and Mellor, Martin and Odell, and Jacobson. Most of the software developers create their own standards and follow them in their organizations. These standards are variations of the basic object-oriented goals and principles. This chapter provides a study of current software development standards. Suggested object-oriented standard guidelines are discussed also.

Study of Current Standards

There are many software development standards available in the industry. These standards originated from the Institute of Electrical and Electronics Engineers (IEEE), Europe, Canada, NASA, and the U.S. Department of Defense (DOD). In fact, almost every sizable computer organization has its own established standard for software development. These standards outline the software development life cycle and the content of required documents. Standards also define software quality assurance, configuration management, and independent verification and validation, as needed for embedded systems.

Software development standards are necessary so that any one of the computer systems can interoperate with the others. Standards establish uniform software engineering techniques that are applicable throughout the system life cycle. These standards incorporate practices which will be cost-effective from a software life-cycle perspective. Standards are intended to be dynamic and responsive to the rapidly evolving software-engineering field. *Data item descriptions* (DIDs) that are applicable to the standards are available and provide a set of complete and concise documents that record and communicate information generated from specified requirements.

The main motivation behind the creation of the IEEE standards is to provide recommendations that reflect state-of-the-art engineering principles for the development and maintenance of software. The U.S. Department of Defense has developed standards that meet the requirements of costly, complex systems regarding quality, performance, and reliability. The purpose of DOD-STD-2167A is to establish and apply requirements during the acquisition, development, and support of software systems.

DOD-STD-2167A is a tightly composed standard that concentrates on software engineering. This standard implies a waterfall, top-down, hierarchical approach, as shown in Fig. 3.1. This standard is not inherently geared toward the object-oriented approach as it is presented in Fig. 3.2. The standard does not provide guidelines for spiral model applications as it is shown in Fig. 3.3. It is difficult to trace system and software requirements to object-oriented design. There is no one-to-one mapping between the software organizational structure of *computer software configuration items* (CSCIs), *computer software components* (CSCs), and *computer software units* (CSUs) and the elements of an object-oriented software architecture. It does not provide guidelines so object-oriented software can be documented.

2B or Not 2B Prophesy

MIL-STD-SDD (498)

This is a revised Military Standard for Software Development and Documentation (SDD). It is the result of harmonization of DOD-STD-2167A with DOD-STD-7935A. The highlights of the revised standard

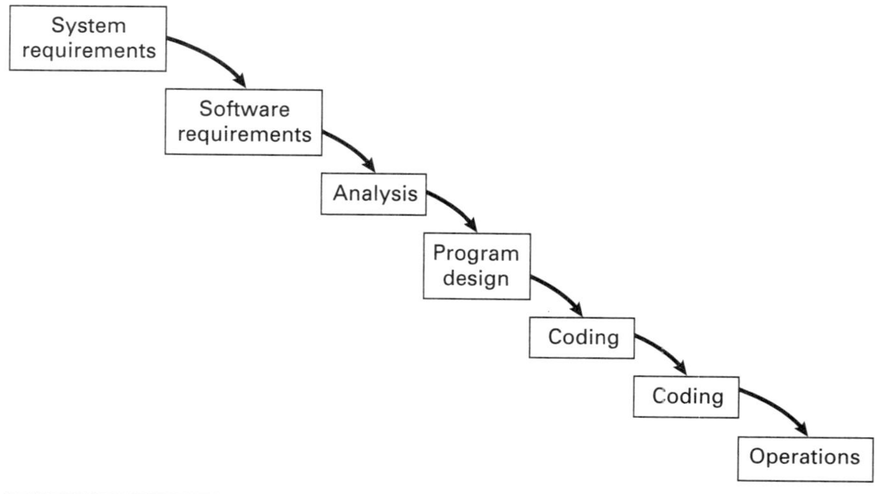

Figure 3.1 Waterfall model.

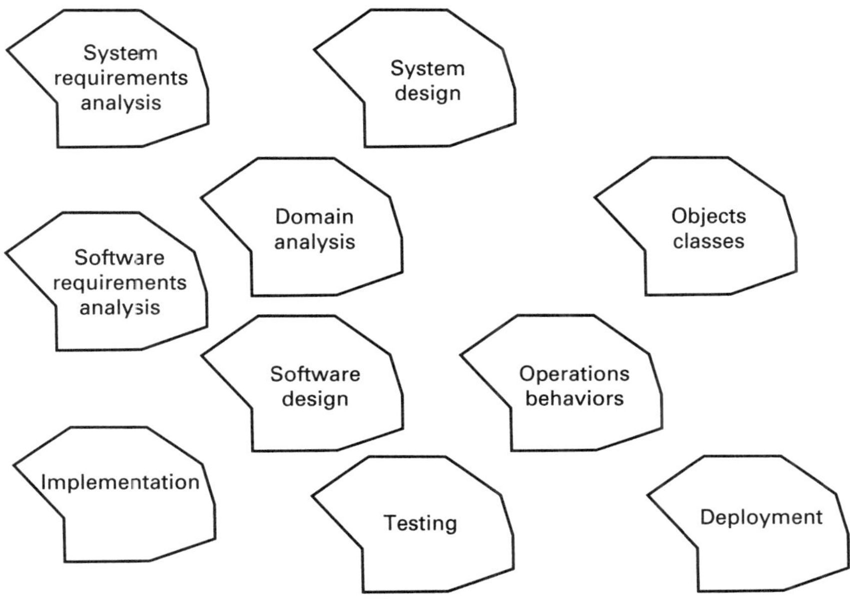

Figure 3.2 Object-oriented method concept.

must be open-ended rather than the specification of any particular software development method. The software developer is responsible for selecting software development methods and *computer-aided software engineering* (CASE) tools that best support the customer's requirements. It provides the means for establishing, evaluating, and maintaining quality in software and associated documents. IEEE 1498 further modifies the MIL-STD-498 so it will be acceptable as an international standard and be a part of the ISO 9000 standard.

Major features

The major features of this standard eliminate the shortfalls of the current DOD standards. It eliminates the waterfall, top-down, and hierarchical implications of DOD-STD-2167A. It eliminates the functional area tracks (software development management, software engineering, etc.), which tend to be waterfall-oriented. It explains several life-cycle models, tells how an incremental or evolutionary development is planned, and provides guidance for the selection of appropriate deliverables in each increment. It eliminates the requirements that partition the CSCI into CSCs and CSUs. This will require only a CSCI to be partitioned into components and will use the method that is proposed in the *software development plan* (SDP). The SDP will be created by the software developers.

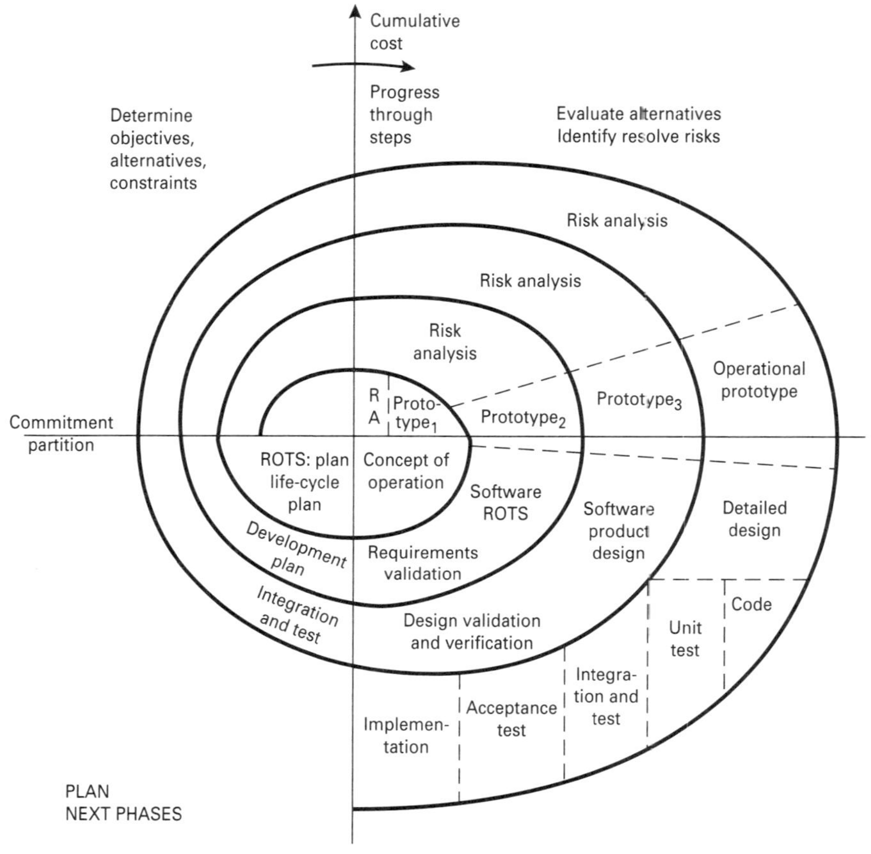

Figure 3.3 Spiral model.

This standard requires that the software developer lay out a software development process which conforms to the life-cycle model established for the software. It acknowledges that each software development activity is an update or refinement of what has gone before, rather than a first-time occurrence. It reorganizes activities that occur at the same time to activities that are concerned with a given software development activity. It explains how each activity is interpreted in the context of builds. For example, how should the planning activity be divided among builds; how should requirements analysis, design, coding, testing, and product evaluation be performed in incremental builds? It covers in-process reviews and supplements or substitutes for formal reviews. It identifies separately system requirements analysis and system design.

This standard eliminates the document-driven implications of DOD-

STD-2167A. The language of the standard has changed from *software and documentation* to the more generic *software development products* which acknowledge nondocument representations, such as data in CASE tools. It separates activity requirements from documentation requirements and emphasizes that software development activities need not result in documents. It clarifies that deliverable documents are the required outcome of an activity only when so specified on the *contract data requirements list* (CDRL). It is explicit in acknowledging electronic representation of information in lieu of documents. It eliminates the developmental configuration as distinct from other software development contractor configuration control. It adds guidance about ordering the executable (and possible source) code via *contract line item number* (CLIN) rather than on CDRL. It adds explicit permission and delivers CASE tool contents for CDRLs.

This standard clarifies and makes the customer's requirements more consistent for each level of testing. This standard provides clear guidelines for software support. It expands and clarifies the requirements which concern incorporation of reusable software. It specifies that nondevelopmental items (possibly modified) are to be incorporated into systems under development if they meet user needs and will be cost-effective over the life of the system. It interprets this policy for software by itemizing considerations that determine whether a reusable software component will meet user needs and be cost-effective over the life of the system. It requires that the software developer analyze candidate reusable components in light of these considerations, report the findings and recommendations to the customer, and incorporate reusable components that meet the criteria. It specifies allowable substitutions for this standard's required documentation when reusable software is incorporated. It makes a preliminary statement about other allowable substitutions, for example, in testing and formal reviews. It defines clearly the interface between software testing and system testing.

This standard has a section for planned software quality assurance requirements. It adds a requirement that will identify, collect, and apply management indicators, and it provides a list of candidate indicators which aid in the selection of a set. It revises the requirement on risk management with emphasis on risk as a guiding principle for planning and managing projects.

Table 3.1 contains a list of 22 individual data item descriptions that are applicable to this standard. There is a set of six consolidated DIDs, which combines the DIDs for plans, requirements, design, testing, user/operator manuals, and support; and there is a single DID for small projects that summarizes all other DIDs. These DIDs describe a set of documents that record the required information by this stan-

TABLE 3.1   List of Data Item Descriptions

Plans:
  Software development plan (SDP)
  Software installation plan (SIP)
  Software support plan (SSP

Concept and requirements:
  Operational concept document (OCD)
  System/segment specification (SSS)
  Software requirements specification (SRS)
  Interface requirements specification (IRS)

Design:
  System/segment design document (SSDD)
  Software design document (SDD)
  Interface design document (IDD)
  Database design document (DBDD)

Test:
  Software test plan (STP)
  Software test description (STD)
  Software test report (STR)

User or Operator:
  Software user manual (SUM)
  Software input/output manual (SIOM)
  Computer center software operational manual (CCSOM)
  Computer system operator manual (CSOM)

Support:
  Version description document (VDD)
  Software product specification (SPS)
  Firmware support manual (FSM)
  Computer instruction set architecture manual (CISAM)

---

dard. Production of deliverable data that use automated techniques is encouraged.

Characteristics of a Good Object-Oriented Standard

A good standard is tightly composed and concentrates on object-oriented goals and principles. The standard establishes uniform requirements for software development that are applicable throughout the system life cycle. The requirements of the standard provide the basis for insight into software development, testing, and customer evaluation efforts. Some characteristics of a good standard are listed in Table 3.2.

Suggested Object-Oriented Standard

Many features of object-oriented methods are new to software developers. It is important that some of its main features and terminology

TABLE 3.2 Characteristics of a Good Object-Oriented Standard

Proper structure: represents clear thinking and a standardized means of communication

Establishes uniformity

Follows software engineering discipline

Fits in accordance with object-oriented goals and principles

Rigorous: follows the processes, standards, and procedures

Can be used along with other standards

Provides guidelines, references, roadmaps, and checkpoints

Involves quantitative feedback reviews and audits

User-friendly

Produces quality products

Includes reasonable documentations

Provides quality activities and evaluations

Provides visibility into software development status

Provides a template model which will introduce a suitable object-oriented method

Provides guidelines that will help in choosing a suitable CASE tool

Encourages use of reusable software

Encourages tailoring aspects

Establishes tests for the object-oriented environment

Standardizes object-oriented software development and management processes

Provides means that will help develop systems that are efficient and cost-effective

---

be understood. During the software requirements analysis phase, objects, classes, their relationships, operations, and attributes should be identified at a high level. A checklist for the suggested object-oriented standard is described in Table 3.3. The checklist can vary according to the suitability of a project. Let us discuss a standardized object-oriented design method that has been in use since 1981 and has been applied to a broad spectrum of problem domains. The method addresses the following:

- Logical and physical decomposition
- Static and dynamic behavior

The method also addresses the two dimensions of system structure that are peculiar to object-oriented systems:

- Parent-child and seniority hierarchies
- Object and class decomposition

TABLE 3.3   Suggested Object-Oriented Standard Checklist

Establish project management standard that includes
   Project progress reporting process
   Statement of work clarification procedures
   Project management graphical representations
   Staff qualifications and experiences
   Cost analysis
   Schedule impacts
   Risk analysis management process
   Metrics
   Review process and procedure
   Tailoring of standards plan
   Documents deliverable process
   Educating and training plan
   Effective dialog and communication between system developers and customers and
     users of process
   Software delivery process
   Software products acceptance schema

Establish system requirements analysis standard that includes
   System requirements analysis diagrams
   Maintenance of system requirements list
   System external interfaces
   Modeling of customer requirements
   Requirements feasibility analysis
   Requirements traceability schema
   Commitment to customer requirements
   Determination of system complexity
   Object-oriented hardware diagram

Establish system design standard that includes
   System design graphical representations
   Allocation of software and hardware requirements
   Object-oriented software development plan
     Selecting a suitable object-oriented method
     Selecting a suitable CASE tool
     Planning for object-oriented software quality
     Planning for increment software development
     Planning for object-oriented software testing
     Planning for configuration management
     Corrective action plan
     Customer reviews and audits process
   System behavioral design
   System architectural design

Establish software requirements analysis standard that covers
   Software requirements analysis diagrams
   Maintenance of software requirements list
   Creation of prototyping models
   Interface requirements
   Establishment of object-oriented database
   Identification of objects' entities
   Definition of class structure
   Development of object-oriented models
   Establishment of real-time impacts
   Determination of sizing and timing requirements

TABLE 3.3 Suggested Object-Oriented Standard Checklist (Continued)

Establish software requirements analysis standard that covers (Cont.)
  Software requirements traceability
  Plan for testing requirements

Establish object-oriented software design standard that contains
  Architecture design diagrams
  Behavioral design diagrams
  Object diagrams
  Algorithms
  Data structure
    Data types
    Associated operations
  Database logical design
  Forming packages, subprograms, functions, and tasks
    Functional cohesion
    Data coupling
  Software design requirements traceability
  Compilation dependencies diagrams
  Identifying, raising, and handling of exceptions
  Setting up of software design file
  Software reuse schema
  Interfaces
  Plan for testing design

Establish object-oriented code style standard that includes
  Coding formatting
    Horizontal spacing
    Indentation
    Alignment of operators
    Alignment of declarations
    Blank lines
    Pagination
    Number of statements per line
    Source code line length
  Readability
    Use of underscores
    Numbers
    Capitalization
    Abbreviations
  Commentary
    General comments
    File headers
    Unit function description
    Marker comments
    Highlighting
  Naming conventions
    Names
    Type identification
    Object identification
    Program unit identification
    Constants and named numbers
  Using types
    Declaring types
    Enumeration types

TABLE 3.3   Suggested Object-Oriented Standard Checklist (Continued)

Establish object-oriented code style standard that includes (Cont.)
  Using types (Cont.)
    Overloading enumeration literals
  High-level program structure
    Separate compilation capabilities
    Subprograms
    Functions
    Packages
    Functional cohesion
    Data coupling
  Syntax
    Loop names
    Block names
    Exit statements
    Naming and statements
  Parameters lists
    Formal parameters
    Named association
    Default parameters
    Mode indication
  Types
    Derived types
    Subtypes
    Anonymous types
    Private types
  Data structures
    Heterogeneous data
    Nested records
    Dynamics data
  Expressions
    Range values
    Array attributes
    Expressions in parentheses
    Positive forms of logic
    Short-circuit forms of logical operators
    Type qualified expressions and type conversion
    Accuracy of operations with real operands
  Statements
    Nesting
    Slices
    Case statements
    Loops
    Exit statements
    Safe statements
    Goto statements
    Return statements
    Blocks
  Visibility
    The use clause
    The renames clause
    Overloaded subprograms
    Overload operators

TABLE 3.3   Suggested Object-Oriented Standard Checklist (Continued)

Establish object-oriented code style standard that includes (Cont.)
  Exceptions
    Disasters versus state information
    User-, implementation-, and predefined exceptions
    Handlers for others
    Propagation
    Localizing the cause of an exception
  Erroneous execution
    Unchecked conversion
    Unchecked deallocation
    Dependence on parameters passing mechanism
    Multiple-address clauses
    Suppression of exception check
    Initialization
  Tasking
    Tasks
    Task types
    Dynamic tasks
    Priorities
    Delay statements
  Communication
    Defensive task communication
    Attributes
    Shared variables
    Tentative rendezvous constructs
    Communication complexity
  Termination
    Normal termination
    The abort statement
    Programmed termination
    Abnormal termination

The fundamental rule for decomposing a system that uses the object-oriented technique is that each module in the system denotes an object or a class of objects from the problem space. Abstraction and information hiding thus form the foundation of the object-oriented method. Actually, abstraction is employed daily and develops models of reality which identify the objects and operations that exist at each level of interaction. Thus, when you drive a car, you consider the accelerator, gauges, steering wheel, brakes, etc., as well as the operations you perform on them and the effects of those operations. When you repair an automobile engine, you consider lower-level objects, such as the fuel pump, carburetor, and distributor. Similarly, the major steps of the object-oriented design method are given in the following list. These steps evolved from an approach that was first proposed by Abbott and should be viewed as an approach that adds value to the identification of objects and classes, as well as the building blocks of complex systems.

1. Identify the objects and their attributes.

2. Identify the operations suffered by and required of each object.

3. Establish the visibility of each object in relation to other objects.

4. Establish the interface of each object.

5. Implement each object.

Step 1.   This step identifies the objects and attributes and recognizes the major actors, agents, and servers in the problem space with their roles in the reality model. The objects are identified from the nouns that describe the problem space. There can be several similar objects. If there are many similar objects, you must establish a class of objects.

The attributes of an object can be characterized by its time and space behavior. The first step (establish the abstraction of the problem space) is the hardest. The problem can be recognized easily, but the location of the abstraction can be difficult. The fundamental challenge lies in drawing the boundaries of each abstraction so that you end up with a set of abstractions that accurately capture the model of reality, are resilient to change, and express interesting behavior. In short, abstractions satisfy the properties of an object.

Step 2.   This step identifies the operations that are suffered and required of each object, and it also serves as the behavior characterization of each object or class of objects. This step draws concrete boundaries around the abstractions that have been identified in the first step. The static semantics of the object are established by the determination of which operations can be meaningfully performed on the object or by the object. Dynamic behavior of each object is established by the identification of time and space constraints that must be observed for each operation.

Step 3.   The visibility of each object in relation to other objects is established. Static dependencies among objects and classes of objects are identified. The purpose of this step is the topological capturing of objects and classes from the reality model. You may begin to see a pattern of objects in this step. At that time, an engineering decision must be made that will create all these objects or continue individual management of yet similar objects.

Step 4.   The interface's establishment of each object (or class) produces the outside view of each object (or class) by the use of some suitable notation. This step captures the static semantics of each object or class of objects established in step 3. This specification also serves as a contract between the clients of an object and the object itself. The interface forms the boundary between the object's outside view and inside view.

Step 5. The final step is the implementation of each object, which involves a choice of suitable representation for each object or class of objects. Implementation of the interface forms the previous step, which can involve either decomposition or composition.

Object-Oriented Design Method Notation

Object-oriented design method notation must be represented clearly, so all relevant details of the analysis and design are visible. Visibility includes logical and physical analysis and design decisions, static and dynamic semantics, and the aspects of both dimensions of systems structure. Also, the notation must be simple enough that you can study the analysis and design, reason about their implications, visualize alternatives, and accurately communicate these decisions to other team members.

A notation consists of four parts. These parts constitute the products of the object-oriented design method.

1. Hardware diagram

2. Class structure

3. Object diagram

4. Architecture diagram

These diagrams are produced in order. Depending on the complexity of the system, production of only one diagram might be necessary, or production of more than one of each diagram might be necessary. These artifacts constitute a project model. For any given system under consideration, there can be many versions of a project model that represent the design of a released version, version in test, and version under development. The important requirement is a self-sufficient model.

Hardware diagram

The hardware diagram asserts the existence of processors, devices, networks, and connections. A processor can run x number of programs. A device is a resource that is used by processors. A network connects processors. And a connection connects processors and devices, processors and processors, and processors and networks. The symbols that appear in a hardware diagram are shown in Fig. 3.4. A hardware diagram appears as a graph, whereas processors, devices,

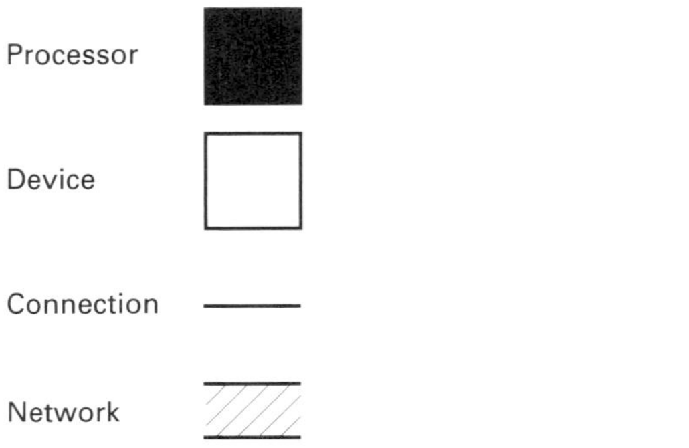

Processor

Device

Connection   ———

Network

Figure 3.4   Hardware diagram symbols.

and networks are vertices of the graph, and connections are directed arcs. For each of these symbols, a name, its semantics, and design notes are provided.

Hardware diagrams outline the underlying target hardware system. After a target hardware architecture is selected, a hardware diagram can be produced. In the simplest systems, there might be a single hardware diagram that contains exactly one processor symbol and no other. However, sometimes complex hardware systems development proceeds in parallel with, or even lags, software development. Thus, generation of a hardware diagram might not be possible prior to implementation of the objects, when you begin making hardware-software tradeoffs in the physical design of the system. The needed capacity of computational resources and load balancing among processors is typically based on empirical evidence from prototypes.

Class structure

The class structure forms the logical design of the software system. It denotes the first dimension of the logical model of the system. From a static semantics class perspective, structures are used and they denote relationships among classes objects. In addition, these diagrams can be used in the capture of the dynamic behavior of individual classes. A project model might contain one or more class structures. Multiple class structures can be used in the grouping of meaningful collections of classes. Each class structure can contain symbols that denote classes and relationships among the classes. The symbols that may appear in a class structure are shown in Fig. 3.5. A class structure takes the form of a graph, where classes are vertices of the graph and relationships are directed arcs.

For each class, a name, its semantics, and design notes are provided. In addition, the static behavior of a class is stored by recording

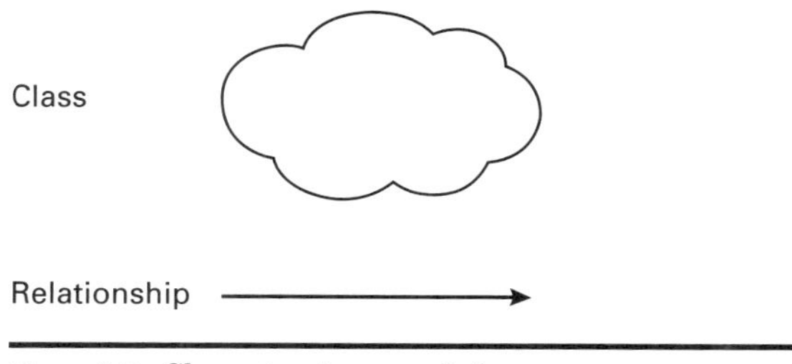

Figure 3.5 Class structure symbols.

certain items. Each item contains a list of some textual information. These items express the resources and are exported by a class. In other words, the abstraction constitutes its outside view:

- Constants
- Types
- Variables
- Constructors
- Selectors
- Iterators
- Exceptions

When a graph of the static semantics of a class is completed, the forms of the class should be denoted with any constraints on the class that might be relevant. A finite state machine, which is another graphlike diagram, can be introduced so that the dynamic semantics can capture a class.

With this diagram, you can express any allowable time that orders operations and the alteration of the state of any cases that are due to interactions among operations. For each relationship, the kind of relationship that exists between two classes is described. The following five relationships are typical among classes of a system:

1. Inherited
2. Instantiation
3. Subtype
4. Derived
5. Synthesis

Inherited means there exists a superclass-subclass relationship. *Instantiation* means that one class is a parameterized instance of another class. *Subtype* means that one class is a constrained copy of another class, or that the two classes are interchangeable. *Derived* means that one class is a constrained copy of another class, while the two classes are not interchangeable, but are treated as distinct classes. *Synthesized* means that one class is a composite of several classes.

Class structures are generally produced during steps 2 to 4 of the object-oriented method process. Classes offer a powerful vehicle for reuse of abstractions.

Object diagram

Object diagrams represent the second dimension of the logical design of a system. Statically, object diagrams are used for expressing the visibility of each object in relation to other objects. Object diagrams are used dynamically as well. They express time and space constraints upon interobject communication, and they express the parallelism that might exist among a given collection of objects.

A project model contains one or more object diagrams. Multiple object diagrams are used in meaningful group collections of objects. Each object diagram can contain symbols that denote objects and visibility. The objects represent distinct objects, and the visibility represents visibility between two objects. Figure 3.6 shows the symbols that might appear in an object diagram. An object diagram takes the form of a graph, which represents the seniority hierarchy where objects are vertices of the graph and visibilities are directed arcs. For each object, a name, its semantics, design notes, and any relevant constraints upon the object are provided. A single object expression of the parent-child hierarchy can be exploded into another complete object diagram, which represents the structure of all its children.

Visibility, as a directed arc, denotes an asymmetric relationship between two objects: Object A might see object B, but is not seen by object B. For each visibility, a list of items is supplied that denotes data or control. The objects can flow between two objects or operations, which might invoke one object on another.

Figure 3.6   Object diagram symbols.

Each flow has its own set of design decisions. For example, the invoked operation must match an appropriate operation and be exported by the class of the designated object. The class travels along the flow, either with or against the direction of the visibility and performance information.

Object diagrams are generally produced during steps 2 to 4 of an object-oriented design process. As objects are identified, they are included in an object diagram. Later, visibility decisions are made, and then the graph is decorated with arcs that denote visibility relationships. As with class structures, an iterative element exists in the design process: You can alter the boundaries of objects for a variety of technical and nontechnical reasons.

Architecture diagram

Architecture diagrams represent the physical design of a system. Thus, they primarily capture static information. A project model contains one or more architecture diagrams. Multiple architecture diagrams group meaningful collections of objects. Each architecture diagram contains symbols that denote components and dependencies. The components represent structural elements that are provided by the underlying implementation language. Dependencies represent compilation dependencies among components. The symbols for an architecture diagram are somewhat language-specific because not all languages provide the same packaging mechanisms, generic units, and tasks. For example, the symbols for Ada are shown in Fig. 3.7.

An architecture diagram takes the form of a graph where components are vertices of the graph, dependencies are directed arcs, and the topology of the graph satisfies the rules of separate compilation for the programming language.

For each component, a name, its semantics, and relevant design notes are provided. Static design decisions are captured by recording the kind of components that use the vocabulary of the underlying implementation language. Each component references a set of classes from class structures of the same project model, or objects from object diagrams of the same project model. This set of entities registers the design decisions with regard to packaging the implementation of individual classes and objects. Typically, there is a one-to-one mapping of classes to components, and there are many-to-one mappings of objects to components.

If the rules of underlying implementation language allow, some components explode and reveal the unveiling of another complete architecture diagram. Dependencies denote asymmetric relationships among components.

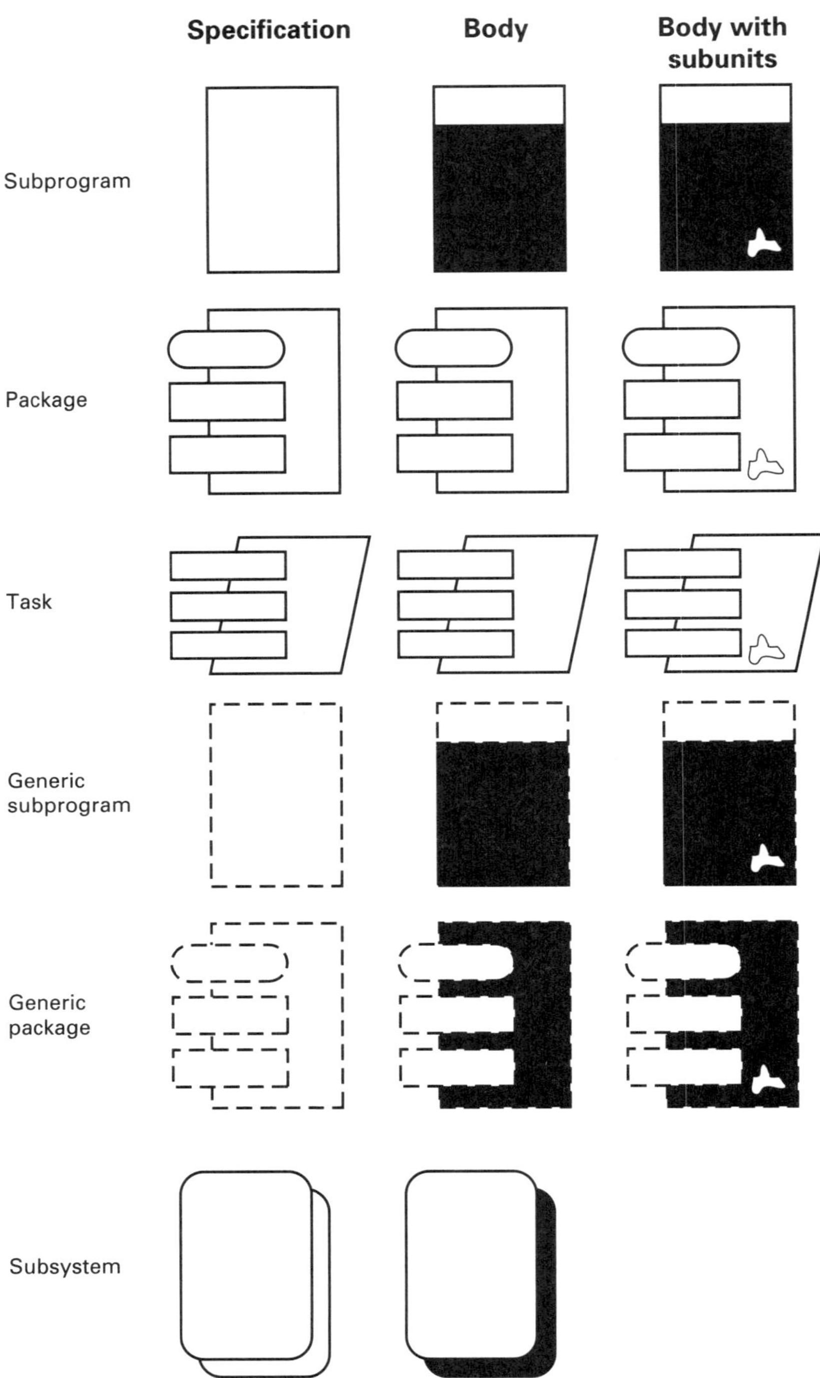

Figure 3.7 Architecture diagram symbols.

Architecture diagrams are generally produced during step 5 of the object-oriented design method process. Production of a diagram motivates changes in corresponding class structures and object diagrams, as the logical design is molded to the physical constraints of the system. These diagrams facilitate the representation and sharing of components among programs, even when such programs execute in a distributed environment.

Object-Oriented Software Development Life Cycle

Customer requirements should be understood and analyzed with an object-oriented method. Proper automated tools (discussed in *Software Requirements Analysis and Specification* by Jag Sodhi, published by McGraw-Hill) must be used that will maintain requirements traceability throughout the system software development. Requirements analysis should be supported by graphical models. These graphical models enhance understandability and clarity. The graphical models depict the customer requirements insight in object-oriented software development. The graphical representations can be diagrams, such as

- Context
- Information
- Object relationship
- State transition
- Event relationship
- Data flow
- Data dictionary

In object-oriented design, graphical representations include data structures and operations that act upon those data structures. These entities are directly derivable from the customer requirements analysis. The requirements are further differentiated in the software design phase. It is important that a trace of the origin of these fragments of a requirement be kept and documented. Graphical representations assist in understanding a design. These graphical diagrams are

- Object architecture
- Object compilation dependencies
- Object hierarchy

- Object communication
- Object relationships with program modules, packages, and components
- Interfaces
- Concurrency
- Object and attribute dictionary
- Timing and sizing constraints
- Testing schema
- Exceptions handling

Tailoring Standards Techniques

Tailoring standards for an individual application is essential. Tailoring means the selection of only those products, activities, and reviews that fit the characteristics of and are essential to a particular project. The purpose of tailoring is to help in the evaluation of requirements in a standard that will save money, prevent duplication, and preserve the schedule of the project. The software developer and customer can recommend tailoring of the standards, but ultimately the customer makes the final decision.

The result of the tailoring process is reflected in the *statement of work* (SOW) that prescribes the tasks and reviews. The contract data requirements list (CDRL) contains all the deliverable documentations. Sometimes clarification is necessary rather than a deletion of requirements. In these cases, the DID for a product can be modified, which will make it unique to the project. When tasks are being added, they may be included in the SOW, which leaves the DID unchanged.

Factors for tailoring.   The following list shows some of the factors that should be considered when a standard is tailored.

- The software development process that will be used
- Software characteristics and intended end use
- Acquisition strategy and type of project management
- Acceptable risk
- Schedule
- Budget
- Development visibility required
- Software maintenance concept

Tailoring of object-oriented standards also depends on the class of software. Software classification includes operational, support, system, diagnostic, and automatic test equipment. The tailoring factor changes for the software that is being developed, modified, and reused. *Commercial off-the-shelf* (COTS) software or *nondevelopmental software* (NDS) also affects the tailoring factor.

Guidelines for tailoring.   The tailoring process is performed many times throughout the life cycle of a system. Many different events trigger the need for tailoring of the standards and DIDs. First and foremost, tailoring should be done every time the system enters a new phase in the life cycle. Phases include concept exploration, demonstration and validation, full-scale development, and production and deployment. The levels and types of documentation that are needed for each phase vary and should be reflected in the tailoring process. The suggested guidelines for tailoring an object-oriented standard are as follows:

- Classify the required software by development or nondevelopment category.

- Select activities and reviews in accordance with applicable standards and DIDs.

- Select deliverable products.

- Tailor the DIDs.

Object-Oriented Database

Object-oriented related standards emphasize that the early identification of a suitable database assists in software development. An *object-oriented database* (OODB) promises that applications will be developed more quickly. Software will be more flexible, more reliable, easier modified, and extended as requirements change. OODB stores objects of any size, which expands the type of data that can be used. Each object is stored as a complete, self-contained entity that has distinct characteristics and behaviors. The basic functional capabilities of an object-oriented database include query capabilities, smooth recovery in case of system failure, secondary storage management for high performance, concurrency control, and persistence. This chapter covers the basis of an object-oriented database. The main features of commercially available Objectivity/DB are discussed.

Object-Oriented Database Concept

The object-oriented database concept centers on applications design environments. In traditional database systems, operations and data structures are table-oriented or hierarchical. This design has proved inadequate in many situations because it places great constraints on application developers who are working with complex data structures. This type of information is generally too difficult to logically map into two-or three-dimensional tables. Achieving and maintaining performance is difficult as the amount of data increases.

OODB management systems technology provides natural mapping. Complex problems that involve many different types of data, which are interrelated in many different ways, are easily modeled when the object-oriented approach is used. This expands the ability of application developers who develop complex applications that model real-world systems and relationships. OODB supports object-oriented software engineering goals and principles. Objects are really self-contained software elements that consist of programs and data. The instructions which give the location and access method of the device are included in the objects. The objects reduce the complexity of OODB management. These objects are written in symbolic languages and executed sequentially. OODB consists of object identity, persistence, concurrency, consistency and recovery, and a query language.

Object identity

Each object has an identity, an existence which is independent of an object's state. Using an object's identifier, you can reference the object without knowing its state. Object identity also allows an application to compare object equivalence in one of two ways: Either the two objects are equal (they have the same value), or they are identical (they *are* the same object).

Persistence

Persistence allows the data in a database to survive the termination of a process so that they can be used by another process later. Persistent objects do exist outside the scope of program execution and do retain all their object properties. For the existence of an object in a database, the object must be an instance of a persistent class. You can create a persistent class that defines it as a subclass of one of several system-defined persistent classes. These classes determine which properties of a user-defined persistent class can be inherited.

Secondary storage management

Secondary storage management facilities allow data to be stored and managed efficiently on secondary storage devices. This is usually supported through index management, allocation of disk storage, and swapping of data between main memory and disk.

Concurrency

Concurrency allows data to be shared simultaneously with multiple users. Support for concurrency allows a highly parallel, cooperative application development process.

Consistency and recovery

The database management system will survive hardware failure (both processor and disk) and software failures (system and application) through recovery. That is, after such failures, the database management system must be able to recover to a coherent and consistent state.

Query language

Query capabilities allow an application programmer or an end user access to specific information in the database; they should be efficient and application-independent. Possible query tools for a multiuser database management system include these:

- Programmatic tools which let application programmers define the data through a *data definition language* (DDL) and access data values through a *data manipulation language* (DML)
- Interactive graphical browsers and menu-driven systems

Characteristics of an Object-Oriented Database

The characteristics of an object-oriented database management system must support teams of people working at different locations with networked workstations from multiple vendors, who use a variety of applications. The major characteristics are as follows:

- Distributed model
- Performance
- Control of operations
- Handling of complex data and association
- Extensibility
- Support for design management
- Database development tools
- Standards

The distributed model provides full and transparent distribution of data and control. It provides the conversion of data that is required by the use of heterogeneous machine architectures. The goal is to provide consistently high performance across the full range of database operations, data distribution, and capacity which is anticipated by application developers. Control of operations allows for the appropriate granularity that is specified to each database operation. This control can be in terms of the amount of data or period of time. Operations that include such control include locking, versioning, recovery, deletion, and creation.

A good database provides complete freedom to define, create, delete, and modify data structures of any complexity. *Associations* are direct interobject links. Association assists in building classes, aggregates, and complex objects. Association can be uni- or bidirectional and can be one-to-one, one-to-many, or many-to-many. Since certain operations can propagate along associations, a set of associated objects can act as a single composite object. Because associations can cross the database, they can be used in the maintenance of dependencies, views, and relationships through the software development process. Association is a construct that logically links objects (class instances).

Extensibility provides mechanisms that can create new objects from existing ones. New objects can inherit the attributes and behaviors of existing objects. You must specify how the new object differs from the existing one, without a rewrite of everything. By establishing associations between objects, you create new composite objects that are logical combinations of existing objects. A good OODB provides the foundation-level functionality for the support of advanced design management systems. Database development tools facilitate the development of a good database. An OODB management system enables broad connectivity between tools and environments and, more importantly, broad interoperability of applications. It supports industry standards.

Objectivity/DB

Objectivity/DB is a commercially available OODB product, and it meets the features and performance requirements typical of many complex applications. It combines the object-oriented approach and the full database management system functionality that is required for real-world applications. Some features are concurrency, security, recovery, versioning, provision of optimal data modeling, performance, and runtime support. Its logical storage model is flexible and allows for concurrent control and access of multiple, physically distributed databases. Figure 4.1 shows various components of the system. These components are as follows:

- Application Software
- Database Tools
- Programming Language Interface
- Type Manager
- Object Manager
- Storage Manager

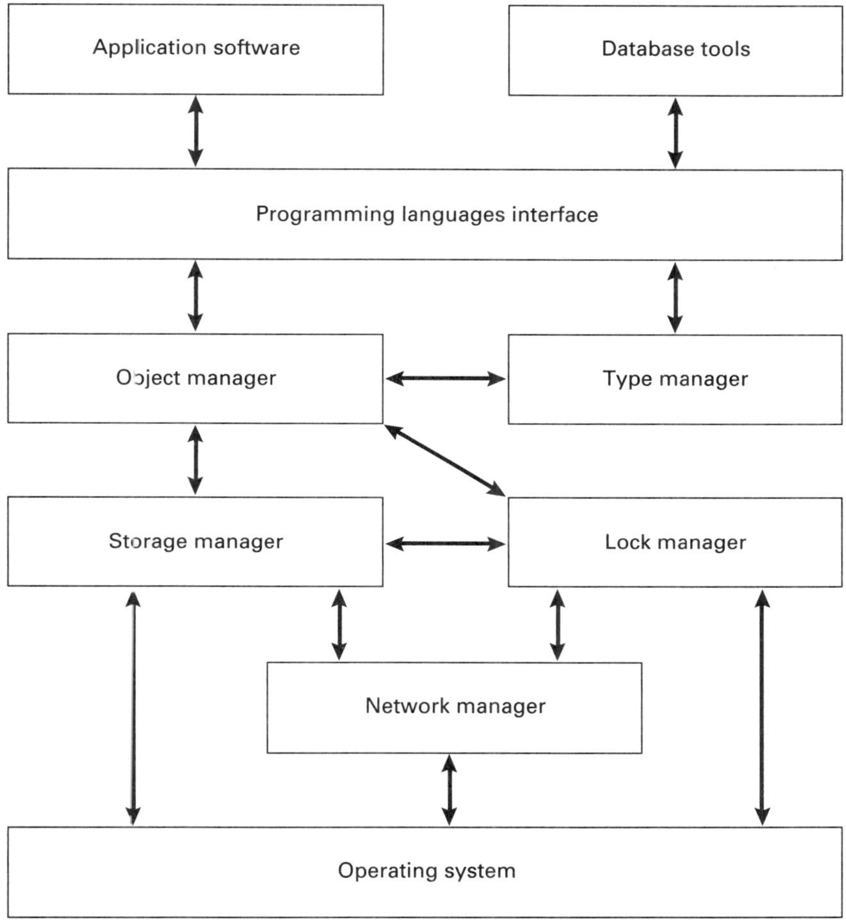

Figure 4.1   System components (*Courtesy of Objectivity/DB*).

- Lock Manager
- Network Manager
- Operating System

Application Software consists of applications that are written with the help of Objectivity/DB Programming Language Interface. Database Tools help program development and database maintenance. Programming Language Interface communicates with Objectivity/DB when applications are being developed. Type Manager stores, retrieves, and maintains descriptions of all classes that are defined in the database. Object Manager keeps track of and manipulates objects within the database. Tasks which are handled by Object Manager include propagation and versioning. Storage Manager is responsible for the physical placement of data in virtual memory and physical storage. Lock Manager oversees access to objects in the database, which manages concurrent access to data. Network Manager coordinates communications between processes which allows "local" processes access to data that are located on "remote" workstations. Your Operating System provides basic services for all other software in the system. Objectivity/DB makes extensive use of its services.

System highlights

Objectivity/DB provides flexible data modeling. It supports encapsulation and inheritance. It provides versioning of objects. It has a *data definition language* (DDL) which is compatible with C++. It has dynamic variable-sized arrays. It provides distributed architecture for fully distributed data storage, control, and processing. Its heterogeneous platform supports heterogeneous machines and operating systems. It has multiuser support—concurrency control, short and long transactions, two-phase commit, and atomic updates. It consists of database tools for graphical data and type browser, database debugger, lock monitor, dump/load utility, and database administrator utilities. It has high performance and capacity for balanced performance, physical clustering, large working sets, and 64-bit addressing. Objectivity/DB acts as an extension of your workstation's operating system, which provides data storage and management at the object level, so application programs can efficiently store and retrieve data as needed. You need not to be concerned with physical location of data; your users can access information that is stored anywhere on the network.

Objectivity/DB concept

Objectivity/DB concept uses four logical storage entities: basic objects, container objects, database objects, and federated database objects. The fundamental unit of storage is the *basic object.* Each basic object belongs to a single *container object,* each container object belongs to a single *database object,* and each database object belongs to a single *federated database object.* These relationships are shown in Fig. 4.2. This figure shows a typical Objectivity/DB system which consists of a federated database object that contains two user-defined database objects.

Basic objects are the fundamental storage entity. Each basic object belongs to a single container object. A container object holds zero or

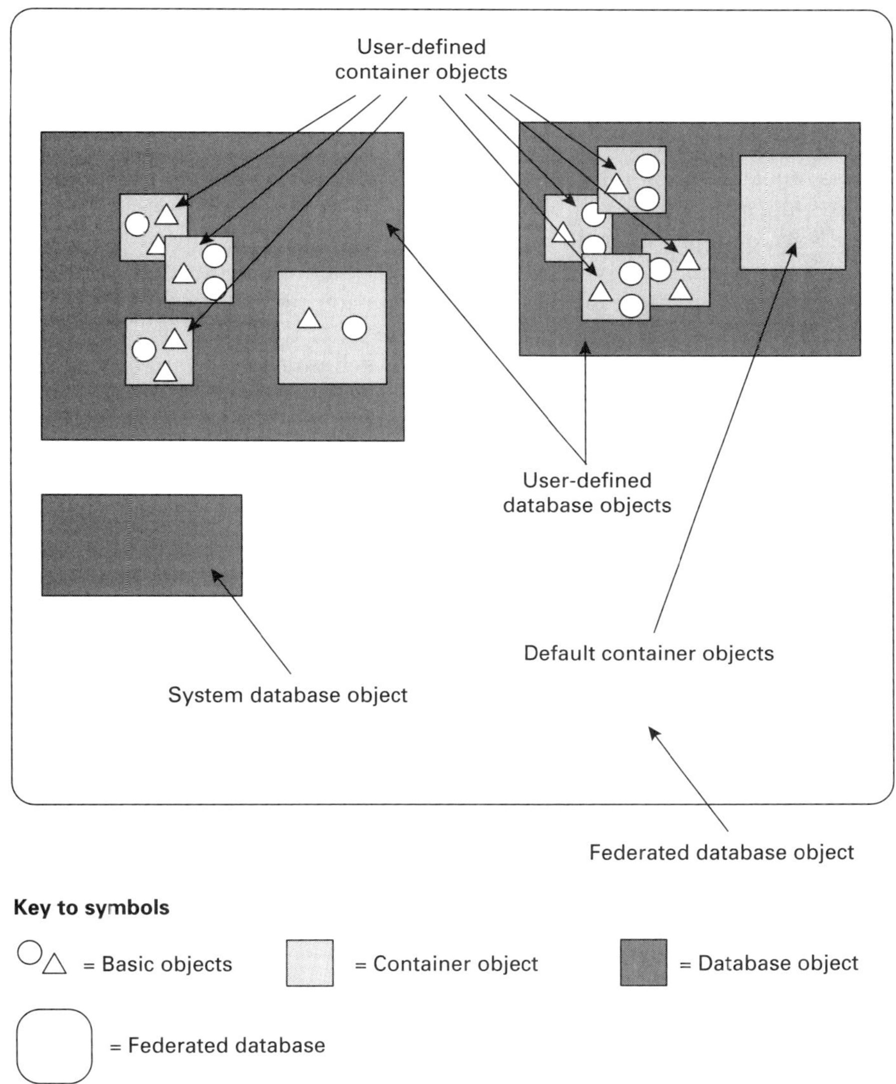

Figure 4.2   Logical storage model (*Courtesy of Objectivity*).

more basic objects and belongs to a single database object. Whenever possible, basic objects in a container object are physically clustered in memory (and on disk) so performance will improve. You can also choose specific basic objects within a container object that are clustered on the same physical page of memory.

A database object consists of a default container object and zero or more user-defined container objects. The default container object holds basic objects that you have not explicitly put into user-defined container objects. An application can simultaneously open and manipulate basic objects in multiple container objects and multiple database objects, which may be distributed on multiple network nodes.

A federated database object consists of a system database object and zero or more user-defined database objects. The system database object is automatically created when you create a federated database object. This system contains the information necessary for the maintenance and administration of the federated database objects. Each federated database object maintains a schema that controls all the publicly visible class definitions. Applications create objects of classes that are defined in this schema. All database objects in a federated database object share the same schema.

Accessing objects

Objectivity/DB applications use pointers which access temporary objects. So that persistent objects can be accessed, Objectivity/DB applications use handlers or pointers, as shown in Fig. 4.3. An *object handler* is a nonpersistent object that serves as an interface between applications and persistent objects. A handle object can reference only

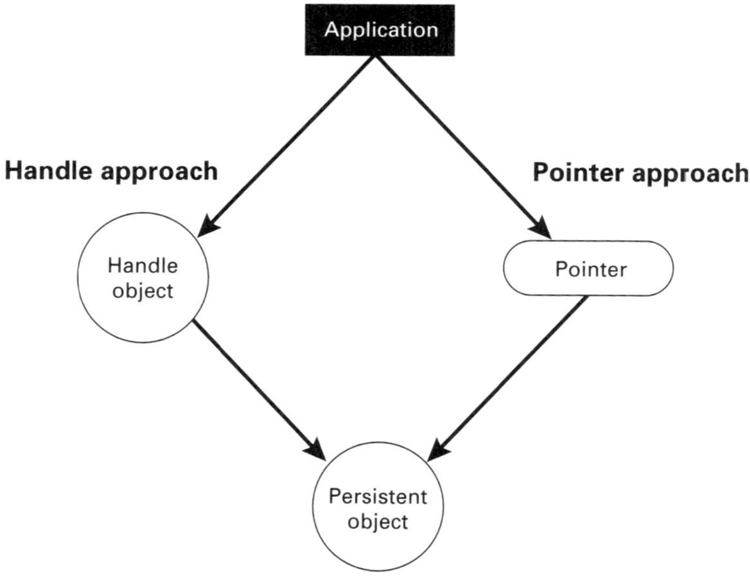

Figure 4.3   Accessing persistent objects (*Courtesy of Objectivity*).

one persistent object at a time. In the handle approach, only handles are used in the application. In the pointer approach, pointers are used in the application.

Physical file organization

For the most part, you need not concern yourself with how persistent objects map to physical files. However, certain persistent classes (federated database objects and database objects) have a direct relationship to physical files, and a general understanding of the subject may help during the testing and debugging process. The physical files that are used by Objectivity/DB are

- Bootstrap files
- Federated database file
- Database file
- Journal files
- Lock file

For every federated database object, there should be one and only one bootstrap file. This file contains the necessary information so that the federated database object can be opened, and includes the full path to the federated database file. The filename of the bootstrap file is specified by the system name for the federated database object. This file must be identical for all applications that use the same federated database object.

For every federated database object there is a federated database file. This file contains the system database, which stores necessary information for maintenance and administration of the federated database object, along with the schema.

The schema is a collection of type definition information that allows a database the allocation for storage and management of objects (that is, instances of classes). The DDL makes class information known to Objectivity/DB. The scope of the schema is the federated database object. That is, a single common schema is shared by all the database objects in a federated database object. Thus, a database may contain an object of any class that is defined in the schema of its containing federated database object.

For every database object, there is a database file. This file contains the database object and all the container and basic objects within the database object. When a database object is created, a path can be specified where the database file should be located. If a path is not specified, the file is placed in the same directory as the federated database file.

During a transaction, Objectivity/DB will create a journal file. The journal file keeps a log of the changes made during the transaction and allows Objectivity/DB restoration of the state of the federated database object if the transaction should be aborted or terminated. Journal files are automatically removed at the end of a transaction. Journal files appear in the same directory as the federated database file.

The lock server process maintains a file that keeps track of persistent locks that are issued to applications which is called a *lock file*. This file exists on the same network node that runs the lock server process.

Developing an application. The development of an application is a five-step process, as shown in Fig. 4.4.

1. Design database schema and create a corresponding schema file. Before the creation of an object, Objectivity/DB must know the object's class structure. The system uses this information for the proper allocation and management of the object that is being created. This user is provided with defined class information by the design of a schema (sometimes called a *data dictionary*) and the creation of a corresponding schema file by the use of the data definition language (DDL).

2. Process your schema file with use of the DDL processor and create an Objectivity/DB database schema, a schema header file, and a schema source code file. The DDL processor generates the appropriate schema information for Objectivity/DB and creates a federated database object, if one does not already exist. The processor also creates a schema header file, so the application program can access the user-defined classes. For C++ applications, the DDL processor also generates a C++ schema source code file that will be compiled with your C++ application program.

3. Write the source code for application in standard C++ or C and include the schema header file.

4. Compile source code file and schema source code file for C++ applications.

5. Link compiled code with the Objectivity/DB runtime library and the compiled schema code.

Association

Objectivity/DB supports binary associations (association between two objects). For associations between objects, an association link must be defined in each object's class. Associations are useful in many situations. For example, a bicycle manufacturer uses an Objectivity/DB-based MCAD system that designs two models of bicycles, the Cezano

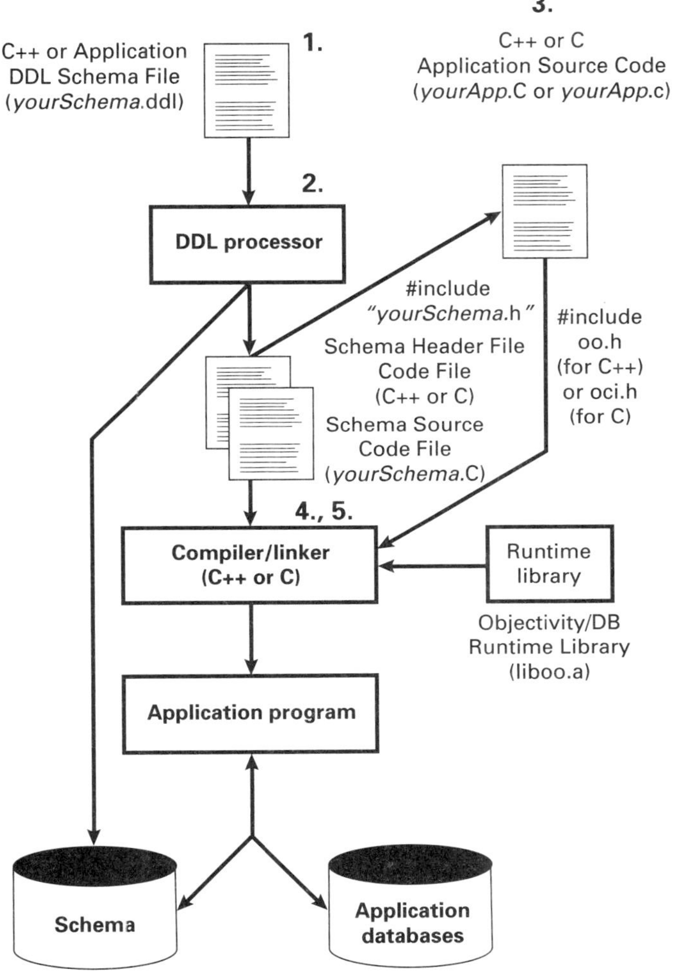

Figure 4.4 Application development flow (*Courtesy of Objectivity*).

and the Piazza, as shown in Fig. 4.5. Each model has the same functional components—a frame, a seat, wheels, and gears. The Piazza uses three gears, and the Cezano uses two gears. In this example, the two models have similar functional components, but the actual components for each model are different. The Piazza's frame is made of carbon fiber, while the less expensive Cezano is made of anodized aluminum. The other components have similar differences.

With the use of associations, the manufacturer associates specific bicycle components with a particular bicycle model. In this example, two bicycle objects (Cezano and Piazza) of class BIKE are associated

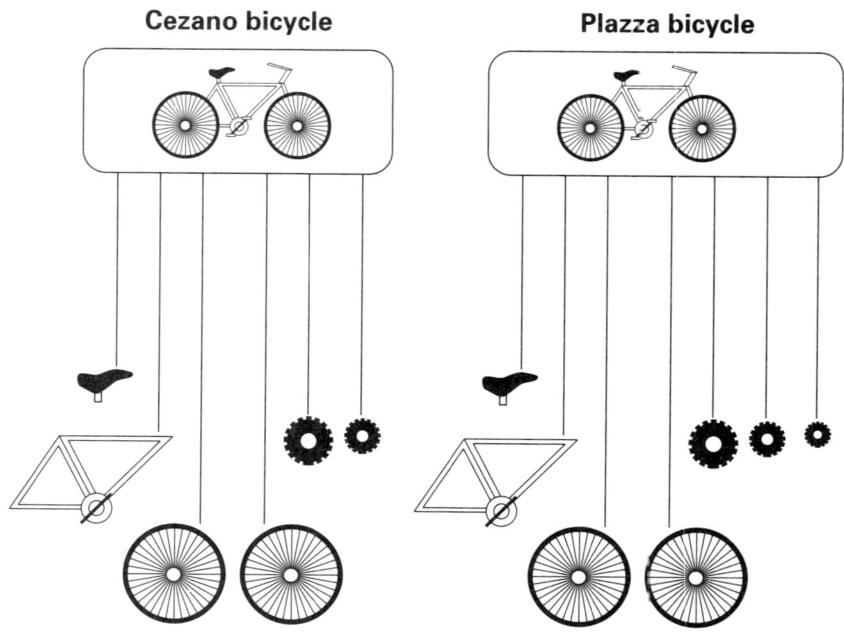

Key to symbols

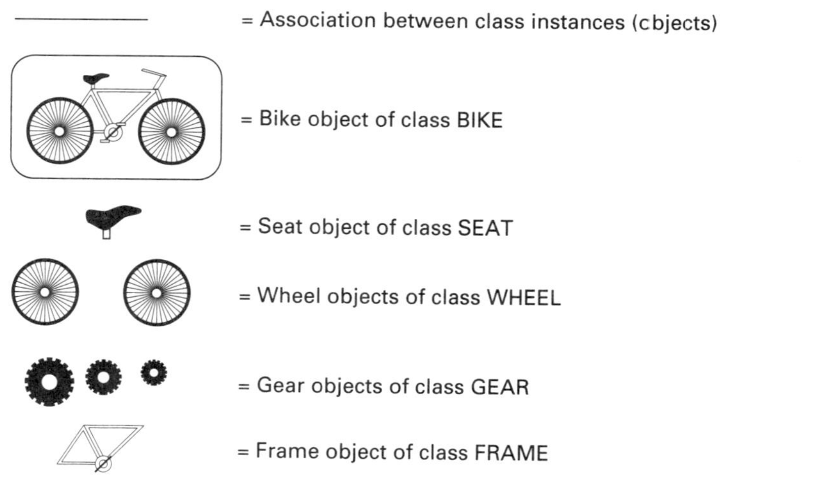

Figure 4.5   Association between class instances (objects) (*Courtesy of Objectivity*).

with objects of classes SEAT, FRAME, WHEEL, and GEAR. So that these associations can be created, we define association links between the five classes. As shown in Fig. 4.6, we need four association links for class BIKE:

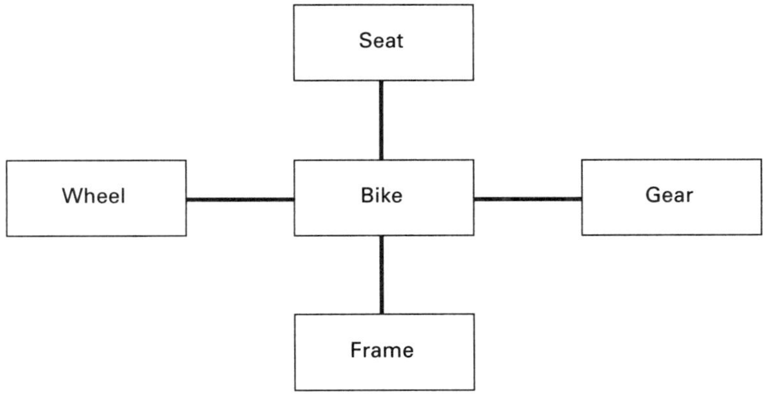

Key to symbols

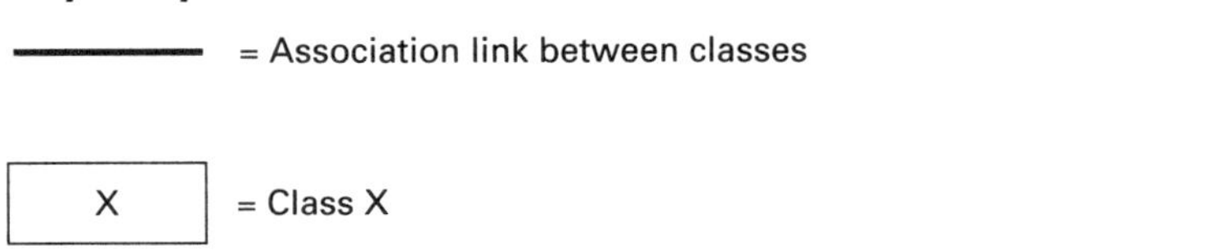

Figure 4.6   Association links between classes (*Courtesy of Objectivity*).

- BIKE-to-SEAT
- BIKE-to-WHEEL
- BIKE-to-GEAR
- BIKE-to-FRAME

Each association link is typed and specified a persistent class with which it is compatible. For example, if the only link defined in class BIKE was to class FRAME, we could not associate BIKE objects to any other objects except FRAME objects.

Concurrency and consistency

Objectivity/DB provides three mechanisms that support concurrency and consistency of the system: locking, transactions, and check-in and checkout.

Locking

Objectivity/DB is a multiprocessing system. It allows simultaneous multiple access to the data. For data consistency, database access is restricted through the use of locks. A process may obtain either a read lock, which allows other processes to read data, or an update lock, which prevents all other processes from reading or modifying the data.

For flexibility in controlling concurrent access to data, Objectivity/DB currently supports locking at the following levels of granularity:

1. Container object

2. Database object

3. Federated database object

Locks are granted automatically and transparently to an application. You can also explicitly set locks. For each federated database object, locks are managed by a lock server process, which is automatically started when Objectivity/DB is initialized. The lock server is a centralized process; there is one and only one lock server process that runs per federated database object on a workstation in your network. All other processes (applications) that access a federated database object must request a lock for the data from this process.

Transactions

When an application works on a database, any changes it makes are buffered by Objectivity/DB and are not actually made until they are specified by the application. Each buffered unit of work is a transaction. Transactions allow a collection of operations to appear as a single atomic operation to the database (that is, either all the operations are performed or none are). Once a transaction is committed (applied) to the database, the changes are permanent. However, an application can abort a transaction at any time up to the commit point. This leaves the database in its original state. Transactions help ensure that the database is always in a consistent (known) state.

Check-in and checkout

Objectivity/DB also provides a check-in/checkout mechanism. This allows a persistent object to be locked for an extended time, rather than for a single session. Checkout obtains a persistent lock on an object for a particular user. The lock may be for either a read or an update access and affects only processes that are owned by other users. Processes with the same user ID as the process that issued the checkout may obtain a regular lock on the object.

Check-in removes the persistent lock from the object and can only be issued by a process with the same user ID as the one issued by the original checkout. If the checkout was for update, then any changes become visible to other processes when the check-in occurs.

Objectivity/DB is the product of Objectivity, Inc. The system works on Sun workstations, DECstation or DECsystem, VAX/ULTRIX, and HP 9000 series 300.

Object-Oriented Database Management

An *object-oriented database management system* (OODBMS) manages OODB systems by storing, sorting, retrieving, modifying, adding, and deleting volumes of database records in a well-organized manner. A *structured query language* (SQL) database management system operates within a client/server architecture. This chapter also covers ObjectStore.

Object-Oriented Database Management System

Object-oriented database management system handles a large volume of data. OODBMS stores objects of any size, which expands the type of data that can be used. OODBMS reduces complexity, manages the objects, and retrieves the information quickly. Objects are self-contained software elements and contain data and operations which are performed on that data. The instructions for locations and access techniques are contained in the objects that reduce the complexity of managing hundreds of network components. OODBMS gives the client a transparent access to objects, regardless of location or storage format.

You can build an object layer on top of a traditional database manager that is used for storage of relational data. Relational network databases store structured data which have a fixed format such as text and numbers. In OODBMS there is no limit to text and numbers. Information can be retrieved quickly. Alternately, you can build an object database from scratch. Most of the OODBMS companies follow this approach. The advantage is that end users can do their own applications development. The application programs are sequential executions of objects. These objects are written in simple object-oriented languages and are easily understood by users.

Distributed Object Management

Distributed object management involves the management of server and client in different host environments. The server and client communicate via a local network when they are running on different hosts, and they operate system facilities such as shared memory and local sockets when they are running on the same host. All distribution supports full concurrency control. Distributed object management consists of server, client, and concurrency control in a client/server environment.

Server

Server is the computer that runs the server process in multiuser configurations. The server process manages physical data on disk and arbitrates among client processes which make requests for the data. The server process maintains locking tables; provides deadlock detection, checkpointing, buffer management, and license management; and handles logging. Servers provide access to data and protect the integrity of those data.

Recovery is based on a log, which uses a write-ahead log protocol. Transactions which involve more than one server are coordinated and use the two-phase commit protocol. The server also provides backup to long-term storage media such as tapes, which allow full backups as well as continuous archive logging. When there is contention for an object, the server overrides the default client behavior of encaching locks for future use and calls back the lock so that the competing transactions can proceed. The server environment includes a directory manager process that handles location transparency for clients who are accessing the database over the network, as shown in Fig. 5.1. Servers ensure that the data are available to all who are authorized so data can be used on demand.

Clients

Clients are the systems that run application processes which access the servers over the network. Client libraries provide the interface between the user's application and the database server. Client manages the logical view of the data and includes collections, queries, versions, transaction management, memory management, and relationships among objects. The majority of the query and OODBMS processing occurs on

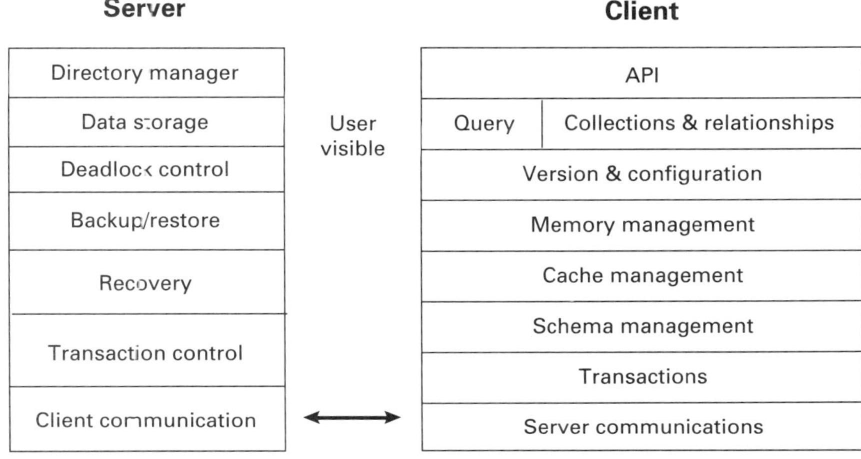

Figure 5.1 ObjectStore provides a powerful distributed client/server architecture for distributed object computing (*Courtesy of Objectivity*).

the client side of the network. When each client does its own work, the aggregate computing power of the network is used, and the server process can be on the same machine as the client processes. This permits great flexibility in configuration. Any potential client machine is also a potential server.

Concurrency control in a client/server environment

This is the prevention control for one set of updates that interferes with another while there is concurrent access by multiple clients. Simultaneous access to objects can be handled either by traditional conventional transactions or by long transactions. A *transaction* is a unit of work that is handled by the application and determined by the user. The act of reading or writing to the database must be within a transaction. The concurrency control scheme that is employed for conventional transactions is based on a serializable transaction management approach. A conventional transaction may be an update or a read only, and either type of transaction can be nested within another transaction of the same type.

The locking model ensures integrity by automatically managing a transaction's write set. Any object that has been updated by a transaction will be written out to a stable storage when the transaction commits. More primitive approaches require that the user program explicitly mark the objects that have changed by the calling of a subroutine for each such object. Neglecting to call this subroutine results in loss of data, because the changes will not be flushed to the disk. Locking information is cached on both the client and server and minimizes the need for network communication when the same process performs consecutive transactions on the same data. A copy of an object in a client cache is marked as either *shared* or *exclusive* mode. The server keeps track of which objects are in the caches of which clients and with which modes. When a client requests an object from the server and the server notices that the object is in the cache of some other client, the server will check whether the modes conflict. If they do, the server sends a message to the client who holds the lock and asks that the object be removed from its cache. This is called a *callback* message, since it goes in the opposite direction from the usual request.

The server checks whether the lock is currently in use when the client who holds the lock receives the callback. If it is not, it relinquishes the object immediately and removes the copy of the object from its cache. If the object is locked, the client replies negatively to the server and the server forces the requesting client to wait until the holder is finished with the transaction. When the holding client commits or aborts, it removes the copy of the object from its cache; then the server can allow the original client to proceed.

In Fig. 5.2, objects are locked for read and write on client demand. Features such as lock probe and timeout are available. The developer can manage the application if these features minimize the probability of conflict. Then the client who requests the lock has the option of setting a timeout on the lock request or can explicitly probe for lock availability. At the end of the transaction, objects are unlocked and modified objects are written to the server log. During this time another client cannot write to a locked object until the lock is released. For example, if client 1 has an object that is required by client 2's transaction, the server sends a callback notice to client 1 who has use of the shared object. Client 2 will receive the object as soon as client 1's transaction is terminated.

On a rare occasion, the system may abort a transaction because of a network failure or because the system has determined that the transaction is involved in a deadlock. By default, the transaction is restarted at the first statement that follows the start of the transaction. The transaction will continually be retried until either the transaction is successful or the maximum number of tries has occurred. A long transaction is a concept rather than a distinct mechanism. A long transaction describes the effect of version use and configurations for the development of applications that allow collaborative concurrency control.

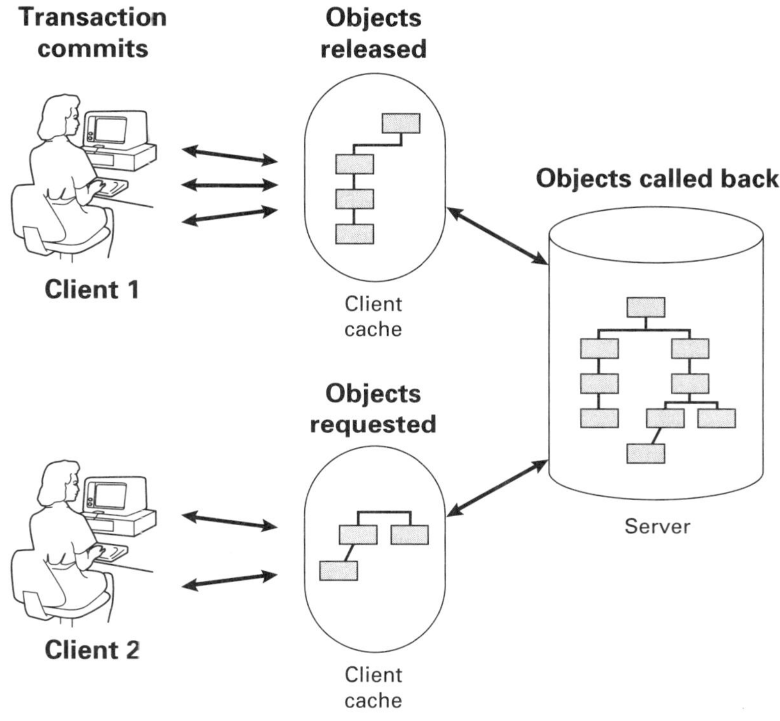

Figure 5.2   Data integrity is guaranteed in distributed environments (*Courtesy of Objectivity*).

Selection Criteria of a Good OODBMS

The selection criteria of a good OODBMS depends upon application requirements, budget, and vendor support. The following factors enhance the selection criteria:

- Performance
- Ease of use
- Migration
- Data modeling capabilities

Performance

Performance of an OODBMS depends upon the way in which it handles the manipulation of complex data models. Manipulation of stored data should be as fast as possible and within the allocated budget and time. The OODBMS operation requires minimum overhead cost per operation. Overhead is related to pointer dereferencing (object traversal), locking, network access, and disk access.

High-performance data manipulation requires that if a pointer or reference to an object is given, then the operation of obtaining data from that object must not incur any undue overhead. This operation is called *dereferencing* a pointer. Objects can be locked on a segment of the database, a page, or in a single configuration that is defined by the user. Only a single lock action is needed for an entire page, segment, or configuration of objects, which provides significant performance gains over other locking mechanisms.

Data caching occurs when a sequence of transactions accesses the same objects. Then there is a high probability that the data which are accessed in the next transaction will already be cached in workstation memory. Since network accesses are expensive operations, the reduction of the number of data transfers is critical to the success of distributed OODBMS. Batching objects that will be transmitted between client and server are typically only one network request and are used when a group of referenced objects is sent into the client cache, as shown in Fig. 5.3. This strategy minimizes network traffic and allows the client to proceed through a transaction without contacting the server until a transaction is committed.

Often an application uses only a portion of a database, and that portion can be stored contiguously in a small section of the database. Related objects can be clustered together in a database. This cluster-

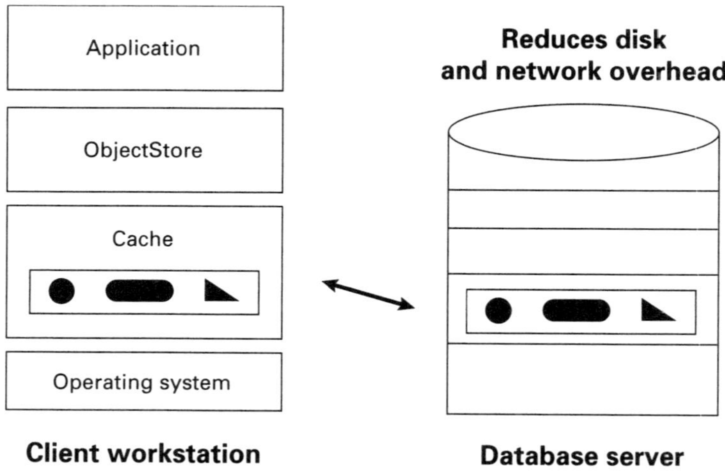

Figure 5.3 When a client requests a group of objects, clustering and data caching minimize disk and network overhead (*Courtesy of Objectivity*).

ing increases performance, since disk access time for contiguous data is faster than random access. The disks can typically read or write many sequential blocks in the same time as the disk head can move to a random location.

Ease of use

Ease of use is reflected in the integration between the database system and the host programming language. There is no inheritance from a special "persistent object" base class. Different objects of the same type may be persistent or transient within the same program. This concept dramatically improves both developer productivity and code reuse. Ease of use further leads to ease of learning. In object-oriented languages, the types, variables, and classes should be declared in the same way; similarly, objects manipulate, access, and set variables, and call functions should all be managed in the same manner.

No translating code is recommended in the ease of use. The programmer should not write code that translates between the disk resident representation of data and the in-memory representation that is used during execution. This is referenced as single-level storage, as shown in Fig. 5.4. In contrast, developers who use the file system storage model must create a linear on-disk representation for their objects and write code that will map its in-memory representation.

Migration

Migration is a convenient means of converting application and customer data to existing code, data stored file, and libraries. Many programmers who are interested in the use of an OODBMS should add persistence to existing applications that deal with transient objects, in addition to new applications that can be built from scratch. This is possible because basic data operations such as dereferencing pointers

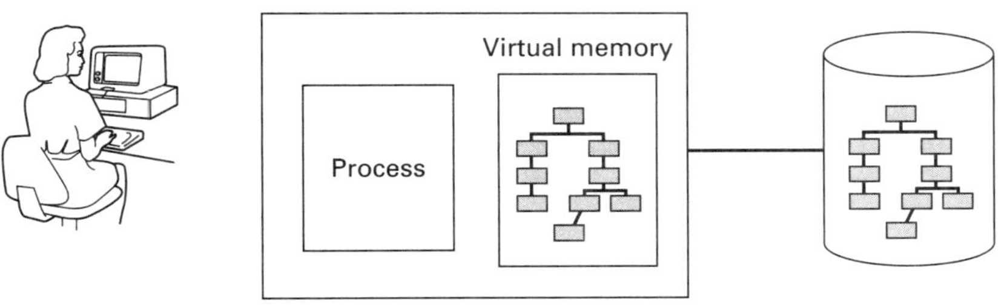

Figure 5.4 ObjectStore's single-level storage provides the programmer with a single view of memory (*Courtesy of Objectivity*).

and getting and setting data members are semantically the same for persistent and transient objects. Variables do not need their type declarations changed when persistent objects are used.

Data modeling capabilities

This means that the OODBMS data model is designed so developers can use the full power of the language for application development. With C++ and Ada, this means full support for the complete language and includes virtual functions, inheritance, polymorphism, encapsulation, and parameterized types. Additional data modeling features include

1. Collections

2. Queries on collections

3. Relationships between objects

4. Versioning of objects

1. Collections are objects that group together other objects. Collections are abstract structures that resemble arrays in programming language or tables in a relational database. Like C++ arrays, collections store many instances of the same type or a derived type. Users may optionally describe intended use by estimating frequencies of various operations (for example, iteration, insertion, and removal), and the collection library will automatically select an appropriate representation. Furthermore, a policy can be associated with the collection and can dictate how the representation should change in response to changes in the collection's cardinality. These performance-tuning facilities simplify the developer's interaction from the coding of data structures to the description of access patterns.

The collection classes for inserting, removing, and retrieving elements of a given collection also provide methods which perform set-theoretic operations such as union and intersection and set-theoretic comparisons such as subset. Often objects have *embedded collections*. For example, a person object might contain a set of children. Collections also store all objects or a subset of all objects of the same type (for example, all employees or managers). Such collections can be arbitrarily large. Access patterns differ greatly among applications and even over time within a single application. A single representation type will probably not provide adequate performance for all such access patterns of support for multiple representations of collections.

2. Queries on collections provide functionality similar to querying a relational database, in that the programmer may not necessarily know how a particular object is found by following pointers. Instead,

the programmer provides a query expression that selects the target object that is based on the values which are contained in it or on the relationships between it and other objects. Many query languages lack the support of multiattribute, multiple-condition, class extents and distributed query functionality.

The best approach treats queries as ordinary expressions in C++ or C. A good OODBMS should provide indexes that permit more efficient implementations. A query optimizer examines a variety of strategies and chooses the least expensive way to execute a query. The OODBMS can index paths through objects and collections and not just fields directly contained in objects. In complex applications where speed is crucial, pointers and embedded collections obviate the need for joins. Therefore a typical query will likely be over a small number of top-level collections. Selection predicates involve paths through objects and embedded collections. These paths express the same sorts of connections which join terms that are expressed in relational queries. Join optimization is of less concern since the path has materialized in the database with interobject references and embedded collections.

3. Relationships between objects are useful when complex objects are modeled such as designs, parts hierarchies, documents, and multimedia information. Each relationship is composed of two or more objects that are constrained and consistent with one another in a particular fashion. The constraints on the data members that compose the relationship are declared by the user. Figure 5.5 shows that the wheel is an object of the class *part*. A relationship exists between the wheel (the parent part) and the components (the child part) that make up the wheel.

4. Versioning objects of OODBMS store and manipulate multiple versions of an object simultaneously. This is useful for modeling many activities, such as writing a document or developing a design, where iterative processes require experimentation with various modifications. A user can check the version of an object or group of objects, make changes, and then check the changes back into the main branch of project development. In the interim, other users continually use previous versions, and therefore are not impeded by concurrency conflicts on their shared data, regardless of the duration of the editing sessions involved.

Its capability includes configurations, workspaces, and version history graphs. Configurations provide a means of grouping related objects that should evolve together. An object which is composed of several objects, such as a document, may constitute a unit for versioning purposes. Configuration provides the user with specified granularity of both evolution and concurrency control. Since versioning is

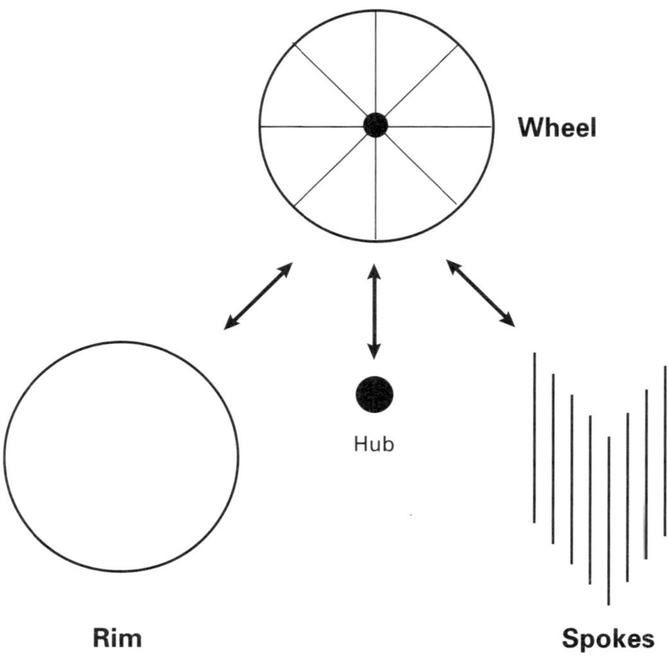

Figure 5.5 ObjectStore can be used to manage the complex relationships typical of design and applications (*Courtesy of Objectivity*).

logical multiple representations of the same thing, a mechanism must allow a process to look at a distinct version.

Workspaces provide a private work area so one or more processes can view a configuration. For each application area, the system designer must determine what types of workspaces must be created. Users can then employ workspaces that selectively share their work in progress. Workspaces can inherit from other workspaces. A designer could specify that a workspace by default inherit "whatever is in the team's shared workspace." Individual new versions can be added as changes are made by overriding this default.

Versioning history graphs provide a model which allows the designer and developers visualization of the evolution of versions. These graphs keep track of the different versions as the entity or entities evolve. The versioning of an object is independent of type, just as the persistence of an object is independent of type. This means that instances of any type may be versioned, and that versioned and non-versioned instances can be operated on by the same user code. Thus you can easily take an existing piece of code that has no notion of versioning and use it on versioned data.

ObjectStore OODBMS

ObjectStore is a commercially available object-oriented database management system that provides a tightly integrated language interface to the traditional database management features of persistent storage, transaction management (concurrency control and recovery), distributed data access, and associative queries. ObjectStore is designed so that it provides a unified programmatic interface to both persistently allocated data and transiently allocated data, with object access speed for persistent data which is usually equal to that of an in-memory dereference of a pointer to transient data.

ObjectStore architecture

The ObjectStore's distributed database architecture makes a transparent access to objects possible for the client regardless of location or storage format. The architecture supports environments in which client and server processes can run on different types of computers and networks. This is called a *heterogeneous operation.* In the client/server environment, it has several implications for the architecture of any software product. The product must be portable, accommodate a variety of networking environments, work with major compilers and software development environments, and allow interaction among systems. An ObjectStore server can support a client of any type regardless of the machine's data format, byte ordering, floating-point representation, or data alignment. It supports heterogeneous operations across major hardware platforms:

- Any client can run with servers of any type (that is, SPARC, Intel, MIPS, RS/6000, HP/PA, Motorola).

- All major networks are supported (that is, TCP/IP, Novell, Banyan VINES, LAN Manager).

- Most of all installed C++ development environments are supported (that is, Sun, Borland, HP, CenterLine, ParcPlace, Lucid).

A Sun server can support Sun, Hewlett-Packard, IBM, and Windows clients simultaneously. ObjectStore applications can be deployed in a wide variety of environments, including

- User interface—Open Look, Motif, Windows

- Networks—TCP/IP, NetBIOS, SPX/IPX

- Operating systems—SunOS, Solaris, AIX,HP-UX, ULTRIX, System V.4, Windows 3.1 (DOS), Netware

- CPUs—SPARC, RS/6000, MIPS, HP-PA, Intel

At the core of the ObjectStore architecture are several revolutionary features so it can be an enabling technology for many applications. These include virtual memory mapping, client caching, database size, relocation, and object-level clustering.

Reusability and Portability Strategy

Reusability means finding ways that existing software can be reused in new software development. Software standards like MIL-STD-498 clearly emphasize reusability. The object-oriented approach provides convenient ways that pretested software can be reused. Software reusability results in increases of object-oriented software engineering goals and principles and reduces cost and schedule of new software development during the maintenance life cycle. This chapter covers software reusability, domain analysis, selection criteria of suitable reuse software, and portability strategy.

The primary objective of the portability strategy is the reduction of difficulty in identifying and changing the parts of the software program that are necessary for acceptance on the target computer. When sound object-oriented software-engineering practices are followed during the design and coding phases, a software results that is easier for porting and reuse.

Software Reusability

Software reusability is a process whereby new software systems are implemented from preexisting software. This is illustrated in Fig. 6.1. The reusable process captures commonalities and differences from the models of systems. It consists of development and acquisition of reusable resources, management, and use of those resources. Reusability can be applied at any scale and any level of abstraction. Software reusability is identified during domain analysis, requirements analysis, design, implementation, and testing phases. Reusability enhances object-oriented software-engineering goals and principles and software reliability. Software reliability is enhanced by

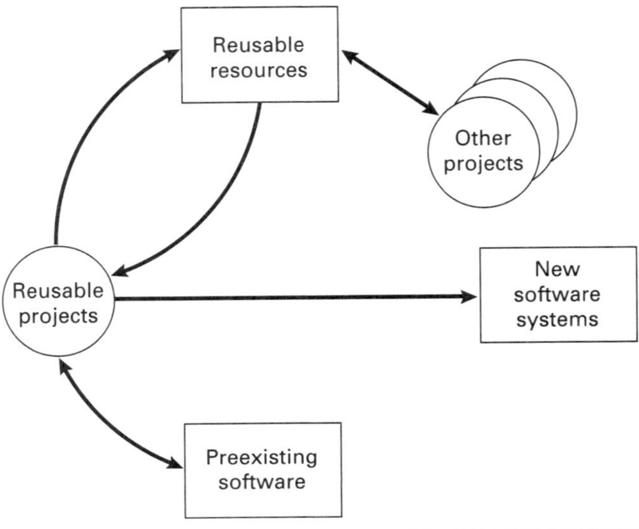

Figure 6.1   Reusability process.

the reuse of software which is seasoned and pretested. New software development schedules are reduced by not rewriting the reusable code and detailed components design. The size and performance requirements of reused components are also known. This includes processor time and memory. Software readability is improved if shared components are well designed. These are examples of reuse:

- Requirements analysis models and documents
- Classes
- Inheritance
- Reuse objects
- Design models and documents
- Code components
- Structure charts
- Test cases
- Test scenarios
- Modules
- Functions

There are always limitations to the reuse of existing software. This depends on customer requirements, which may prevent the reuse of existing software. These limitations occur because the software design is not clear enough or it does not provide any guidelines for software reuse. Or this can occur when software reuse documentation is not clear enough for effective reuse in a particular software. It is then more economical for a new software to be written than to reuse an existing one.

Software Reusability Process

Software reusability process steps are to construct, collect, catalog, classify, comprehend, and customize. Construct means the reuse of existing methods and products. Collect is the reuse of the existing library and continues building it. Catalog is the reuse of descriptive information. Classify is the reuse of semantic and functional information. Comprehend means the reuse of resources identification and analysis. Customize is the development of applications from reusable resources.

Software Reusability Process Activities

Software reusability process activities are listed in Fig. 6.2. The components of the process model are adaptive, parameterized, and engineered. The adaptive model for reuse is the process of modifying a system or component so that it will perform its function in a different manner or on different data from what was originally intended. In an adaptive model, to *construct* in this context means that modular software is built while software-engineering techniques are applied such as information hiding and data encapsulation. Here, *collect* means that the database is organized of projects and project software. In this case, the *catalog* is the description of projects and software modules. In this model, classifying uses architecture models and applies reverse engineering. *Comprehend* means the maintenance of bench-

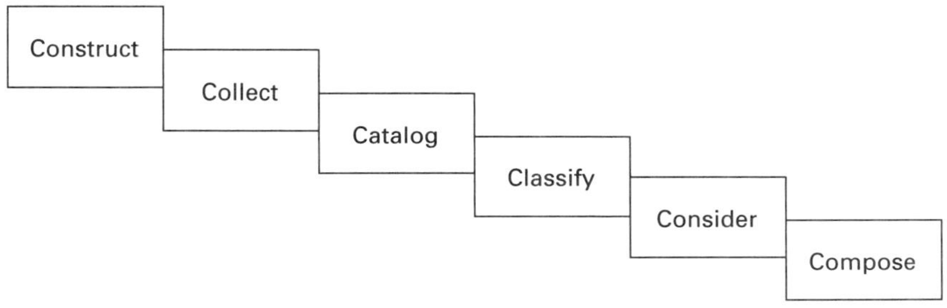

Figure 6.2   Major activities in reusable process.

marks and other performance information that includes test data. *Customizing* means the use of CASE tools and reengineering support for maintenance.

Constructing in the parameterized process model for software reuse means building software as standard products and continually refining them, just as in a software factory. Here collecting means establishing inventory for the software factory. In this case, cataloging gives descriptive information about standard products. Classifying is semantic and functional and tailors information to products. In this model, comprehending has rapid prototyping capability; customizing is automated customization and system generation. The engineered process for software reuse is shown in Fig. 6.3.

Basically, three activities occur in the reuse process, as shown in Fig. 6.4: domain engineering, applications engineering, and reusable assets. Domain engineering identifies and develops reusable assets within a domain, for example, requirements, design, and coding. Applications engineering then uses the assets from domain engineering when new applications are developed within the domain. Applications engineering also identifies assets for reuse after they have been used and modified for new applications. Those are then transferred into the domain engineering mode. Domain engineering can be categorized as engineering for reuse, because it represents the supply side of reuse, whereas application engineering is the demand side. These two processes are linked by the reusable asset management process that serves as the middleman (or supplier) of reuse. This includes one or more of the repositories, the tools, and the procedures required so reusable assets can be managed.

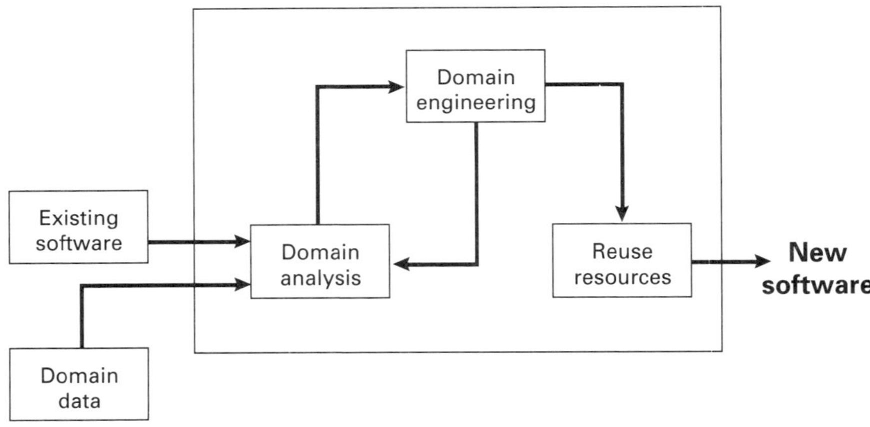

Figure 6.3   Software reuse engineering process.

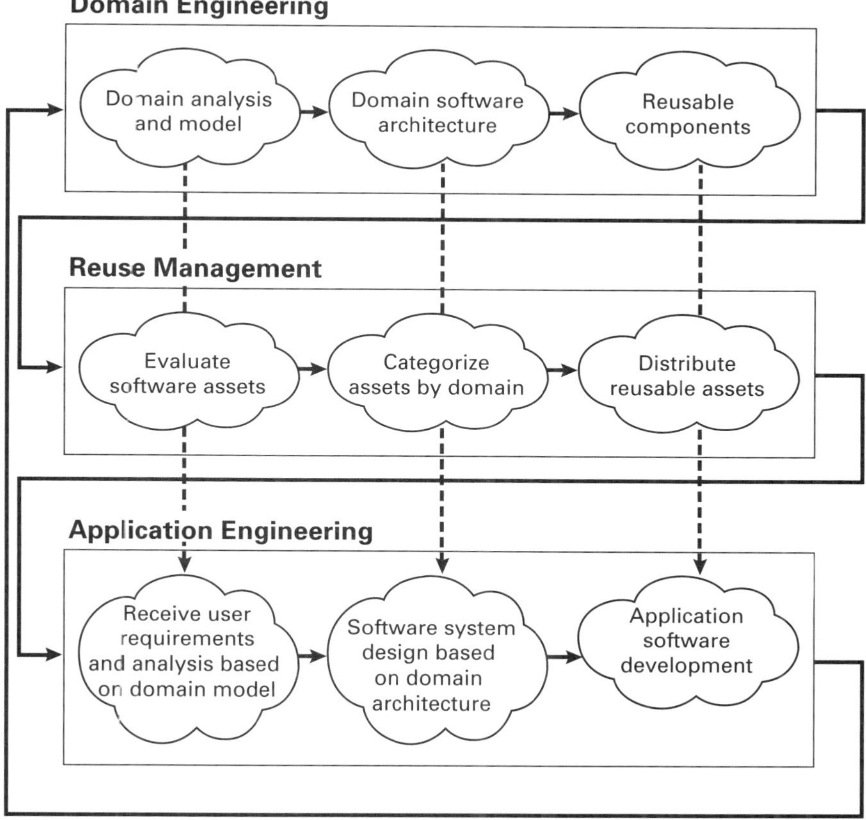

Figure 6.4 Software reuse activities.

Domain Analysis for Reusability

Domain analysis for reusability is the systematic exploration of related software systems that discover and exploit commonality. Domain analysis produces a set of features that are common to a class of systems and represents them in an exploitable form. It also provides a method that maps commonality to specific instances. The objectives help develop domain analysis products and support implementation of new applications by an understanding of domain, supporting user-developer communication, and providing reuse requirements, as illustrated in Fig. 6.5. The domain analysis consists of these components:

- Context modeling
- Domain modeling
- Architecture modeling

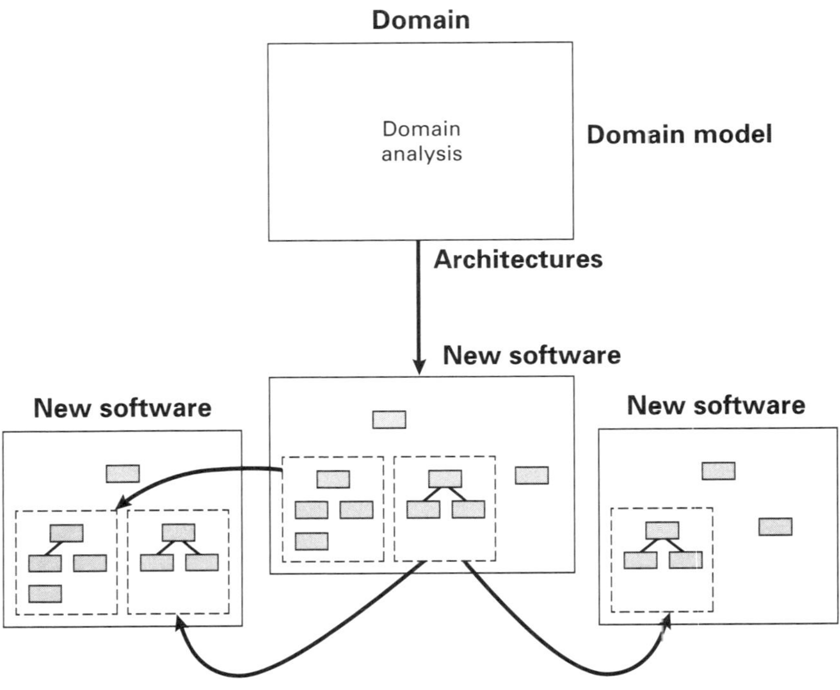

Figure 6.5 Domain analysis products.

The methods which are used in the domain analysis are reused in the software development process. The domain analysis products can be further used in software implementation. Figure 6.6 shows the major features of the domain analysis methods process.

Context modeling

Context modeling is domain scoping and analyzing the variables of external conditions. Context analysis consists of structure diagramming and context diagramming. The context model is a structure diagram that shows how the domain is placed in relation to other domains. It is a top-level data flow diagram that shows external entities and data flows between the domain and the external entities. A sample context diagram is shown in Fig. 6.7. The context diagram provides an end-user's perspective of the capabilities.

Domain modeling

Domain modeling is the analysis and modeling of domain problems. Domain modeling consists of an entity relationship model, feature

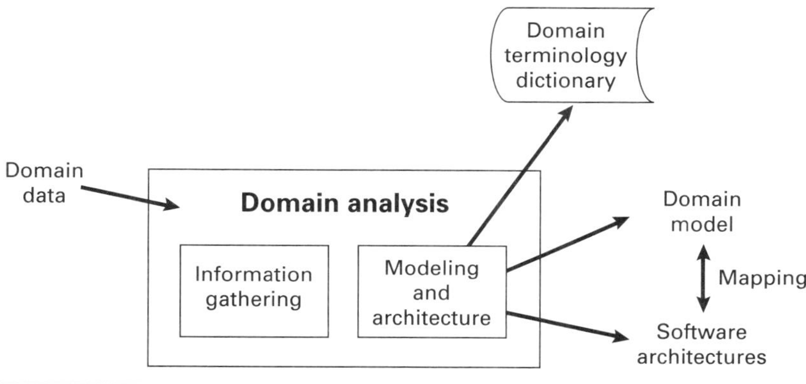

Figure 6.6 Domain analysis methods.

model, functional model, and domain terminology dictionary. The entity relationship (ER) model is the combination of Chen's entity relationship model notation and the semantic data models. The semantic data model consists of "is-a" and "consists-of" notations. A sample ER model is shown in Fig. 6.8.

The feature model provides an end user's perspective on the capabilities of applications in a domain. These capabilities are mandatory, optional, and alternative. The capabilities of an application are defined as an instantiation of the feature model. This model is for the use of parameterizing other models. The major components of the feature model are a features diagram, composition rules, issues and decisions, and records of existing system features.

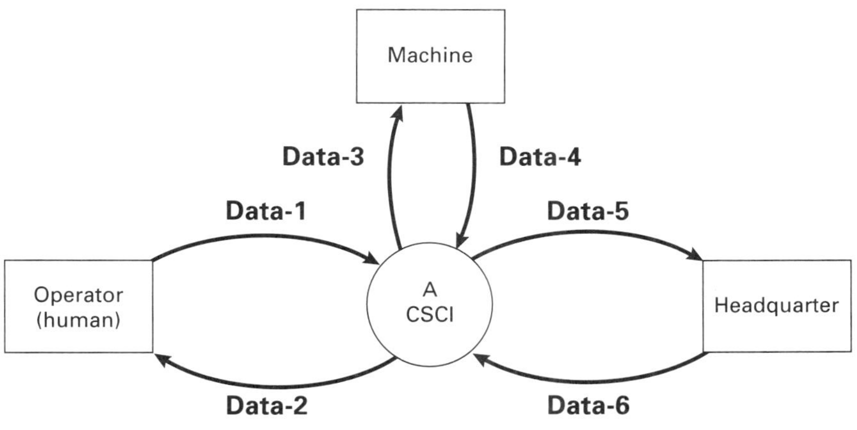

Figure 6.7 A sample context diagram.

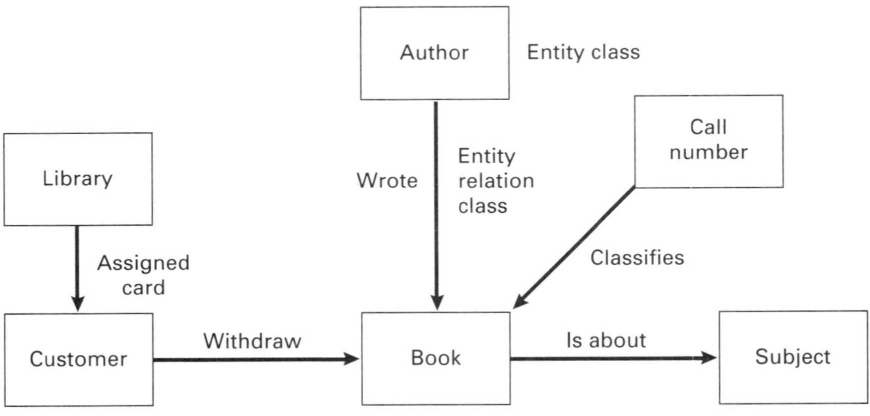

Figure 6.8   ER model.

Data flow models show the logical flow of data among the processors and data stores. The data flow model describes the internal interfaces among the components of the software system. It consists of rectangles which are the source or destination of data outside the system. A data flow symbol (arrow) represents a path where data moves into, around, and out of the system. A process symbol (circle) represents a function of the system which logically transforms data. A data store is a symbol (open-ended rectangle) which shows a place in the system where data is stored.

The domain terminology dictionary standardizes baseline terminology. It provides the result from information gathering in all phases. The domain terminology dictionary is essential in an evolving domain.

Architecture modeling

Architecture modeling is the analysis and modeling of application architectures for domain problems. Architecture modeling is a process that involves an interaction model and a module structure chart.

Selection Criteria of a Suitable Reusable Software

Selection criteria of a suitable reusable software begins in the early stages of software development during the domain analysis, software requirements analysis, and design phases. Significant savings can be realized if the products of these phases can be reused. Software reuse is considered to have great potential as a source of productivity that can be gained in software development. Object-oriented analysis and design make the reuse of isolated architectural elements more practical in the long run. Many commercial off-the-shelf (COTS) packages are available for such purposes. Table 6.1 lists some of the selection criteria of a suitable reusable software.

At the lowest granularity level, a typical subroutine library of mathematical functions or subroutines code is available for reuse. The choice of granularity involves a tradeoff. A large granule of code can yield a very high productivity gain when it is reused, but a close fit is generally not easily found between a user's requirements and a large aggregation of code. However, a library of many small granules generally provides chunks of code that match a user's requirements, but the productivity gain is smaller and the problem of indexing and search is greater. Mathematical subroutines have been used for a long time, and they yield benefits despite their general fine granularity because they are relatively easy to comprehend, standardize, and index.

Object-oriented languages center on the creation of abstract data types. Ada is often described as a software language that is particularly suited to, and will take advantage of, code reuse. Ada has features, generics, and packages that make it easier to design code for reuse. One of the design goals of Ada is to facilitate the creation and exploitation of reusable parts in recognition of the potential productivity improvements that reuse can bring.

Packages, visibility control, and separate compilation support modularity and information hiding allow the separation of specific application parts of the code, which maximizes the general-purpose parts that are suitable for reuse and enables the isolation of design decisions within modules that facilitates change. The Ada type system supports localization of data definitions so that consistent changes can be made easily. Generic units directly support the development of a general-purpose adaptable code and can be instantiated so that spe-

TABLE 6.1   Selection Criteria of a Suitable Reusable Software

Reusable software should belong to a reputable repository library.
Reusable software should be of the highest possible quality.
Reusable software should be correct, reliable, and robust.
Reusable software should be easily portable.
Reusable software should be clear enough that it is easily understood.
Reusable software should be well documented.
Reusable software should be adaptable.
Reusable software should be easily modifiable and should fit the requirements of
    current applications.
Reusable software should be easily maintainable.
Reusable software should conform to well-established design principles such as
    information hiding.

cific functions can be performed. The careful use of these features will produce code that is more likely to be reused. Some of the common examples of reuse are classes, functions, and modules.

Establishing a Reusable Repository

Establishing a reusable repository is the right approach in an organization. The repository consists of workable and defect-free software components that meet the organization's software reuse needs. Believe it or not, every possible line of code that could be written, has been written in a language. Only a software engineer with experience and knowledge can find whether that code is in existence. Many organizations have established centralized reusable software repositories. The repository evaluates, accepts, maintains, and makes reusable assets available for use and reuse on any specific software project. As the primary support tool for software reuse, the repository supplies reusable software assets. These are similar to a retail outlet store, thus it is a software reuse facilitator. The items for consumption can be based on vertical domains, horizontal domains, the types of components it contains, and the software language used. At present, there are a few well-established software reuse repositories:

- Asset Source for Software Engineering Technology (ASSET)
- The Booch components
- Central Archive for Reusable Defense Software (CARDS)
- The RAPID library of reuse Ada code
- Portable Reusable Integrated Software Modules (PRISM)
- The Grace Components
- Defense Software Repository System (DSRS)

A repository library assists in the work by the reuse of existing pretested software, so that it does not have to be reinvented. It is important that this repository be structured so as to be useful and easily accessible. Table 6.2 lists some of the guidelines for the software reuse repository. It is expensive to establish an effective software reuse repository.

The challenge of reusability will provide software engineers with the capability of finding what they want, when they want it. Time and cost are of the greatest essence. There should be information available in catalog form that will look for such information. It should be easily found and accessible. Key words and phrases should be used so the user can identify a group of software components that may

TABLE 6.2   Software Reuse Repository Guidelines

Establish a separate repository for each computer language.
Include only needed and reusable software components.
Software components should be small with less than 100 lines of code.
Software components should be robust and standardized.
The repository should be properly cataloged.
Selection criteria should be properly structured so that the components are easily
  accessible.
Software components should be indexed.
Software components should contain minimum comments in the code for explanation.
  (Detailed explanation should be included in the design documents.)
Identifier for the software components should be self-explanatory.
Easy-to-use electronic search capability for the reuse components should be available
  and included in the repository.

---

meet the need. Many repositories include various kinds of software components. It is equally important that necessary training be provided to software engineers who look for such information.

It is the design effort that builds a reuse software. The reuse repository should be properly built, and it is a software engineering effort that will keep on building such a repository. The custodian of the repository should be an expert and should provide proper index, catalog, and update the repository with the latest versions of the software components. The data included with such reuse software components should contain the date of creation, author, any proprietorship information, comments, date of test, and reference to tested data with any modification. This information is needed before this component can be reused. Selection of components that can be reused readily is not an easy job.

Software engineers should be trained in the reuse capability. Necessary training should be provided so the best use of the software reuse repository can be made. Management should establish goals and the use of reuse repository. Those who do reuse the software should be rewarded. It is a management commitment that all should be involved in the reuse software repository.

Portability Strategy

Portability means that a code written anywhere is potentially reusable and is not just written for a specific system. The primary objective of the portability strategy is to reduce the difficulty of identifying and changing the parts of the software program necessary for acceptable program behavior. By design, an object-oriented code is well suited for the integration of system components from multiple sources. The strategy of portability depends upon sound software-engineering practices used during software design and coding phases.

Ada language provides considerable aid in the portability of Ada programs. Recognition of some of the major features of Ada enhances portability. Recognize those Ada constructs which have an adverse impact on portability and avoid them. Localize and encapsulate non-portable features of a program if their use is essential. Highlight use of constructs may cause portability problems. There are always trade-offs between efficiency and portability. Target compiler selection is an important portable issue. User-defined types for "float" enhance portability. Ada Compiler Validation Capability (ACVC) checks the compiler and sees that it conforms with the Ada language standard. ACVC does not test to see how well it is implemented. A creative solution to compiler inconsistencies is to have the developer compile the software on three different compilers. This schema is made easier when the software is fully portable.

Portability also depends on hardware implementation. By encapsulating hardware and implementation dependencies into a package or packages, the remainder of the code can ignore such problems and thus be fully portable. This also localizes the dependencies and makes it clear as to which parts of the code must be changed when porting the program. Some implementation-dependent features may be used to achieve particular performance or efficiency objectives. Documentation of these objectives ensures that the software engineer will find an appropriate way and will achieve portability when porting to a different implementation or recognize that they cannot be achieved. Carefully recognize the order dependency which affects the program on certain implementations; when the program is ported, the code might not execute correctly. Avoid incorrect dependencies, but also recognize that even an unintentional error of this kind could prohibit portability.

Ada features, particularly numeric types and expressions, must be used with great care if full portability of the resulting program is to be guaranteed. An implementor can freely define the range of the pre-defined numeric types. Porting code from an implementation with greater accuracy to one of lesser accuracy is a time-consuming, error-prone process. Many errors are not reported until runtime.

The graphical environments of various hardwares are vastly different. They use totally different concepts and sometimes force changes onto the computer interface software which will require some redesign of the screens for portability.

Many hardwares use different memory addressing schemes. Therefore it is better that addresses be modified in shared-memory packages to avoid errors. The use of global variables violates good software-engineering practices, and their extensive use in the original design drastically affects portability.

Part

2

Object-Oriented Software Architecture

"Method will teach you to win time."

GOETHE

Object-Oriented
System Engineering

A computer system consists of both hardware and software requirements. These requirements come from a customer or user. This chapter covers topics for the software developer so the customer's requirements can be properly analyzed and understood before system design and other object-oriented software development phases are started. Planning for object-oriented software development will also be discussed and will include the selection criteria of an object-oriented method. The requirements specification process captures and records the requirements that have been defined by the customer. The user's environment and needs are modeled so that the domain for reuse components can be identified. A requirements specification document is created and signed as an agreement between the customer and the software developer. This document ensures that the software developer has understood the requirements that are the basis for developing and testing the system. This document contains the baseline for functional, performance, interface, and design constraints. Any unresolved items should be reviewed, discussed, and resolved at this time.

System Requirements Analysis Process

A system requirements analysis process ensures that the software developer has understood the customer's requirements. The software developer will carry on the task while the completion of software requirements is reconfirmed. Proper communication is set up between the customer and the software developer so that when any question is raised, it can be satisfactorily answered. Many exchanges of information pass between them. If there is the need for clarity, the customer's view model is presented. This model can be a graphical representation of the customer's view by the software developer; thus ambiguity can be avoided.

The software developer identifies any states or modes in which the system must operate. The states and modes include idle, ready, active, postuse analysis, training, degraded, emergency, backup, etc. The software developer itemized the requirements which are sufficient for acceptance with regard to each of the following as are applicably annotated and identified variations in different states and modes. These are listed in Table 7.1. At this time, it is important that the system requirements be listed in the order of precedence. If a system is developed in multiple builds, its requirements may not be fully defined until most of or all builds are complete. The software developer should identify the subset of system requirements that will be defined in each build and the subset that will be implemented in each build. In case of shortage of time or budget constraints, important requirements are satisfied first in the object-oriented software development.

System Environment

A system environment includes everything that is not in the system. These are the circumstances under which a system will be employed.

The software developer models the customer's or user's environment. The model can be graphical and describe the system capabilities and functionalities in the environment. The environment identifies at a high level the reuse component candidates that can be imported from other related domains. These components need further domain analysis for software reuse.

System Boundary

A system boundary separates the system from the environment. The software developer models the boundary of a system. The models can be graphical representations of the system within the boundary. The boundary describes the operational and functional capabilities of the

TABLE 7.1   A System's States or Modes

A system's capabilities and associated parameters such as time and accuracy
Databases or data banks that must be incorporated into the system
Interfaces with other systems, equipment, software, databases, and users
Physical characteristics such as weight limits, dimensional limits, and color
The system quality factors such as reliability, maintainability, and availability
The environment within which the system must operate
Transportation and materials handling, portability, flexibility, and expansion
Design and construction standards, including safety, security, and privacy
The system documentation, logistics considerations, and personnel and training

system. The software developer interviews the customer or user in order to understand the system requirements and create the boundary for the system. This process is enhanced when the software developer conducts domain analysis and prototyping of the system. The software developer also conducts tradeoff studies and activities and explores system requirements feasibility, cost-effectiveness, and risk reduction analysis.

Identify Domain

A domain is a group or family of related systems. All systems in that domain share a set of common capabilities and/or data. The domain's identification for a system is an important issue at this time. The domain should be within the system's environment and boundary. A domain may be made up of subdomains. The software developer selects a domain expert who does further research so that a subset of the domain subdomains can be set up. The selection of domain and subdomains successfully leads to software reuse components identification during the domain analysis. For example, it is practically clear that the system requirements belong to Financial Accounting System. Hence, it is clear that domain is Financial Accounting, and subdomains are General Accounting, Bookkeeping, Accounts Payable, Accounts Receivable, Payroll, etc. A domain expert has good knowledge of domains and subdomains and explores candidates for software reuse components as he or she progresses in the next phases of the object-oriented software development.

System Requirements Specification

The system requirements specification helps the software developer understand exactly what the customer desires. The understanding of the requirements establishes the basis for an agreement between the customer and the software developer and about what is required. The system requirements specification provides a clear, concise, precise, and unambiguous statement of the requirements. It covers all aspects of the functionality, performance, interfaces, and design constraints. The requirements are stated so that verification can be made objectively as to whether the delivered software will meet the requirements:

- Performance requirements (operation concepts) specification (PRS)
- Design requirements specification (DRS)
- Interface requirements specification (IRS)
- Testing specification

Performance requirements specification

The PRS specifies system operation capacity, response times, system management, and availability. The capacity depends upon the number of simultaneous users and networking requirements. The response times are especially for inquiry functions and on-line updating. The availability or usability depends upon fault recovery which includes fallback procedures and data reconstruction. The availability also includes the exception handling.

Design requirements specification

The DRS includes constraints upon specific technical design solutions so that certain requirements are met. These requirements cover software, hardware, and user design constraints. The software design constraints are applicable standards and languages. The DRS also includes the standards for domain analysis, object-oriented requirements analysis, object-oriented design, object-oriented programming language, data naming, audit tracing, communication, and interfaces. The constraints include program size and data handling capabilities. The hardware design constraints include requirements that use specific types of hardware, details of the working environment, hardware reliability requirements, and mechanical and physical constraints. The user design constraints include the features of the operator or user and the environment in which the system will function.

Interface requirements specification

The IRS describes the hardware and software interfaces across which the system communicates or interacts with its environment and with other systems. The IRS clearly defines the boundary between functional inputs and outputs and interfaces. In addition, the boundary between the requirements and design should be explored. Basically there are three interfaces, and they are specified as follows:

- Human-machine interfaces (HMIs)
- Hardware interfaces
- Software interfaces

Human-machine interfaces support and enhance human capabilities. The interactive devices are user dialogues, graphics, and screen formats. The conversation between the person and the system is a complex protocol. These should be defined in terms of what response is created, to what inputs, and in what combinations of the situation. This covers ergonomic (human engineering) requirements for equipment and hardware devices.

Hardware interfaces include all kinds of interfaces via hardware to the external world. This covers maintaining precise timing requirements, analog measurements, and analog control. Communication interfaces are special cases of hardware interfaces. These include input and output communication ports, communication protocols and procedures, and message formats and throughput. Their specific problem is the combination of a complex protocol with the timing and parallelism of other hardware interfaces that must maintain continued communication and data integrity under all circumstances.

Software interfaces are the procedure-call or language interfaces to other pieces of software. This includes any requirements for a specific operating system, database management system, and application package. The interfaces clarify the logical connection between data constructs that will be generated within the system and those in any other interacting system.

Testing specification

This identifies the risks and presents a process that can be followed to reduce these risks. Tests are designed for identification and risks reduction. Types of risks are as follows:

- Technical
- Programmatic
- Supportability
- Cost and schedule

Technical risks are associated with the evolution of a new design which will provide a greater level of performance than was previously demonstrated because of constraints. These technical risks are testing, modeling, integration interface, software design, requirement changes, operating environment, system complexity, unproven technology, fault detection, safety, and related properties. There are programmatic risks which are associated with obtaining and using applicable resources and activities, such as personnel skills, requirement changes, communication, security, safety, and environmental impact. Supportability risks are associated with fielding and maintaining systems which are currently being developed, such as reliability, maintainability, training, technical data, and safety. Cost and schedule risks arise when there is the setting or meeting of an unreasonably low cost and schedule objective. Cost risk sources are technical, programmatic, supportability, schedule, and error estimating. Schedule risk sources are technical, programmatic, supportability, schedule, number of critical paths, and error estimating.

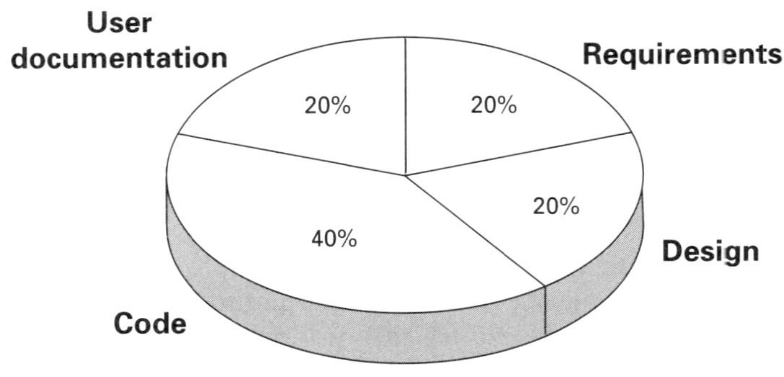

Figure 7.1   Occurrences of software defects.

Risk can be high, medium, and low. Solving high-risk problems is difficult. High-risk problems are important. They can cause serious disruption in schedule, increase in cost, and degradation in performance. The medium-risk problems are less significant and are solvable but with consequences. The medium-risk problems can cause disruption in schedule and degradation in performance. The low-risk problems are easily solved. They can cause some minor disruption in schedule, increase in cost, and degradation in performance. Risks and defects are directly related. It is cost-effective to identify defects which can cause risks at early stages during the requirements specification. Requirements defects are very expensive if they are not detected before the formal or system test. Such defects lead to various degrees of risks. The percentage of software defect occurrence is depicted in Fig. 7.1. The correction of defects will cost more if they are not corrected when they occur and thus will cause risks.

Requirements Specification Document

The *requirements specification document* (RSD) is prepared by the software developer. It specifies the complete requirements for a system. Upon approval by the customer, this document becomes the functional baseline for the system. The format of the document is outlined in Table 7.2.

The title page contains the necessary information with regard to system name, number, preparer of the document, and receiver of the document. This page also contains the signatures of the person who approves it and the person who is authenticating it.

The table of contents contains the title and page number of each paragraph and subparagraph. It also contains a list of page numbers of each figure, table, and appendix.

**TABLE 7.2   Requirements Specification
Document Structure**

1. Cover
2. Title page
3. Table of contents
4. Scope
5. Applicable documents
6. System requirements
   - *a.* Definition
   - *b.* Characteristics
   - *c.* System quality factor
     - Reliability
     - Maintainability
     - Availability
   - *d.* Environmental conditions
   - *e.* Transportability
   - *f.* Flexibility
   - *g.* Portability
   - *h.* Design and construction
   - *i.* Documentation
   - *j.* Logistics
   - *k.* Personnel and training
   - *l.* Qualification
7. Quality assurance provisions
8. Preparation for delivery
9. Notes
10. Appendixes

The scope section consists of identification number, title, and abbreviation, if applicable, of the system to which this document applies. The system overview contains a brief summary, purpose of the system, summary of the purpose, and contents of this document.

The applicable documents section contains specifications, standards, drawings, and other publications such as manuals, regulations, handbooks, and bulletins.

Upon acceptance of the RSD, the requirements are tentatively frozen by the customer or user. The software developer's understanding of these requirements and design of the system are expected and should start. This chapter presents the highest level of system engineering. The software developer identifies hardware and software that will be used and allocates the requirements to computer software configuration items. Requirements traceability and CASE tools will be discussed in this chapter and will supplement the process.

Characteristics of System Engineering Requirements

System engineering consists of requirements for the hardware and software. Their characteristics specify their uniqueness and completeness. The software developer ensures that the requirements do not duplicate or overlap. The requirements are necessary in the development of system engineering. They are feasible and implementable. The requirements must not be outside the capability of current technology. They must be consistent and stated unambiguously. These requirements must be evaluated. There will be a feasible way that will determine which requirements have been satisfied and are traceable forward and backward. The requirements must state *what* will be implemented, and not *how* it will be implemented.

Three types of requirements are generally identified from the RSD, which is the system's functional baseline and contains the requirements—explicit, implicit, and derived. The explicit requirements are part of the functional baseline whereas the implicit requirements are implied by nature or by special knowledge of the system, although they are not stated or expressed in the functional baseline. These may include requirements which are derived from a specified technical understanding of the system. The derived requirements are also unstated in the functional baseline but may be deduced from the structure, relationship, or nature of the system. These requirements will be correctly and seamlessly mapped in the system design.

Building a System

The building of a system requires identification of hardware for which the software will be developed. The requirements for the system will be derived from the RSD. Identification of hardware depends on the customers. They provide the necessary tools and instruments that will be used by the software developers. This process assists the software developers so the software is tested in accordance with the requirements. Any further discussion of hardware is beyond the scope of this book.

Identification of software depends on whether it is a new development, reuse of available existing software, reengineering of the software, or a reverse engineering process. Many commercial off-the-shelf (COTS) software packages are available which can suit the requirements. Knowledge and experience of the system analyst and/or engineer play a major role in this selection. This selection must be the right software with the right requirements.

New development

In new development, various software development phases are customary. These are illustrated in Fig. 7.2. The major phases are domain analysis, requirements analysis, design, and implementation.

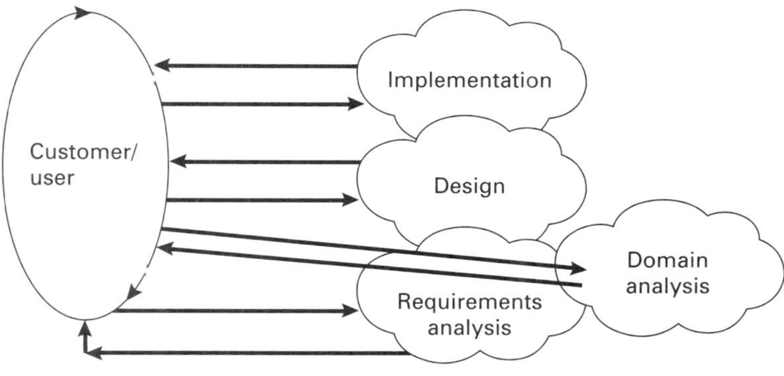

Figure 7.2   Object-oriented software development major phases.

Commonalities and differences are identified in domain analysis. These can be further divided into subphases, as shown in Fig. 7.3. Most of these phases are reiterative. This is an example of a typical waterfall model. Various models have been discussed in detail in my book *Software Engineering Methods, Management, and CASE Tools.*

The new development normally follows a set of prescribed standards, methods, and CASE tools. Traditionally, the process moves

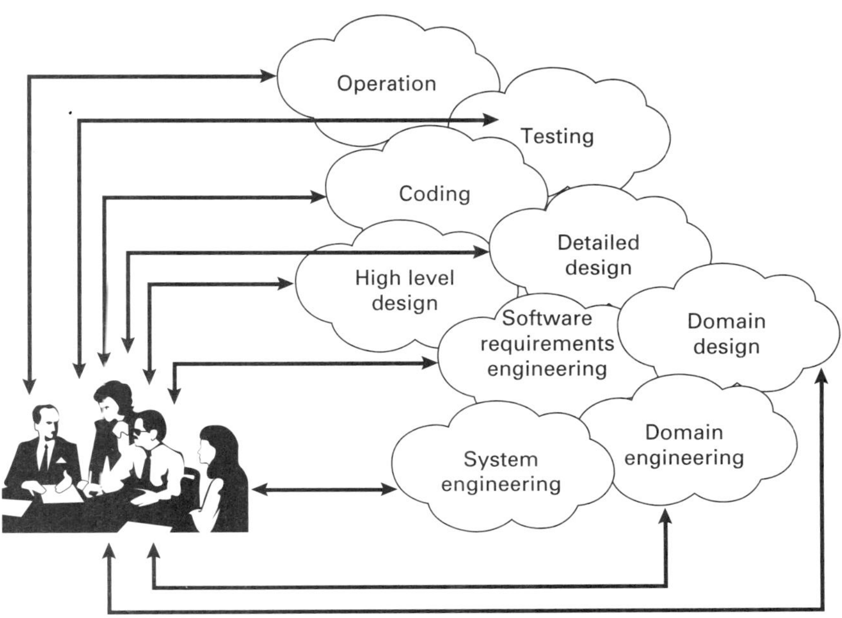

Figure 7.3   Object-oriented software development subphases.

from high-level abstractions and logical implementation-independent designs to the physical implementation of a system. It follows a sequence that goes from requirements through the design of the implementation. It leads to new development of software throughout the life-cycle phases. It starts from the initial phase of analysis of the new requirements and moves forward to the development of all phases of analysis until the project is completed.

Reusable software

Reusable software is software that is developed in response to the requirements for one application and can be used in whole or in part for the satisfaction of requirements of another application. The domain analyst must find a way that existing software which is pretested and cost- and time-efficient can be reused. The basic approach involves configuration and specialization of preexisting software components into viable application systems. Cited studies suggest that initial use of reusable software during the architectural design specification is a way in which implementation can be speeded up.

Reverse engineering

Reverse engineering extracts design artifacts and the building or synthesizing of abstractions that are less implementation-dependent. This process implements changes which are made in later phases of the existing software and automatically brings back the early phases. It starts from any level of abstraction or at any stage of the life cycle. It covers a broad range that starts from the existing implementation, then recaptures or recreates the design, and finally deciphers the requirements that are actually implemented by the system.

Reengineering

Reengineering is the renovation, reclamation, examination, and alteration of the existing system software for changing requirements. This process will reconstitute the existing system software into a new form and the subsequent implementation of the new form. This dominates during the software maintenance life cycle. It helps identify and separate those systems that are worth maintaining from those that should be replaced.

Computer Software Configuration Item Selection Criteria

A computer software configuration item (CSCI) is not easily selected. The software developer conducts a proper analysis and selects one or more CSCIs. The selection criteria depend on the following factors.

- System requirements
- Hardware
- Software
- Requirements allocation
- User acceptance
- Schedule
- Cost

It is better for the system requirements to be partitioned and allocated to the smaller number of CSCIs for effective use of cost and time. If there are a larger number of CSCIs, then there will be more work in the creation of the volume of documents, which will further lead to more workers needed to check the documents. This schema will definitely need more time and cost. The ideal is from one to three CSCIs.

Allocating Requirements to CSCI

The software developer determines the best allocation of system requirements to a CSCI. The software developer defines a set of engineering requirements for each CSCI by showing the system's architecture and interfaces. The operational concepts of the system will be explored. Its functional and operational environments will be discussed.

A sample system architecture is illustrated in Fig. 7.4. It represents the allocation of system hardware and software resources. Graphically it represents the picture of the system when built. It is the top-level model that shows all the interfaces with external entities. The context of the system is presented graphically. If more than one CSCI has been selected, it is better that the system's architecture be shown for each CSCI for clarification. It is important that meaningful names be given to the CSCI and interfaces. These names will be carried out throughout the software development life cycle. This top-level graphic becomes the foundation of the system software development.

It is time that the requirements be segregated between automated and manual ones. Only the automated requirements will be allocated to the CSCI for software development. The automated requirements also consist of environmental and operational requirements. All these requirements are derived from the RSD.

System Engineering Design Document

The *system engineering design document* (SEDD) contains the highest level of design information for the system. The SEDD describes the allocation of system requirements to CSCIs. If a system is developed in

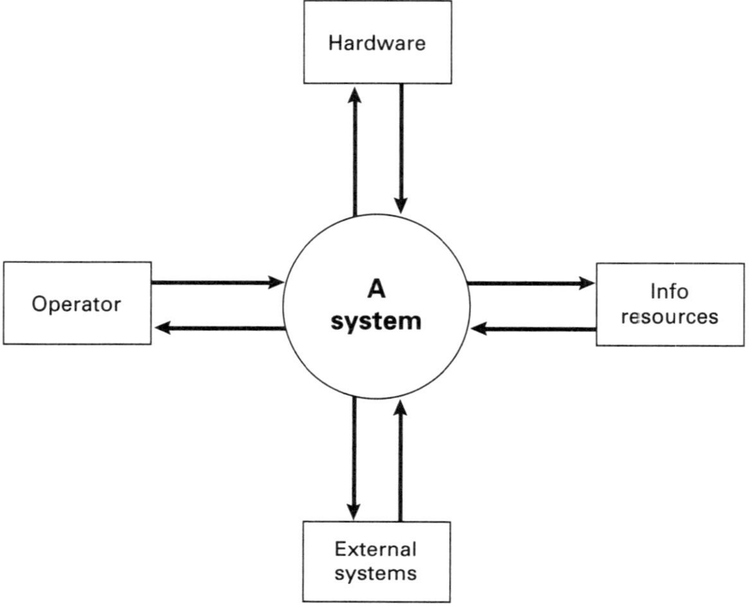

Figure 7.4   A system architecture.

multiple builds, then its design may not be fully defined until most of or all builds are complete. The major outline topics for the SEDD are

- Behavioral design
- System architect
- System design
- Processing resources
- Requirements traceability

Behavioral design describes the overall system appearance and behavior in response to system requirements. The behavioral design covers the internal structure of the system. Examples may include decisions about how the system will appear to the user, how the system will behave, how displays or reports of the system will appear, what console keys of the system mean, and how other choices for meeting the system requirements are made.

System architecture describes the internal structure of the system. The CSCIs and *hardware* configuration *i*tems (HWCIs) will be identified, and their purpose will be summarized. The purpose of each external interface will be explained. A graphical system architecture will be included for clarification.

System design consists of the identification of each HWCI, CSCI, and manual operation of the system. A description of the relationships of HWCIs, CSCIs, and manual operations within the system will be given. Each CSCI will be named uniquely. Each requirement from the RSD to the CSCI will be identified. Each external interface to the system that is addressed by the CSCI will be recorded as follows:

- Bits per second
- Word length
- Message format
- Frequency of messages
- Priority rules
- Protocol

Include any design constraints, system interfaces, system state, and mode on the CSCI.

Processing resources cover hardware, programming, design, coding, and utilization characteristics of the processing resource. These characteristics include the following parameters:

- Memory size—amount of internal memory (absolute, spare, or both) of the computer
- Word size—number of bits in each computer word
- Processing speed—computer processor capacity (absolute, spare, or both)
- Character set standard
- Instruction set architecture
- Interrupt capabilities of the hardware
- Direct memory access
- Channel requirements
- Auxiliary storage
- Growth capabilities of any part of the processing resource
- Diagnostic capabilities
- Allocation of pertinent processing resources to each CSCI

System Engineering Design Review

System engineering design is a formal review that accepts the SEDD by the customer. The software developer conducts and presents the

TABLE 7.3   SEDD Review Parameters

System engineering
Operations
Maintenance
Test
Training
Software
Facilities
Personnel
Logistic support
Security
Safety
Risk
Optimization

necessary SEDDs for formal review. The software developer conducts the review. The customer evaluates the correctness of the allocation of the requirements to the CSCI. The review encompasses the system engineering parameters, shown in Table 7.3. Once the SEDD is reviewed by the customer and accepted, the software developer uses this design information in the following phases as the basis for developing software.

Multiple Views of Software Requirements Model

Once we segregate software requirements from hardware requirements, multiple views of the software requirements model are necessary so that the process of software development can be understood. The models should reflect as many aspects of the software requirements as possible. The goal is twofold. First, the customer is satisfied and understands the implementation of the requirements. Second, the software developers are helped by these models, so the software design can continue. The commonalities among these models are the types of products they eventually produce. The model differs depending upon the software development process used. The abstract life-cycle model assumes these types of products:

- Requirements model

- User view and operational model

- Information flow model

- Implementation model

Specifications describe all subsets of the aspects of a software process. It also describes a product at some level of abstraction and from some point of view that uses some degree of formalism. The desirable aspect, the desirable level of abstraction, the proper perspective, and the desirable degree of formalism are determined by the purpose and context of the particular process or product type within the software life cycle.

The *requirements model* provides a view at various levels of the software refinement process for the entire system, subsystem, or modules. This shows what requirements are essential for the software development. What needs should the proposed software system fulfill?

The *user view and operational model* provides the requirements which are concerned with the software problems. What functions, from the customer's point of view, must the system perform so that these needs are met? Its main function is to communicate with the customer and the software developer. The goal corrects any omission in the early stages, improves the productivity, and increases the quality of the produced software. The model provides assistance and guidance to the customer and to the software developer. It provides an understanding of the requirements in greater detail and of how they will be implemented in the software development.

The *information flow model* provides the necessary detail requirements information for software development. This supplements the flow of information and what is essential for the customer's point of view. The type of information should be specified and based upon the purpose and context of the specification product.

At this time you are looking for commonality and differences. Commonality captures common states and transition in the state charts. It also captures the common activities and data flows for input and output in activity charts. The difference parameters are captured by conditions in control flow in the state charts. The difference parameters are also captured by the optional data flow in activity charts.

The behavioral aspect shows the way that the system responds to specific inputs, the states it will adopt, and the outputs it will produce. And it will meet the boundary conditions on the validity of inputs and states. This includes a description of the environment that produces the inputs and consumes the outputs. It includes constraints on performance that are imposed by the environment and are a function of the system. The information model includes finite state and data or object models.

The implementation model products actually lead and build the system in accordance with the customer's requirements. This provides details of how a system will be built and behave, as it has been described in the software requirements analysis and specification. The code is written and tested so it can be actually implemented on the computer while a particular object-oriented method is used. Any change requests will be entertained and executed in the process. An existing system should be changed and some inherent errors corrected, should better fulfill changed requirements, or should be adapted to a changed environment of both hardware and software. Depending on the severity of the change, change requests can trigger the creation of new product versions at various levels in accordance with the changed requirements.

In the maintenance phase, the intended changes to the system must be specified. In addition, new, updated versions of various levels of existing products should be developed. Specifications of processes and products permit the incorporation of changes in a formal way.

Requirements Traceability

The requirements traceability process tracks the specified requirements of the RSD throughout the object-oriented software life cycle. Requirements traceability provides traceability of the requirements which were allocated to the HWCIs, CSCIs, and manual operations back to the requirements of the RSD. Traceability should be tabulated in a requirements traceability matrix. This traceability will carry forward and backward throughout the object-oriented software development documents.

Requirements traceability means that specified requirements are mapped onto deliverable components throughout the software engineering. The mapping process is called *allocation.* Allocation means that a particular software component should satisfy a particular requirement. The well-defined requirements are allocated to targets properly. The requirements allocation assigns each requirement to targets which should satisfy it. Ideally, every target has at least one allocation. Targets with no allocations are unnecessary.

Object-Oriented Software Development Plan

A *software development plan* (SDP) is started once the requirements for object-oriented software development are understood. The plan includes object-oriented standards that will be followed for analyzing requirements, design, coding, testing, and producing necessary documentations. The plan incorporates schema for identification of OODBMS and for reusable software products. The SDP includes other plans for software development such as scheduling, staffing, budgeting, resources, tracking requirements, managing software development, the selection criteria of an object-oriented method for the software development, software testing, software quality assurance, configuration management, software product evaluation, and the acceptance criteria by the customer.

An important decision is the selection of an object-oriented method from those available, such as Rumbaugh, Shlaer and Mellor, Booch, Coad and Yourdon, and Martin and Odell. As mentioned before, there is no one standard object-oriented method, and each of these methods has pluses and minuses. The selection of the best one that is suited to your requirements and environment is not easy. Let us briefly study each of these methods and explore their strengths and weaknesses. We will study these methods in the context of object-oriented semantics, such as inheritance, aggregation, and association. Explicitly, we mean here by *inheritance* "is a kind of," by *aggregation* "is a part of," and by *association* "is related to." We prefer that the object-oriented method cover both analysis and design phases and support other phases of the object-oriented software development life cycle. The method should be easily understood and followed. The method should be mature and well tested on various object-oriented software development environments. The method should be supported by a CASE tool. Proper education and training should be available for this method.

The Rumbaugh method is known as the *object modeling technique* (OMT) and is one of the easy techniques for object-oriented analysis and design. The OMT consists of object model, dynamic model, and functional model. The object model is like an entity relationship diagram. The object model shows classes and their attributes, which include operations and relationships among classes. The relationships include inheritance, aggregation, and association. The object model provides the data view. The dynamic model contains a *state transition diagram* (STD) for each class in the object model. The functional model is the *data flow diagram* (DFD) and provides the link to objects by partiticning so that the lowest level of DFD bubbles contains operations on classes.

This method has been tested on various applications. The symbolic notations for these models are easily followed. The method is well documented in the book by Rumbaugh et al. The method is supported by many CASE tools. Several training courses are available for this method. OMT was originally developed in the General Electric Research and Development Center, New York. The strength of this method is that it is easily followed and consists of familiar notations. The weakness is that it is still in evolving.

The Shlaer/Mellor object-oriented method is a recursive system development process. This system process consists of domain partitioning, domain analysis, application domain, service domains, software architecture domain, and implementation domain. *Object-orient-*

ed analysis (OOA) is the derivation of any of these domain analyses. The OOA provides three viewpoints—information model, state model, and process model. Classes are modeled in data view, which provides association and subtyping. Each class is then given a state transition diagram. Here actions are described by a DFD. Classes are connected by messages, and this initiates architectural view. Different notations are used that describe design for classes and their interactions; that is actually a weakness for this method in transitioning from analysis to design. This method is documented in a book by the authors. There are many CASE tools available for this method.

Many training courses are available for this method. The strength of the method is that the recursive design will change the design model to a working system. The weakness of this method is that there is no smooth transition from analysis to design.

Grady Booch's object-oriented method is well known in the industry. Booch describes *E*ntity *R*elationship *D*iagram (ERD) features in the data view as *class diagram*. Dynamics are illustrated with an STD within a class. Booch shows interactions between objects by timing diagrams and object diagrams. The method shows logical architecture with object diagrams and class categories that use object partitioning. The method shows the physical design with module and process diagrams. The method covers object diagrams which provide object partitioning, and the relationship between object behavior. The method is well documented in a book by the author. There is a CASE tool available for this method. Many training courses are available, too. The strength of this method is that it is more mature than any other object-oriented methods. The weakness is that the notations are unfamiliar and are not easily put into practice.

The Coad/Yourdon method relates to data view with ERD. It shows aggregation, association, and subtyping. The method shows behavior by naming operations on the classes and defining them within the class by service charts. The service charts consist of state transition charts and flowcharts. The method shows the behavior among the objects by the placement of message connections on the ERD. The classes are grouped into subjects in an architecture. There are many training courses available for this method. The method is documented in a book by the authors. CASE tools are available also. The strength of this method is that the whole system can be described in a single diagram, which is considered to have many layers. This diagram makes it easy for a user who views different layers of the system. The weakness is that for a large system, the various-layers view may not work well.

The Martin/Odell method describes data view as a binary rather than entity relationship. The method explains that the objects change class during their lifetimes. The method supports subtype, class expression, and dynamic classification. The method states behavior in ERD. The events are linked with the data view. A CASE tool compiles an event diagram into executable code. The method defines architecture with the help of object flow diagrams that use a functional partitioning schema. The method is documented in a book by the authors. CASE tools are available for this method. The strength of this method is the analysis phase which involves an event-driven approach that identifies the event first and then these events define objects. The weakness of this method is that it is not easily followed.

The choice of an object-oriented method depends upon the environment and the nature of your system requirements.

Object-Oriented Software Life Cycle

Finding a system software that will stand alone these days is hard. An object-oriented software is always a part of a domain, and it consists of other systems software. The life cycle of an object-oriented software consists of a specific set of activities and phases during the development, maintenance, and retirement of that software. This chapter presents system object-oriented software life-cycle models. It also covers domain engineering and domain analysis for software reuse that will be used in object-oriented software.

Object-Oriented Software Life-Cycle Issues

Object-oriented software evolution represents the cycle of activities in the development, use, and maintenance of software systems. Systems software comes and goes through a series of passages that account for its inception, initial development, productive operation, upkeep, and retirement from one generation (version) to another. In turn, models of software evolution date back to the earliest projects where large systems software was developed. The apparent purpose of these object-oriented software life-cycle models was to provide an abstract scheme which accounts for the "natural" or engineered development of systems software. Such a scheme could therefore serve as a basis for planning, organizing, staffing, coordinating, budgeting, and directing software development activities, as shown in Fig. 8.1. These fourteen activities are discussed:

Activity 1. *System initiation and adoption* identify the system's origin. Many new systems replace or supplement existing processing mechanisms.

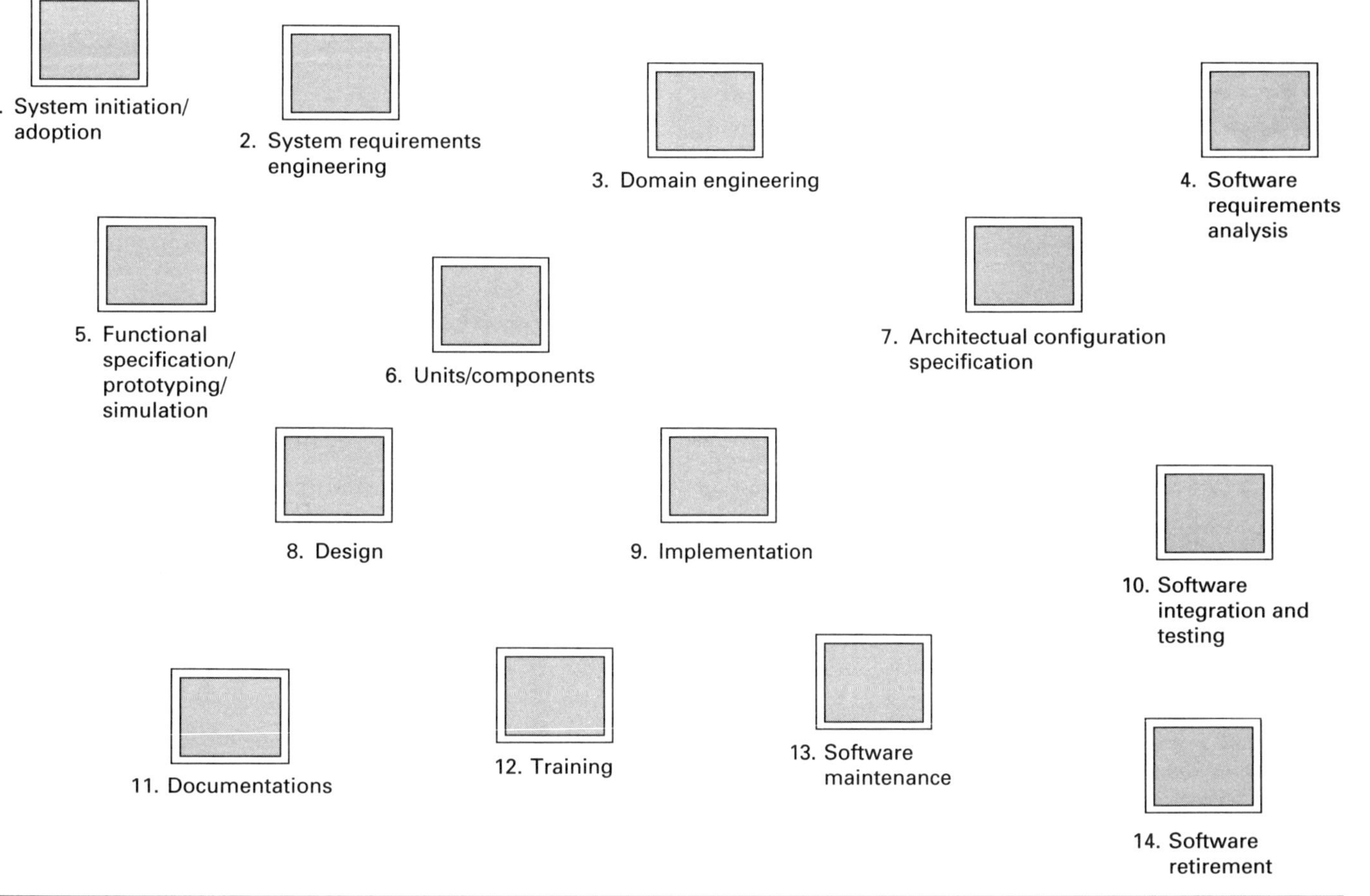

Figure 8.1 Object-oriented software development activities.

Activity 2. *System requirements engineering* involves separating requirements into hardware and software. The specified software requirements are allocated to CSCIs. OODBMS is identified as object-oriented software.

Activity 3. *Domain engineering* addresses domain analysis and architecture engineering as well as the creation and evolution of particular assets or components for reuse in object-oriented software development.

Activity 4. *Object-oriented software requirement analysis and specification* identify the problems which should be solved. The software architecture process determines what will be produced. This involves requirements identification, analysis, representation, communication, and development of acceptance criteria and procedures. A suitable object-oriented method is selected for software development.

Activity 5. *Functional specification, prototyping, and simulation* identify and potentially formalize such subactivities as the objects of computation, their attributes and relationships, the operations that transform these objects, and the constraints that restrict system behavior.

Activity 6. *Partition and selection* for the given requirements and functional specification divide the system into manageable pieces that denote logical subsystems. Then it is determined whether new, existing, or reusable software systems correspond to the needed pieces.

Activity 7. The *architectural configuration specification* defines the interconnection and resource interfaces between system modules in ways which are suitable for their detailed object-oriented design and overall configuration management.

Activity 8. *Detailed component object-oriented design specification* defines the object-oriented, procedural methods through which each module's data resources are transformed from required inputs to provided outputs.

Activity 9. *Component implementation and debugging* codify the preceding specifications into operational source code implementations and validate their basic operation.

Activity 10. *Software integration and testing* affirm and sustain the overall integrity of the software system architectural configuration through verification of the consistency and completeness of implemented modules, verification of the resource interfaces and interconnections against their specifications, and validation of the performance of the system and subsystems against their requirements.

Activity 11. *Documentation revision and system delivery packages* rationalize recorded system development description into systematic documents and user guides. This is all in a form that is suitable for dissemination and system support.

Activity 12. *Training and use* provide system users with instructional aids and guidance for understanding the system's capabilities and limits for effective system use.

Activity 13. *Object-oriented software maintenance* sustains the useful operation of a system in its host or target environment which provides requested functional enhancements, repairs, performance improvements, and conversions. Maintenance represents ongoing incremental iterations throughout the life-cycle activities that precede it.

Activity 14. *Software retirement* is not very common. Most of the retired systems software has been deemed useless and hence not in existence. These retired systems were once created for some special purpose with a special language and for a special computer. It is better to use those components which are well tested and efficient to create new ones. Understanding and identifying the reusability and viability of software components for the new systems are important. The model of a new system can be compared with the existing model of the retired system to identify suitable software components. The reuse of these pretested software components will definitely save time and money and will increase the quality of the software products. The model concept, which is taken at a high level of abstraction and applied to software development, is called the *software life cycle*. This life-cycle notion exists beyond the design and programming stage of development. The life-cycle concept implies that software exists even in the conceptual stages of problem definition, that it needs to be maintained after formal development has been completed, and that it functions until retirement.

Modeling Concepts

Models are abstractions which assist the conceptualizing of the object-oriented software development process. A software model represents the components of the development process. The finite phases of a model are not realistic. Models are constructed with the builder's ideas of what is important. This idea must determine the greater visibility of a certain set of concerns. Some of these concerns are not clearly defined. Models can be an object-oriented software development process, software itself, or a software management process. Models ensure that the object-oriented software product matches the customer's requirements. Assurances correlate to other considerations, such as

- Type of system that will be developed
- Technical orientation of people involved in the development effort
- Tools that are used in the effort

The customer can validate the system. A model can incorporate the concept through a structured formalism which ties requirements to the end product.

Models exhibit various ways of viewing the object-oriented software development process. This viewpoint contributes to the formulation of other models, much like a chain reaction. Models can assist in managing object-oriented software, testing, maintenance, and retirement. Some of the popular models are briefly discussed now.

Object-Oriented Software Life-Cycle Model

Object-oriented software life-cycle model encompasses many concepts throughout the software development. These concepts are from the project management through system design and software coding to maintenance. Software requirements may change with the times. There may be a bug which is identified in due time. With the advent of modern technology, the software must be reengineered. Thus the life cycle provides a way of looking at various phases of object-oriented software development for a system. The phases assist in going through various aspects of software development into a common language, which may be graphical, so that the effects of changes to the development process can be determined. A software life-cycle model is either a prescriptive or descriptive characterization of software evolution.

Prescriptiveness is the level of detail which is supplied by the method insofar as a direction is provided on how the various activities will be accomplished. A prescriptive life-cycle model can be developed more easily. Many software development details can be ignored, glossed over, or generalized. This, of course, should raise concern about the relative validity and robustness of such life-cycle models when different kinds of application systems are being developed in different kinds of development settings. A descriptive life-cycle model, however, characterizes how software systems are actually developed. For them articulation is less common and more difficult for one obvious reason: One must observe or collect data throughout the development of a software system. This development period is an elapsed time that is usually measured in years. Also descriptive models are specific to the systems that are observed and only generalized through systematic analysis.

Waterfall model

The classic waterfall model was introduced by W. Royce in 1970. This software evolution proceeds through an orderly sequence of transitions

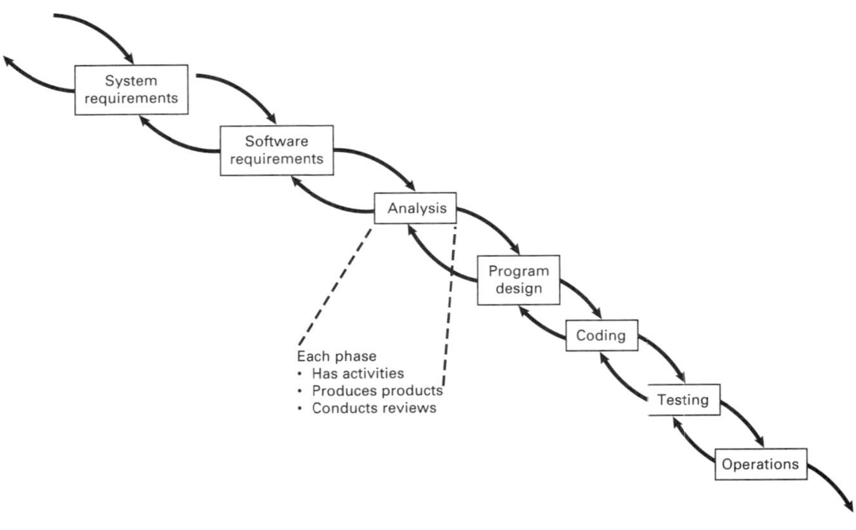

Figure 8.2　Software development using waterfall model.

from one phase to the next in linear order. The model divides the software process into the following phases, as illustrated in Fig. 8.2:

- System requirements
- Software requirements
- Analysis
- Program design
- Coding
- Testing
- Operations

Each phase is described in terms of input, process, and output. The software process proceeds through a sequence of steps with iterative interaction between phases which are confined to successive steps. A deliverable software is usually produced and then is used as input to the next phase.

In reality, system or software development is never so clean. As shown in Fig. 8.2, there exist feedback loops between phases. Because of these feedback loops, the deliverable products at each phase need reviews and changes prior to acceptance. The design phase may be subdivided into many phases with an increase in level of detail.

The model derives its strength from its classical steps which are taken successively. It provides a structured template for software development. This model is not popular among the object-oriented software developers due to its weakness. This weakness is that more interactions between nonsuccessive steps are needed. Identification of all the requirements for an object-oriented software is not an easy job.

The model has been most useful. It has helped structure and manage software development projects that are large, medium, and small in organizational settings.

Incremental model

In the incremental model, an initial subset of the system is fully developed. Then in successive steps more elaborate versions are built upon the previous ones. The architectural design of the total system is envisioned in the first step, but the system is implemented by these successive elaborations. The object-oriented software is developed in increments, as shown in Fig. 8.3, which represent degrees of functional capability. Object-oriented software is built in small, manageable increments. Each increment adds a new function to the system.

The strength of incremental development is that the increments of functional capability are much more easily understood and tested. Use of successive increments provides a way to incorporate user experience into a refined product at lower cost.

This model combines the classical software life cycle with iterative enhancement at the level of system development organization. It also provides a way to periodically distribute object-oriented software

Software development in increment

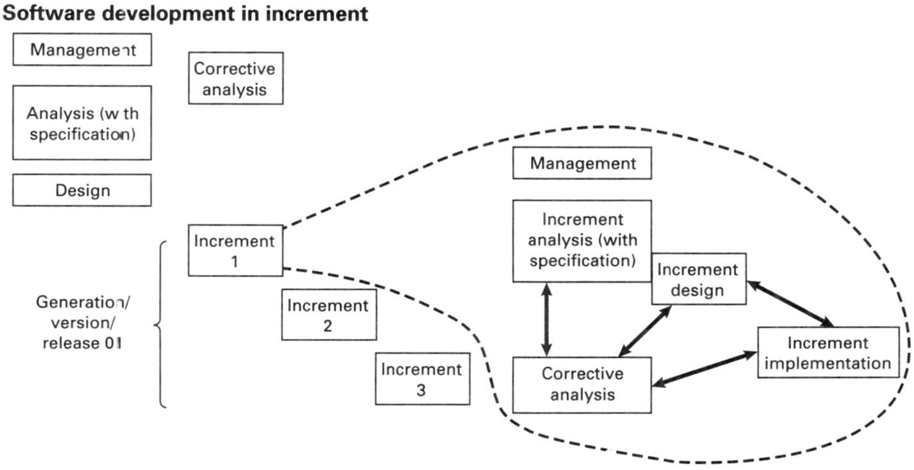

Figure 8.3   Incremental model.

maintenance updates and services to dispersed users. This is a popular model of object-oriented software in the computer industry.

Prototyping and simulation model

The prototyping model advocates the early development of components that represent the eventual system. Often these components represent the user's interface to the system. A skeletal implementation of this interface is developed with the idea of its being an opportunity to provide feedback from the object-oriented software user before the final system is specified and designed. While the clarification of the user interface is one goal, prototyping may also be employed as a concept within the context of another model. In this case, the second model of the object-oriented software process may regard prototyping as but one component of the process which will be used for clarification of the behavior of the system at an early point in the development.

Prototyping technologies usually accept some form of software functional specifications as input, which in turn are simulated, analyzed, or directly executed. As such, these technologies let software object-oriented design activities be initially skipped or glossed over. In turn, these technologies can allow rapid construction of primitive versions of software systems that users can evaluate. These user evaluations can then be incorporated as feedback which refines the emerging system specifications and designs. Depending on the prototyping technology, the complete working system can be developed through a continual process of revising and refining the input specifications. This model has the advantage that it always provides a working version of the developing system, while object-oriented software design and testing activities are redefined for input of specification refinement and execution.

Assembling reusable components model

The basic approach of reusability will configure and specialize preexisting object-oriented software components into viable application systems, as shown in Fig. 8.4. However, the characteristic of the components depends upon their size, complexity, and functional capability. Most approaches attempt utilization of components similar to the common data structure with algorithms as their manipulation. Other approaches attempt utilization of components resembling functionally complete systems or subsystems which are user-interface management systems. There are probably many ways that reusable software components in evolving software systems can be used. However, cited

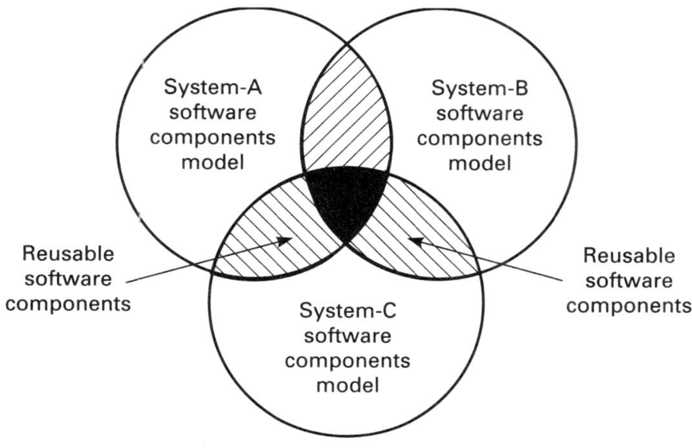

Figure 8.4 Assembling reusable components model.

studies suggest their initial use during architectural or component design specification is a way to speed up implementation. They might also be used for prototyping purposes if a suitable software prototyping technology is available.

Spiral model

The spiral model was developed at TRW by B. Boehm in 1988. The model involves multiple iterations through cycles with the intent of analyzing the results of prior phases by determining risk estimates for future phases, as shown in Fig. 8.5. At each phase, alternatives are evaluated with respect to the objectives and constraints that form the basis for the next cycle of the spiral. Each cycle is completed with a review that involves vested interested parties. Boehm states, "The model reflects the underlying concept that each cycle involves a progression that addresses the same sequence of steps for each portion of the product and for each of its levels of elaboration from an overall concept-of-operation document down to the coding of each individual program."

The radial dimension represents the added incremental cost incurred in completing the developmental steps. The angular dimension represents the progress made in completing each cycle of the spiral. The basic premise of the model is that a certain sequence of steps is repeated while a software is being developed or maintained. The steps are first done at a very high level of abstraction, then each loop of the spiral represents a repetition of the steps at successively lower levels of abstraction. The strength of the model lies in its flexibility

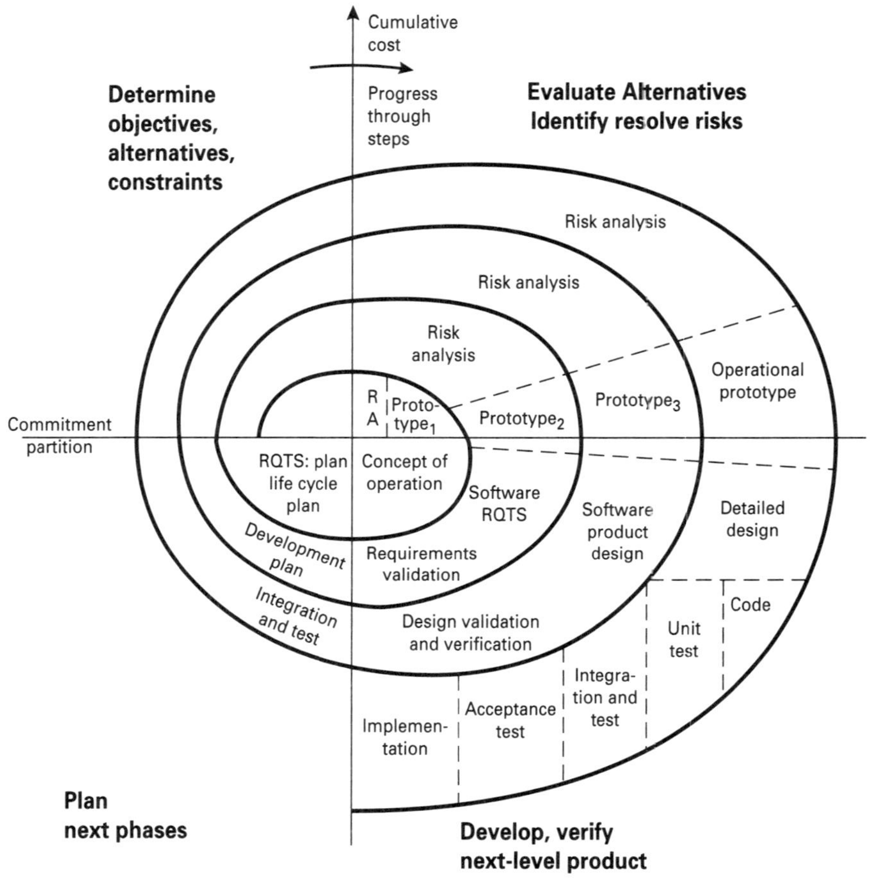

Figure 8.5 Spiral model.

for the management of a system object-oriented software development life cycle. One can plan an examination of risk at each major abstraction. The model accommodates any mixture of specification-oriented, process-oriented, object-oriented, or other approaches to software development. This model is the most favored by the object-oriented software developer because of its strengths, as defined above. The weakness of the model is that it does not match any existing standards. The model depends upon identifying and managing sources at project risk. The model needs more uniformity and consistency.

Operational model

Behaviors particular to the problem domain are modeled and simulated in the beginning stages of the operational model. This is done so the software customer can explore the way and order in which events happen. Exploration is made possible with the construction of an operational specification of the system. Concern at the specification level with how the system behaves is in contrast to other models whose specifications define the system in terms of a black box that maps the inputs to outputs.

While the behavior of the problem domain is emulated in the specification, the object-oriented software structures that will eventually be used in the actual system which produces this behavior are determined later in the development process.

Transformational model

The transformational model starts with a program specification and ends with a program. The transformational model's progress between the two points is made through an automated series of transformations. H. Partsch and R. Steinbrueggen: "Transformation rules are partial mappings from one program scheme to another so that an element of the domain and its image under the mapping constitute a correct transformation. Transformational programming is a software process of program construction where successive applications of transformation rule. Usually, this process starts with a (formal) specification of a formal statement with a problem or its solution and ends with an executable program."

The benefit that is associated with the transformational model is the reduction of labor intensity of software production through the automated transformation. This model assists in preserving correctness through the application of formal transformations and replaces the final product testing by verification of the program specifications. One of this model's abilities produces a desired transformation through a combination of small units from specialized programming knowledge.

Object-Oriented Life-Cycle Model and MIL-STD-498/IEEE 1498

An object-oriented life-cycle model can represent a combination or a single model, as discussed above. The main features of an object-oriented model are that objects should be identified in the problem space during the requirements analysis activity. The same objects are mapped in the solution space during the design activity. And the same objects are implemented with the help of object-oriented programming language during the implementation activity.

MIL-STD-498 identifies three examples for life-cycle models. The *grand design* model is essentially a once-through model. Simplistically:

determine user needs, define requirements, design the system, develop the system, test, fix, and deliver. In this model all the requirements are defined first. The *incremental* model determines user needs and defines the system requirements, then performs the rest of the development in a sequence of builds. The first build incorporates part of the planned capabilities, the next build adds more capabilities, and so on, until the system is complete. Multiple developments are permissible in this model. All the requirements can be also defined first. Field interim products may be possible in this model.

The evolutionary model also develops a system in builds, but it differs from the incremental model in acknowledging that the user need is not fully understood and all requirements cannot be defined up-front. In this model, user needs and system requirements are partially defined up-front, then they are defined in each succeeding build. In this model, multiple development cycles are permissible. Also field interim products are possible in this model.

Domain Engineering Model

Domain engineering is an iterative process for the design and development of a product of a family and an application engineering process for producing members of that family. The domain engineering life-cycle model addresses domain analysis and architecture engineering as well as the creation and evolution of a particular asset or components. Domain engineering consists of domain analysis, domain repository, and domain implementation, as shown in Fig. 8.6. The

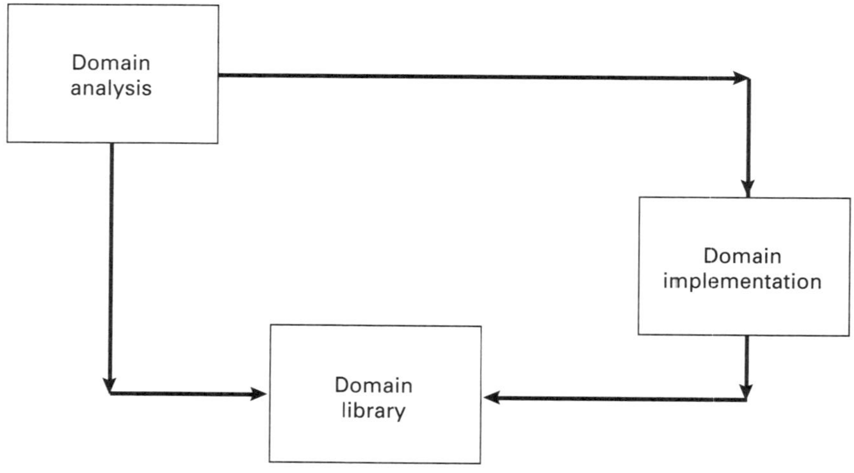

Figure 8.6 Domain engineering model.

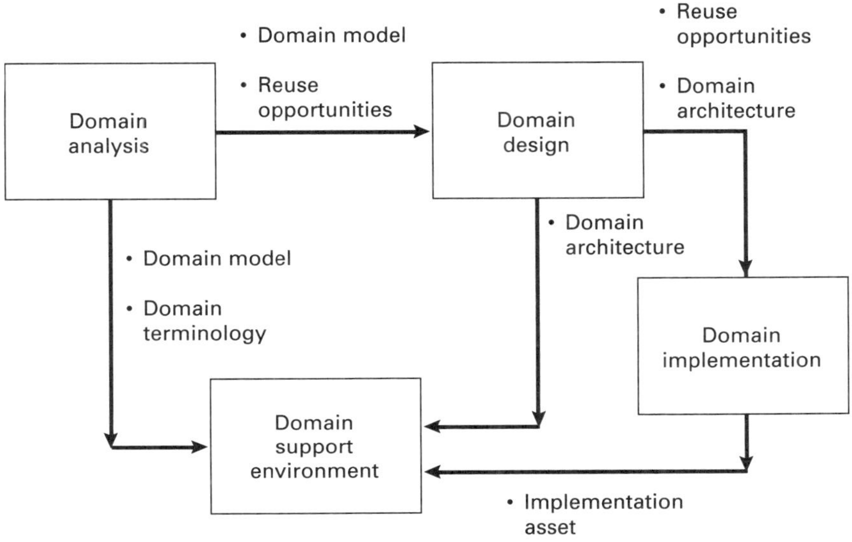

Figure 8.7 Domain engineering components.

goals are to identify, derive, organize, abstract, and represent commonalities and differences of a particular domain. These further facilitate reusability of life-cycle work products within an organization's body of domain knowledge.

Figure 8.7 further illustrates the concepts of domain engineering. Domain engineering is not a part of any one project, and it cuts across all projects. Applications engineering makes use of the products of domain engineering, as illustrated in Fig. 8.8. The application engineering life cycle addresses the construction of new or reengineered systems by the use of generic requirements, domain architecture, and components. Figure 8.9 distinguishes between domain engineering and application engineering and treats them as separate life cycles. In the top row of processes, a series of domain engineering activities starts with domain analysis and produces a domain model. The next is the software architecture development activity that produces a domain software architecture. Finally the reusable asset component and generator development activity produces the components and generators.

The bottom row of processes, which can produce a family of application systems, is a series of application engineering activities, which involve analysis that is based on the domain model that produces application requirements. The next is the design that is based on a domain architecture, and it produces an application architecture and design. Finally, implementation which is based on the set of imple-

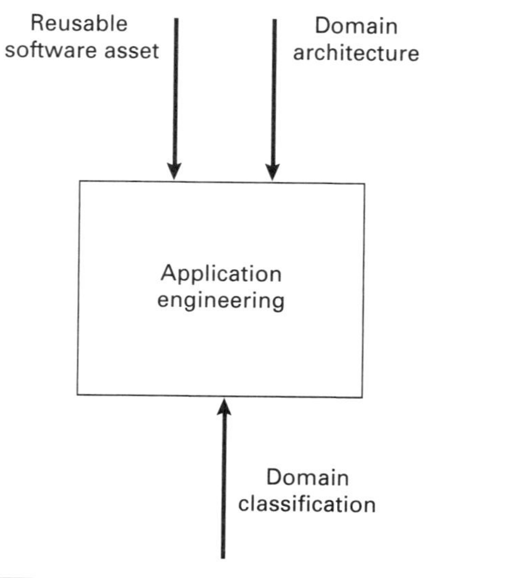

Figure 8.8   Application engineering.

mentation assets available produces an application system. At each stage there is feedback from application engineering to domain engineering that assists in the evolution of the reusable domain products. Sitting between the domain engineers and application engineers is a reuse repository that would house all the domain assets that could be shared across applications. Figure 8.9 implies that reuse must be integrated throughout the application engineering process. The domain model provides generic domain requirements which must be considered as part of the system requirements analysis. The application architecture should be derived from the domain software architecture or generic architecture.

Domain Analysis Model

Domain analysis examines a portion of the domain engineering process which will identify reuse components. The process of domain analysis collects, organizes, analyzes, and presents information which will identify reuse opportunities within the domain. Traditionally problems are formulated and defined as requirements for specific software systems or parts of systems. By contrast, domain analysis identifies and models problems for a group of related systems in a domain and develops generic requirements that address recurring problems in the domain and ensure that domain capabilities remain viable over changes in technology, time, needs, people, and budget.

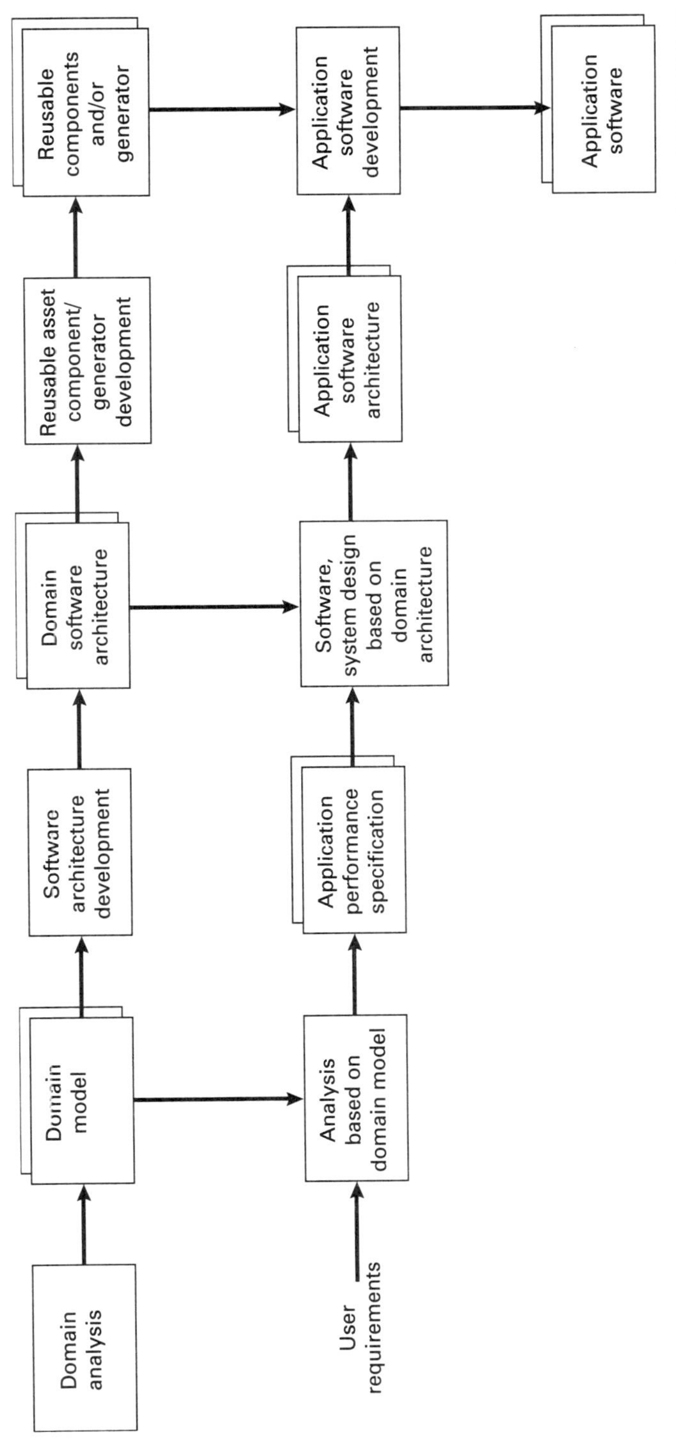

Figure 8.9 Domain engineering approach.

Domain analysis is conducted as an iterative process that consists of four logical processes: identify the domain, scope the domain, analyze the problem space, and design the solution space. Each logical process can be further partitioned and its associated responsibilities and activities can be described. This method of structuring the problem and solution is called *abstraction*. Abstraction helps manage complexity by hiding details until they are relevant and necessary for understanding.

Benefits of domain analysis

There are many benefits of domain analysis, and these are some: Domain analysis minimizes redundant object-oriented software development efforts, improves process productivity, and improves product quality during system, object-oriented software development and maintenance life cycle. Domain analysis reduces costs, risks, and schedules. Domain analysis increases user suitability and opportunities for competition by lowering domain-knowledge-based barriers.

Domain Design Model

Domain design constructs generic domain-specific solution architectures that facilitate the development of a new application in the domain. Domain design evolves generic solution architectures for domain-specific lines and facilitates user validation of solutions to the existing problems. Domain design serves as an adaptable or configurable framework for similar application software evolution.

The primary objectives of domain design are to construct a design that reflects the requirements of a product line within the domain and to provide a generic solution architecture. Domain analysts and designers capture and structure domain-relevant information for reusability and use process guidelines. The necessary information is provided by the planning documents, existing system documentation, domain experts, and other reuse analyses or studies.

Integrated Computer-Aided Manufacturing (ICAM) DEFinition (IDEFo) Process Model

IDEFo is a top-down diagramming technique that starts with a general process and decomposes it into subprocesses. IDEFo starts with a single *context* diagram that represents the entire process. This is decomposed into successively more detailed diagrams collectively and is called an *IDEFo model*. Each decomposition level is represented by an activity diagram called an *actigram*. Each box in the model repre-

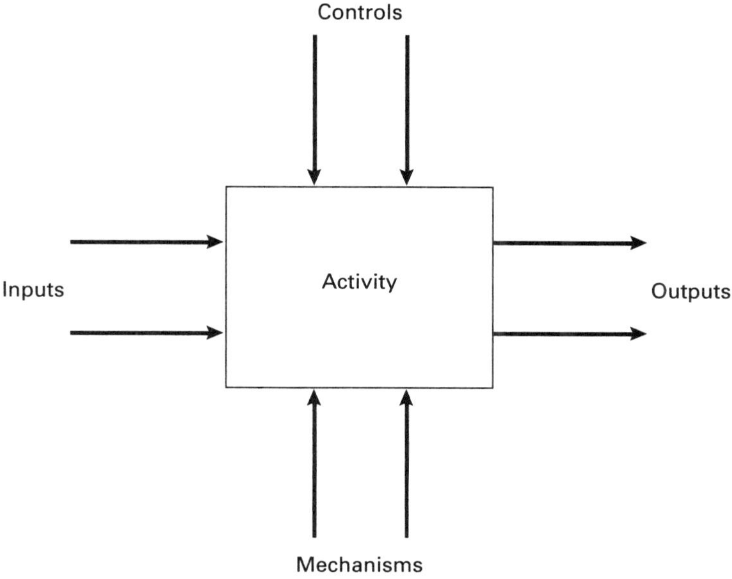

Figure 8.10 IDEFo process model.

sents a process which consists of a group of activities that accomplish-
es the process. The necessary information or data that will carry out
the activities of the process and the information or products which
are generated by the process are represented in an IDEFo diagram by
arrows. Figure 8.10 illustrates an IDEFo process model.

The IDEFo diagram consists of boxes and arrows. The box represents activities or functions. Arrows denote objects or data. The placement of the arrows on the boxes has a specific meaning. Arrows on
the left that are going to the box are inputs which initiate the activity
and are transformed. Arrows that are coming from the box on the
right are the outputs, the results produced by the activity. Arrows
that are coming to the box from the top are the controls which regu-
late or guide the activity. Arrows that are coming to the box from the
bottom are the mechanisms which perform the activity.

The IDEFo process model is a technique that lets professionals
understand systems and communicate their understanding to others
in a simple way. The IDEFo process model is a series of diagrams that
represent the understanding that has thus been gained. The diagrams are organized in a hierarchical method and decompose the
main box into more detailed boxes as its components in a top-down
fashion. Each part which is shown on a detail diagram is again partitioned and so forth until the desired level of detail is reached. The

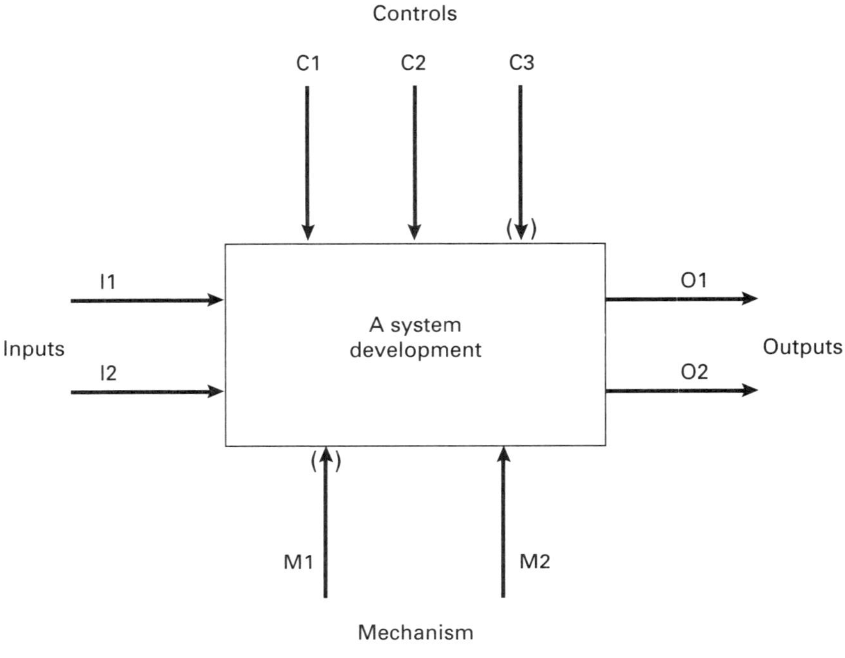

Figure 8.11   An object-oriented system development sample.

higher-level diagram is called the *parent* of the lower-level *detail* diagram. The lower-level diagram balances for inputs, outputs, controls, and mechanisms with its parent diagram. The lowest level of IDEFo models leads and identifies *objects*.

Figure 8.11 shows an example of IDEFo's main box for an object-oriented system development. Figure 8.12 illustrates the lower-level diagram. If an arrow end has small brackets, then there is no match on the detail diagram for that arrow, and this arrow will not be shown in the lower level. If an arrow beginning has small brackets, then there is no match on the parent diagram for the arrow, and it will be shown in the lower level. If an arrow splits, then the same data are going in two different directions. If two different data are merging into one arrow, then one datum is combined with the other datum. Node numbers begin with the letter A (for *activity*) which is followed by a digit for every node traversed. Each decomposition has the node number of its parent with the specific appended box number. The "top" is designated A0. A single box diagram summing up the A0 diagram and stating the purpose and viewpoint is designated A−0 and is usually the starting point for a model. The context diagrams show the environment of the model and can have negative numbers.

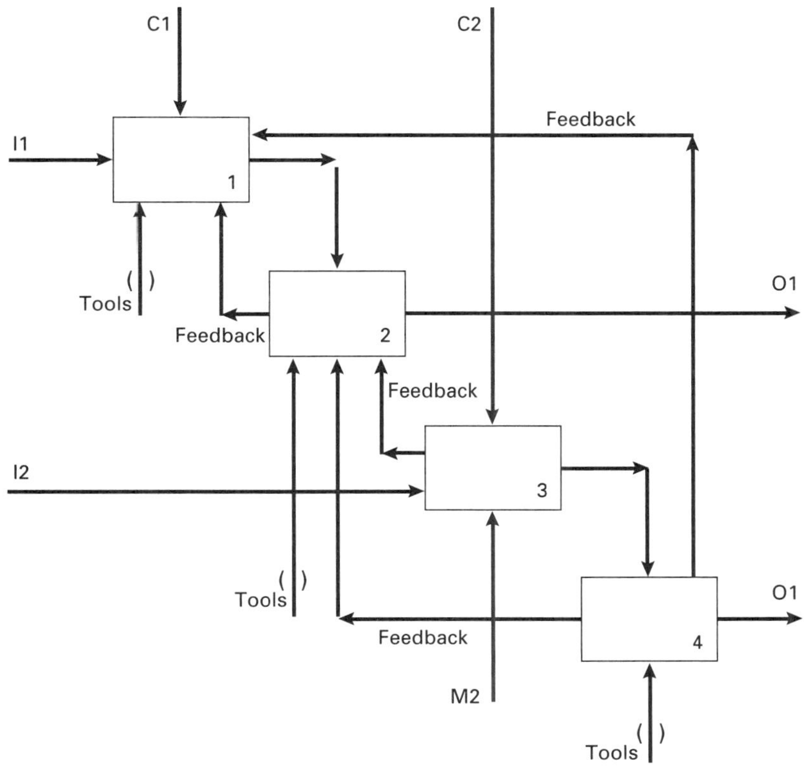

Figure 8.12 Detail diagram.

Example

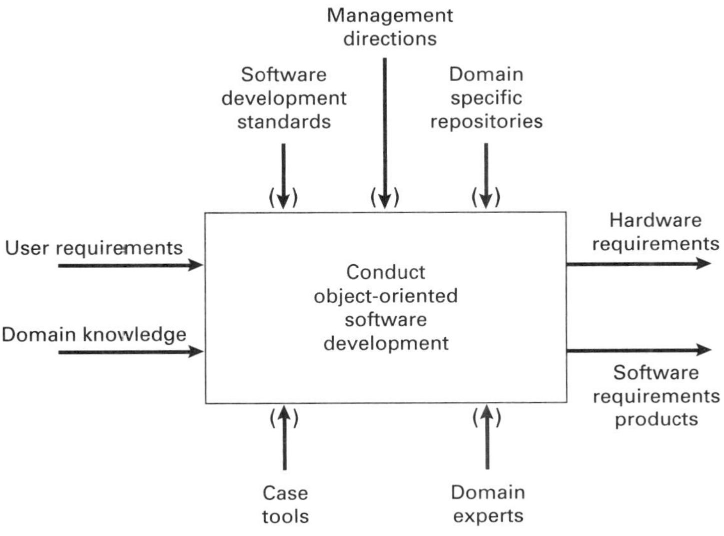

Figure 8.13 IDEFo object-oriented software development.

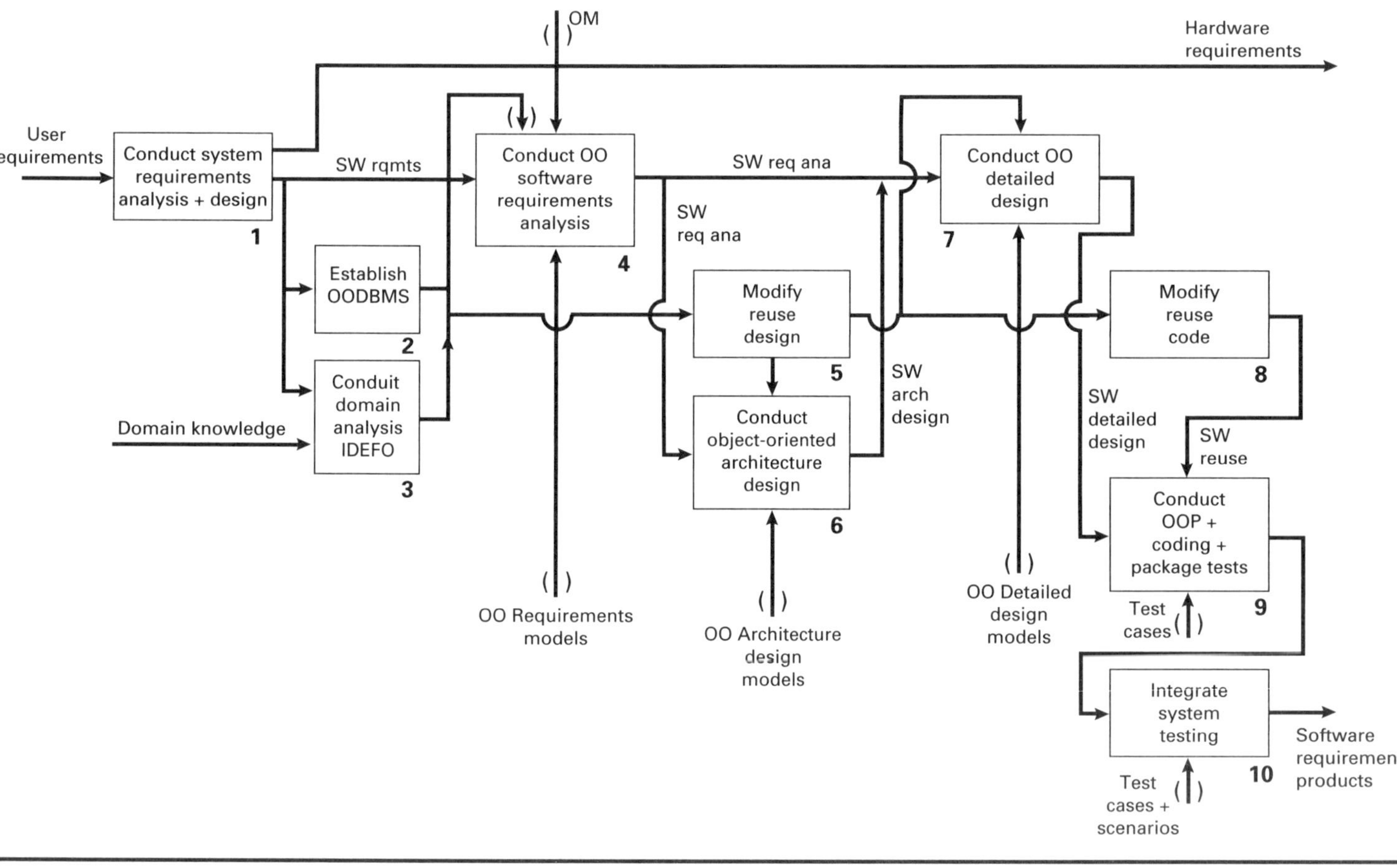

Figure 8.14   IDEFo lower level.

Object-Oriented Software Requirements Analysis Method

There are many object-oriented software requirements analysis methods available, and some have been briefly discussed in previous chapters. The *object-oriented method* (OOM) is developed toward the DOD standard particular for the development of object-oriented software. The concept of OOM is to understand customer requirements, and then it graphically shows the customer requirements by logical models. The OOM determines objects and establishes relationships between objects. The instantiation criteria for objects and their relationships are determined, and functional processes are developed. The OOM covers all phases of the software development life cycle. The OOM is in evolution.

OOM Overview

The OOM is the combination of an object-oriented approach, a data structure approach with entity-relationship modeling, and a functional process approach. It provides a systematic methodology for problem analysis of real-time, scientific, and business systems. Changes are propagated through all relevant steps and are reviewed at each phase of software development in accordance with MIL-STD-498. The OOM simplifies transitions between various phases of software development. It enhances communication among the system and software engineers and among management and users at all stages of the software development. It supports analysis and understanding of the requirements. The methodology is supported by many CASE tools. The OOM makes the evolving software a quality product that is visible and controllable at all stages of software engineering. The OOM is an open-ended, teachable, and easily transferable methodology.

OOM Goals

OOM goals capture in detail the domain-specific knowledge of the application in a form that lends itself to careful point-by-point verification by domain experts. The methodology provides, through formal models of the problem domain, a detailed and well-documented foundation where requirements decisions are made. The methodology transfers the domain knowledge accurately to the software engineers and communicates the requirements analysis in a form that is easily understood and mapped into an object-oriented design.

OOM Concepts

OOM is to understand the customer's requirements, graphically show the logic to the customers, and understand the stated requirements. They determine objects, establish relationships between objects, determine instantiation criteria for objects and their relationships, and develop functional processes. An object is a mental abstraction of a set of real-world things. This methodology uses concepts from object-oriented and structured approaches which include abstract data types, inheritance, and module coupling and cohesion. It uses graphical models with proper documentation which transfers the requirements from one phase to another for implementations. The OOM couples its analysis into object-oriented design (OOD) and is implemented in any suitable object-oriented programming language, including Ada. This concept maintains the traceability of the requirements for embedded systems. The methodology provides the project controls and communication tools for management, quality assurance, and documentation formats. Such systems can be developed cost-effectively and efficiently, and they can be effectively maintained for a longer time. Table 9.1 shows the basic models which comprise the OOM.

Object analysis model

The *object analysis model* (OAM) consists of all the analysis needed so the customer's requirements can be understood. It also contains information with regard to all the identified external interfaces. This step

TABLE 9.1   OOM Basic Models

Object analysis model (OAM)
Object information model (OIM)
Object behavior model (OBM)
Object process model (OPM)
Requirements definition model (RDM)
Object-oriented design (OOD)

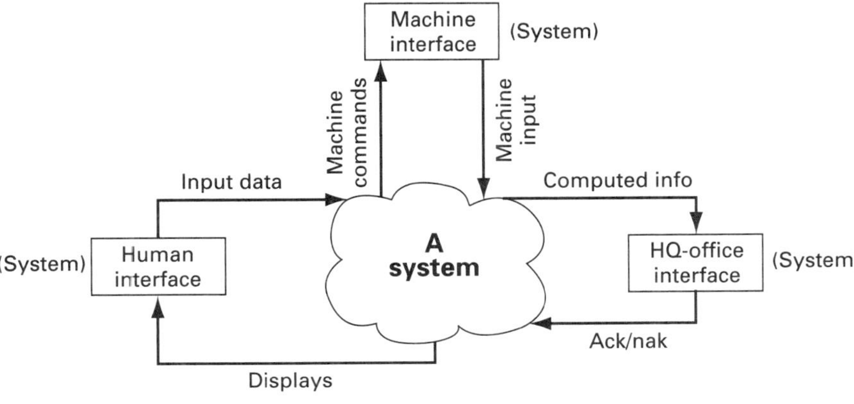

Figure 9.1 OAM diagram.

is especially important for the embedded systems. These interfaces
are linked with external systems as illustrated in Fig. 9.1. The point
of drawing this graphic is so that the customer's requirements are
understood in an unambiguous way and the customer understands
her or his stated requirements. Enough material about requirements
analysis has been discussed in previous chapters. The model can be
extended by identifying processes, data storages, and data flows. The
goal is that the requirements will be mutually understood and recorded in the proper document before proceeding to any further analysis
or design activity. The notations used in the graphic should be clearly
defined and properly recorded in the document for understandability.
The object data dictionary (ODD) can be initiated at this level by the
recording of this essential information.

Object information model

The *object information model* (OIM) identifies the conceptual entities
of the problem and formalizes them as objects and attributes.
Complete and unambiguous understanding of the problem is the goal.
OIM is the beginning of the analysis phase. It identifies things about
the problem and their relationship. Things and associations are modeled here. The model is simple enough to be easily read and understood. Significant emphasis is placed upon formalization of the relationships between objects. A model is developed and depicted
graphically, as shown in Fig. 9.2. The textual descriptions are used in
the definition of the model's semantics.

In Fig. 9.2, abstraction of "like things" is grouped together into sets.
Things are alike if they behave in the same way and can be described
by the same characteristics. This recognition of grouping leads to the

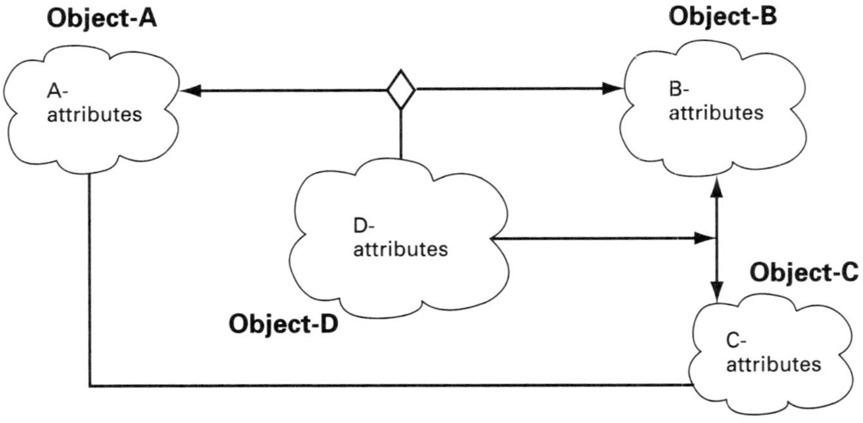

Figure 9.2 OIM diagram.

first cut by naming an *object*. The characteristics which all elements
of the set have in common are called *attributes* of the object. An
attribute is the abstraction of a single characteristic which is possessed by all entities and was abstracted as an object. The set of
attributes must be complete, fully factored, and mutually independent. There is a dot notation for attributes. Here is an example:

```
"Object.Attribute"
```

The types of attributes are descriptive, naming, and referential. The
descriptive attributes provide facts that are intrinsic to each instance
of the object. The naming attribute provides a fact about the arbitrary
name carried by each instance of the object. The referential attribute
links an instance of one object to an instance of another object.

Object-A

Attribute-A1	Attribute-A2	Attribute-A3	
Instance-A			

Figure 9.3 OIM table.

Tables are used for defining the types of questions which can be answered by inspection of the objects. The table name is the name of the object. Each column of the table is an attribute of the object. And each row is an instance of the object. The instance is the specific element of the set and is denoted by that object name. As illustrated in Fig. 9.3, every box in a table contains exactly one value. Attributes of an object should not contain internal structure. Tables are the basic formal structure of the OIM because they are simple and adequate. The object representation by table assists in the identification of the objects and attributes. The table also helps in the representation of instances of objects.

There exist "associations" between "things" in the real world. These associations must be formalized in this model. These can be recognized by verb phrases in the descriptions, for example:

```
The car has tires
```

Thus a relationship is named by a verb phrase. It can be phrased in both directions of the relation, for example,

```
A class is composed of students
```

and

```
Students compose a class
```

The same two objects may have more than one relationship between them. This depends on their type of relationship. An object may be related to itself. There can also be a relationship between multiple objects, for example,

```
Floppy Disk was formatted on Disk Drive
Floppy Disk is owned by a student
Floppy Disk contains disk files
```

This type of relationship which involves two objects can be classified into three fundamental forms and called *multiplicity* as shown in Table 9.2.

TABLE 9.2   Multiplicity Forms

Multiplicity	Notation	Example
One-to-one	(1:1)	Husband has a wife
One-to-many	(1:M)	Student owns books
Many-to-many	(M:M)	Capacitor is a component of a computer

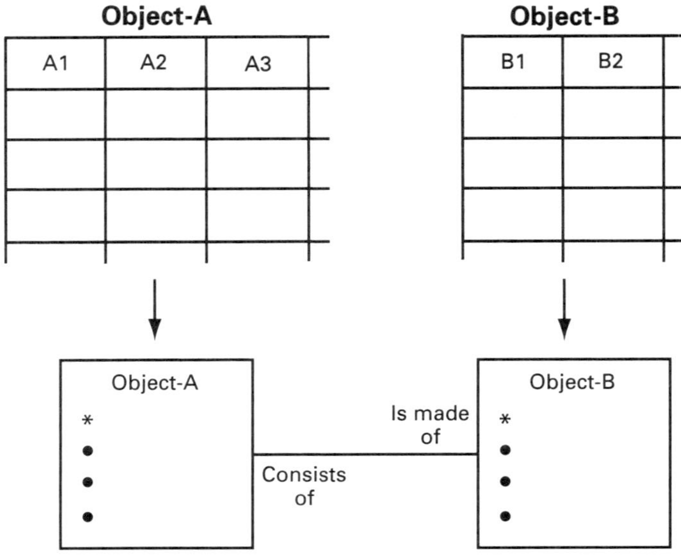

Figure 9.4 OIM table and object relationship.

A graphical notation is necessary for the replacement of a table for complex objects, as shown in Fig. 9.4. The graphical notation eases handling of complex systems. This graphical notation represents spatial compression of the model. Thus OIM notation representations are illustrated in Fig. 9.5. A supertype and subtype construct is shown in Fig. 9.6. The correlation relationship symbol is illustrated in Fig. 9.7.

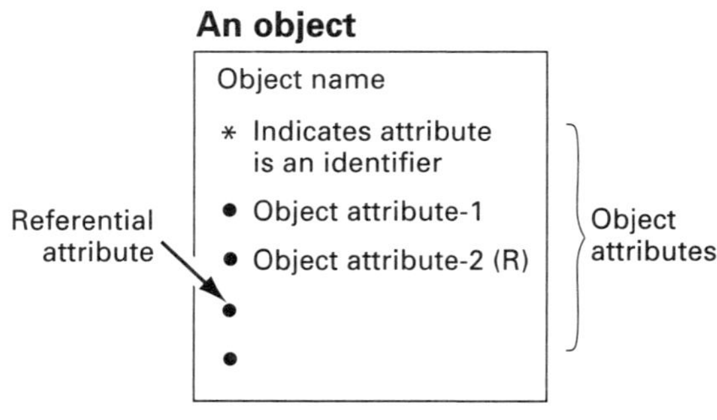

Figure 9.5 OIM notations.

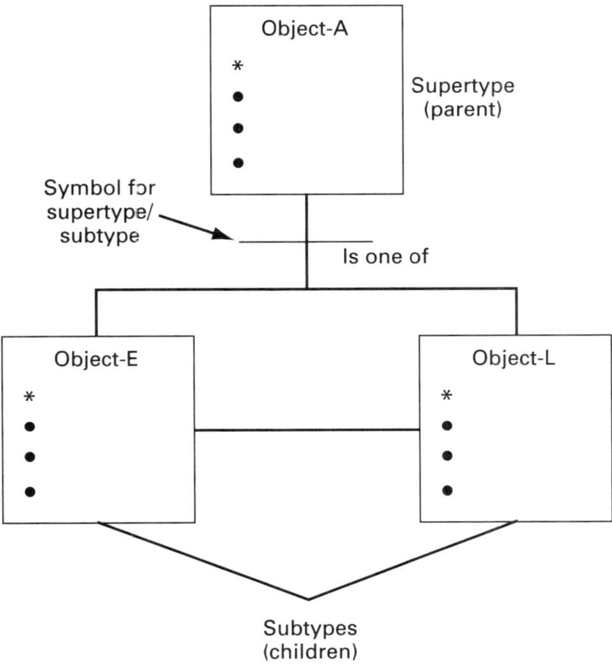

Figure 9.6   Supertype/subtype constructs.

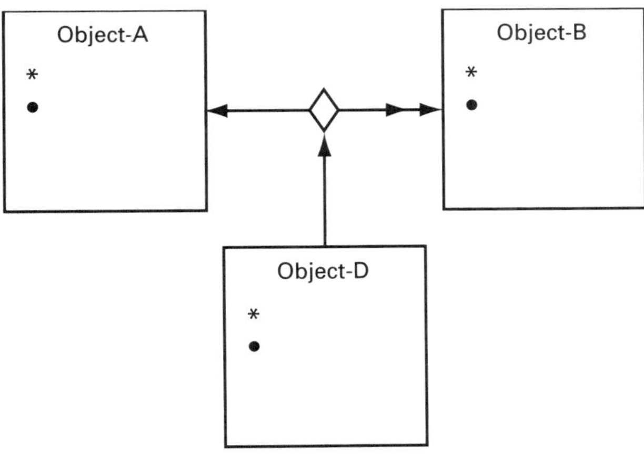

Figure 9.7   Correlation symbol.

Object data dictionary.   The objects, attributes, and their relationships are documented in an *object data dictionary* (ODD). This document consists of a written description of objects, formalizes the identification of objects, forms part of the formal system specification, and separates descriptions that are written for each object. This is a live document and should start at the beginning of the software engineering and grow throughout the software development and maintenance phases.

Selection criteria for a correct object.   There are four major tests which help by not accepting false objects. These are listed in Table 9.3.

The *uniformity test* is based on the definition of an object; each instance of the object must have the same set of characteristics and be subject to the same rule.

The *more-than-a-name test* is applicable to those objects which cannot be described by attributes. This object has no characteristics other than its name. Probably it is an attribute of another object. It is already defined that every object has attributes.

The *OR test* is conducted on the object description. If the inclusion criterion in the object description uses the word *or* in a significant manner, then you probably have a set of diverse things rather than an object.

The *more-than-a-list test* is conducted on the object description. If the inclusion criterion is in the object description, then it is simply a list of all specific instances of the object, and it is most likely not a true object.

Object behavior model

The *object behavior model* (OBM) formalizes the life or event histories of objects and relationships, as was identified in OIM. "Things" go through various stages during their lifetime in the real world. The life cycle of an object is therefore the behavior of an object during its lifetime. An example of an object lifetime diagram is presented in Fig. 9.8.

TABLE 9.3   Testing Objects

Uniformity test
More-than-a-name test
OR test
More-than-a-list test

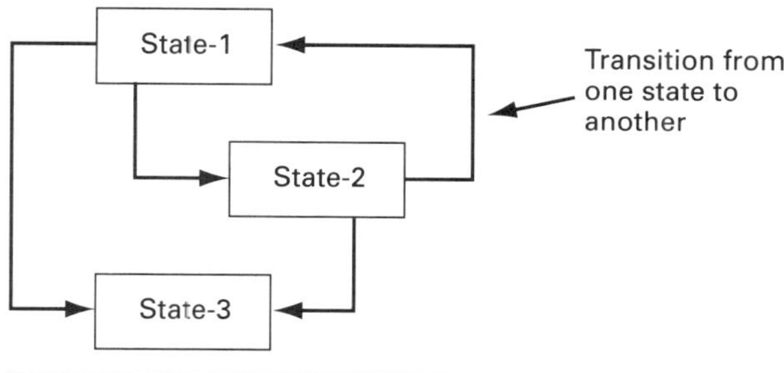

Figure 9.8 Object lifetime diagram.

An object may be in *only* one stage at a time. The stages are mutually exclusive. These stages are discrete, and transitions can occur instantaneously. Transitions from any stage to any other stage are not always allowed. Incidents cause the transition of things between stages. Some incidents cause a progression only when the thing is in certain stages of its life cycle. Similar characteristics of real-world "things" have a common life cycle. Thus the OBM is a formalization of the life cycle of an object in regard to the following parts:

- States
- Events
- Transitions
- Actions

The *state* of OBM corresponds to the state of an object's life cycle. An *event* is an incident or action that causes a progression to another state or to the same state. The *transition* is the new state of an object if a particular event occurs while the object is in a particular state. The *action* is the function that is performed immediately upon entering a new state. Each state can have only one action, but that action might consist of many processes.

A sample OBM is shown in Fig. 9.9. The boxes represent the states. The lines represent the events. The event causes the transition to the new state.

Figure 9.10 represents an alternative version of a state transition diagram (STD), which is a kind of OBM. An alternative form of state model representation is the state transition table (STT), shown in Fig. 9.10. In the STT, the rows represent states, the columns represent events, and the cells represent the effect of each event in each state. When a particular event cannot happen for a particular state of

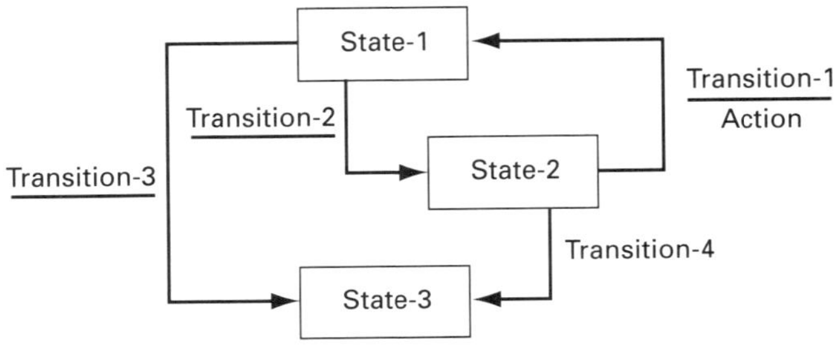

Figure 9.9 OBM sample.

the object, then the cell entry cannot happen. The event may be prevented from happening for many reasons, such as a physical impossibility, definition of the object, and constraints. If a particular event can happen for a specific state of the object, but the object does not respond to the event, then an "event ignored" entry is made in that cell. If the event is ignored, then the object stays in the same state. The advantage of STT is that it can be extended by adding another column for action and is associated with entering each state. The information contained in the STT or STD is the same. But the development of the STT from the STD will catch one of the most common errors in developing an OBM. This is illustrated in Fig. 9.11.

OBM is built for each dynamic object in the OIM. The following are suggested guidelines for constructing an OBM.

- Take one instance of the model, and analyze and record the life cycle of that instance.

- Write down the various states for that instance.

- Find the states which consider all relationships of the object.

- Build an STT.

	Event-1	Event-2	Event-3
State-1	Effects of event-1 in state-1		
State-2		Effects of event-2 in state-2	
State-3	Effects of event-1 in state-3		

Figure 9.10 State transition table sample.

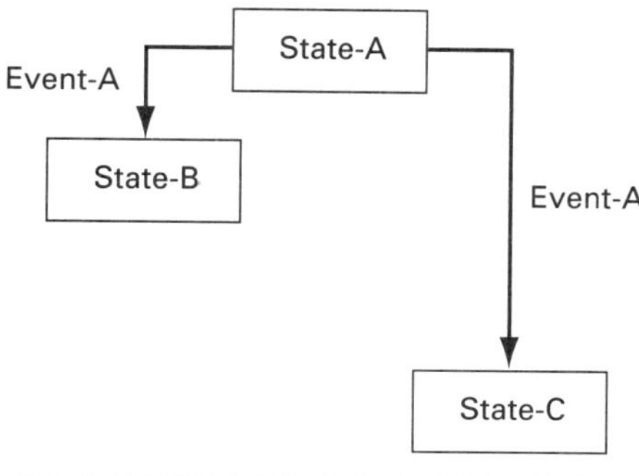

Figure 9.11   STT check.

- Check the table for new or additional states.
- Define the action which will be executed upon entry into a state.
- Identify nonfinal states.
- Identify events which the object must generate so it can exit non-final states.
- Expand actions which generate these events.
- Add the new events to the STT.
- Complete the STT.
- Complete the STD.

Object process model

The *object process model* (OPM) makes use of data flow diagrams and develops the required processes which drive the objects through their event chains. The principle of data flow diagrams has been discussed in the book *Software Engineering Methods, Management, and CASE Tools,* by the author. Only a few concerns with objects will be discussed here.

The following is a suggested list of processes for the development of a data flow diagram of a single object.

- Develop an OBM which formalizes the behavior of an object over time.
- Analyze the action which is performed when the state is entered.
- Break the action down into a sequence of processes.
- Depict each process as a data flow diagram.
- Place each action data flow diagram on a separate page.

The data of an object are represented as a data store in the data flow diagram. The data store will be recorded in the object data dictionary. The data store for the object contains all the attributes of the object. The instances of the object are created and stored in the data store. The data store holds all data and all attributes of all instances of the object. The data store is shared by all action data flow diagrams. The data flow diagram involves data stores which are made up of attributes of those data. These processes are discrete.

Requirements definition model

The requirements definition model determines what information and processes will be used within the automated system as opposed to those which will be carried out by operators or other external agents. It describes the boundary statements and clarifies the system specification.

Object-oriented design

Enough material for OOD will be covered in the next chapters.

OOM and DOD-STD-2167A or MIL-STD-498/IEEE 1498

OOM fits in DOD-STD-2167A or MIL-STD-498 requirements for software development. A set of formal reviews and audits is necessary at different phases of the software development and testing. The standard should be tailored and should produce necessary documentations. Some OOM notations should be identified with respect to the standard. The object and its life cycle should be considered as a capability. Each capability should be correlated with the matching requirement in the system specification. Its purpose should be stated clearly, and its performance should be described in measurable terms. The data item description specifically refers to an established relationship of capability to the state and modes of the system.

The external interfaces are established, and the internal interfaces are further identified by OOM models. The data elements of the standard can be recognized by the organization of objects and attributes. A computer software configuration item corresponds to the system or problem domain of the OIM. The computer software components correspond to the identified objects, and the computer software units related to the processes.

OOM Benefits

The OOM is stable under changing requirements. It does not require a system boundary. The notations used are simple and understandable. This method aids in minimizing code.

OOM Weaknesses

The OOM is evolving and not yet mature. There is a lack of standardization. External stimuli and responses are not apparent.

Object-oriented methodology represents the emergence of an object-oriented approach, a data structure approach with entity-relationship modeling, and a functional process approach. The OOM is an open-ended, teachable, and easily transferable methodology. OOM is stable under changing requirements. The notations used are simple and understandable. OOM fits in the standard for DOD-STD-2167A and MIL-STD-498 software development.

Object-Oriented Software Development Methods

This chapter covers the evolution of an object-oriented software methodology called ObjectOry and an object-oriented structured design (OOSD).

ObjectOry

ObjectOry is an object-oriented software development methodology. It covers the analysis, design, and test phases of the software development cycle. It supports object-oriented features such as objects, classes, and inheritance during both analysis and design. The development steps are unified in a seamless way. It defines a process that is considered a factory. This factory is installed in a systems development department where the analysts, designers, and programmers become the mechanisms for operating the process.

System development

The scenario assumed when one is building a system is similar to the manner in which construction is carried out in many other disciplines such as house construction, design of electronic systems, or, in simplified form, a system built of a set of application modules called *blocks,* as shown in Fig. 10.1. A block itself may be made up of other lower-level blocks or by *components.* Components are standard modules which can be used for many different applications. The lowest-level blocks are made up of components only. Blocks as well as components are naturally implemented as classes which use object-oriented programming.

The input to ObjectOry is the customer requirements, and the output is a system description which includes the complete program

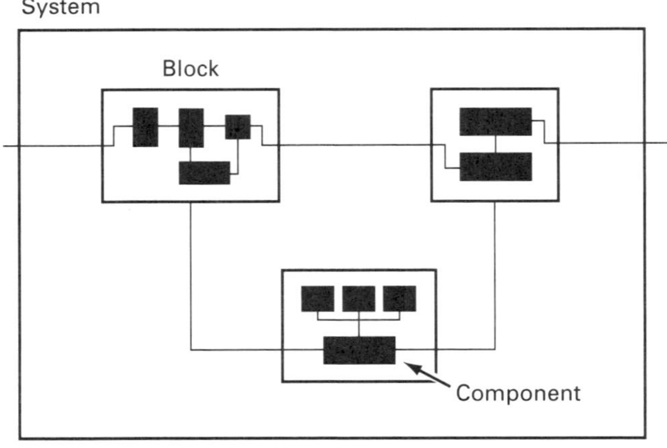

Figure 10.1   A system is composed of blocks. Blocks are designed with components.

code, as shown in Fig. 10.2. The customer requirements and the system description are two different, yet related, models of the behavior of a system. The requirements should be met by the system description. The program code which is included in the system description has a formal meaning and can be interpreted unambiguously. In between these two "endpoints," a number of other models are designed. The objective is partitioning of the complex work on a large system into steps and allows more developers to participate in the work. Developers make proper decisions for getting closer to the final model—a well-formed system. Every new model gives more formal structure to the system than the previous model did.

In order to make the transfer of the different models as simple and errorfree as possible, one model of the system must relate to the next. The models are seamlessly related to one other if concepts introduced in one of the models can be found in the other model through simple mapping.

Most systems in the industry must have a long life. During this lifetime, they undergo constant changes. System development is an

Figure 10.2   The system development process ObjectOry its input and output.

activity that changes a system from being one thing to another different thing. The first development cycle is a special case—a change from nothing to something. Software development is done incrementally, rather than concurrently. The main items in the system are modeled first, the items of less importance next, and so on. Work on different models can be described as sequential. Normally modeling is done in parallel.

Because modeling is viewed as a changing process, this technique also is useful for rapid prototyping. A particularly interesting part or feature can be studied in advance. A prototype of the system is made which can be easily changed.

ObjectOry consists of two processes, as shown in Fig. 10.3. These processes correspond to the real-world-oriented analysis phase and implement the oriented design phase of system development. These processes encapsulate the activities as well as the objects manipulated by the activities. Processes can be concurrent. They communicate with one another by the use of messages. A process is also an object, but an object as an enterprise model, not as a computational object.

System analysis

System analysis (SA) uses the customer's requirements and produces a specification of the requested system in cooperation with the customer. It consists of five subprocesses, which are shown in Fig. 10.4. There is only one instance of a specification process created for each identified object in the system.

Use cases

A *use case* is a special sequence of transactions performed by the system interacting with a user in dialogue. A user can be an object which represents anyone that is external to the system and interacts with it in some way, that is, by exchanging information with it. This means

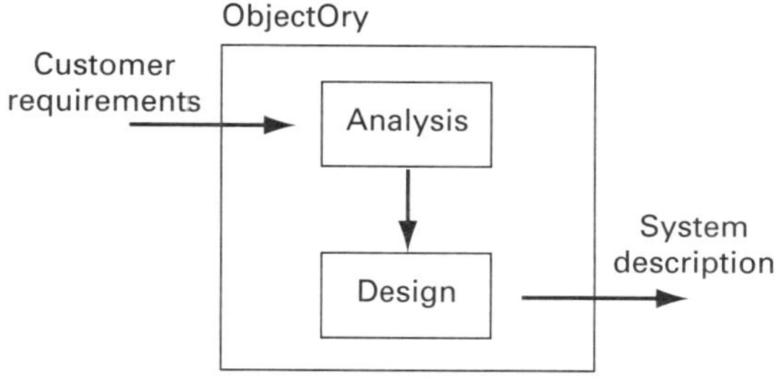

Figure 10.3 ObjectOry consists of two subprocesses: analysis and design.

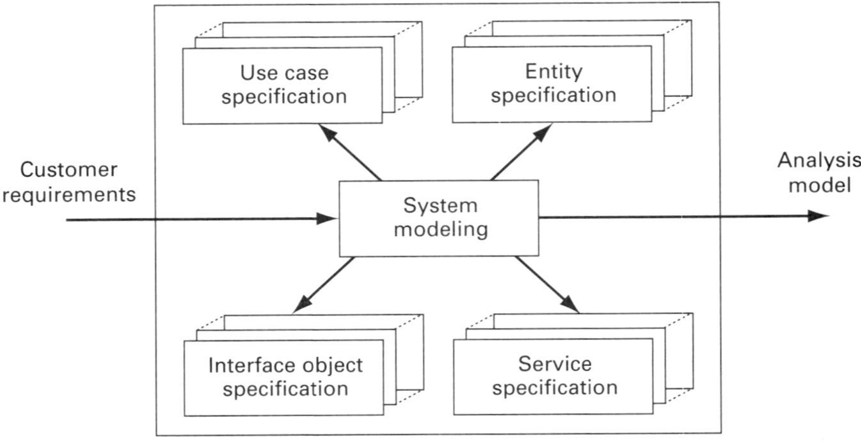

Figure 10.4 Analysis with its subprocesses.

that a user can be another system or another computer that communicates with your system via network as well as a human user. A transaction is initiated by a stimulus and may in turn create new stimuli or transactions. When no more stimuli can be generated, then the transactions will finally end and the use case is finished. A use case is always initiated by a user, and in general there can be several use cases which perform in parallel in the system.

The basic idea of ObjectOry is design for users. The system is described as a black box by the description of a number of its aspects. Each of these different aspects corresponds to a behaviorally related sequence and is called *use case*. In order for users to be guaranteed the system they want and need, the system's total behavior is structured in aspects, where each aspect corresponds to a use case. The collected description of the set of use cases then constitutes the total behavior of the system and is the main part of the input that is designed. The guarantee then becomes a matter for the designers so that the requested ways of using the system are implemented by means of design elements which are blocks. Tracing of a given use case is now possible throughout the entire design.

The use cases (UCs) are illustrated in Fig. 10.5. They consist of nodes and arcs between the nodes. The nodes correspond to use cases, and the arcs represent associations between the use cases. The dotted arrows indicate that they associate classes of objects rather than instances. Figure 10.5 contains two types of associations:

1. The *isA* associations mean that the associating use case inherits all the behavior, which is defined in the other use case. It also contains

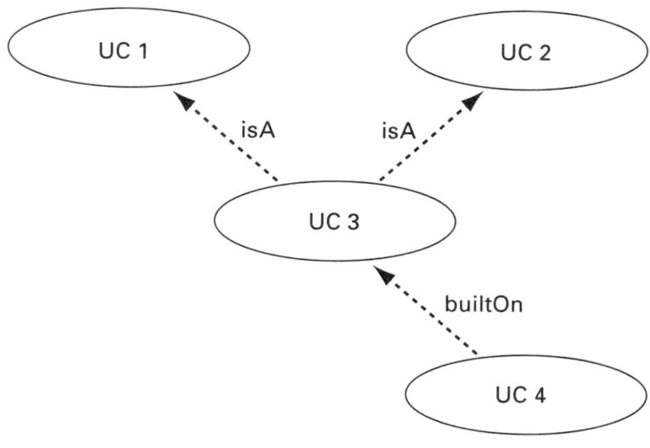

Figure 10.5 A schematic conceptual model of the system's use cases.

more behavior that is added to the inherited parts. Therefore, this use case can be seen as a specialization of the inherited one. Multiple inheritances are common.

2. The *builtOn* associations indicate that the associated use might be extended by the behavior in the associating use case. In this manner, only the extending part has to be specified in the associating use case. The behavior in the associating use case will be added and will also be specified.

Each use case is described in a semiformal manner by the use of structured English or by using graphics—a data flow diagram or a state transition diagram. The use cases are handled during a great number of activities. Therefore, they have unique identities that follow them throughout these different activities.

Entities

In ObjectOry information data are modeled in terms of entities together with operations on these data. Entities are things, often close to reality, about which you make assertions and about which you want information. The reason for some specific piece of information that is being modeled as an entity is a use case that you have already identified, and it needs to fulfill its responsibilities. Since the entities mirror objects in reality, it is of utmost importance that the entities reflect in the developed system. Then the system can follow reality, and changes in reality can be transferred in a simple manner to changes in the system.

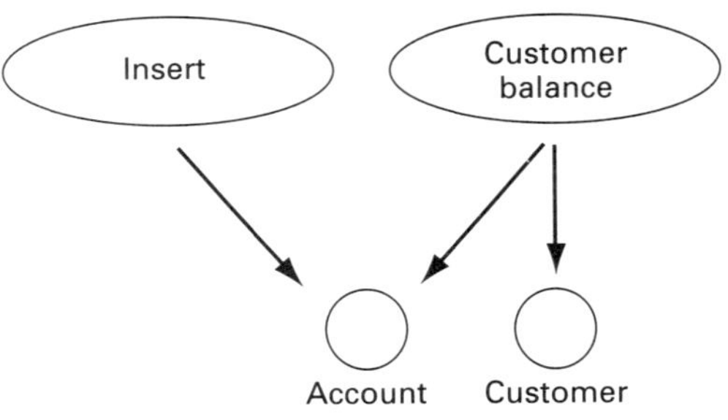

Figure 10.6 An example with some use cases, entities, and access associations.

A use case is one that needs inspection or manipulation of data stored in an entity and has an access association to this entity. The access associations correspond to operations on the information in the entity. Operations are defined in the entity. Entities together with these access associations are shown in Fig. 10.6. The access associations are represented by a full-drawn arrow. This is an indication that they associate instances of the objects and are unlike the isA association, for example.

Entities are associated with one another in many different ways. Like use cases, entities may inherit each other and are modeled by an isA association as well. There are two more associations that associate instances of entities. The *acquaintance* association is used in describing how the different entities depend on one another and show their relations to one another. This association is called *acquaintance association* since it indicates an instance of an entity and knows of instances of another entity. An entity can have access associations to other entities as well as use cases which can associate entities in this way. As in the use case, it represents a permission for an instance of the associating entity in accessing data stored in an instance of the associated entity. In this way a lot of the "intelligence" in the system is located in the entities; behavior that is closely related to the entities is attached to the entities directly. Information is never used independently by the use cases but is always accessed via an entity and is modeled as an *attribute* to this entity. The total amount of information of an entity is made up of its attributes and its acquaintance associations. Entities with their isA and acquaintance associations are shown in Fig. 10.7.

Interface objects

A complete description of the interaction between users and the system is given in terms of *interface objects*. All communication between

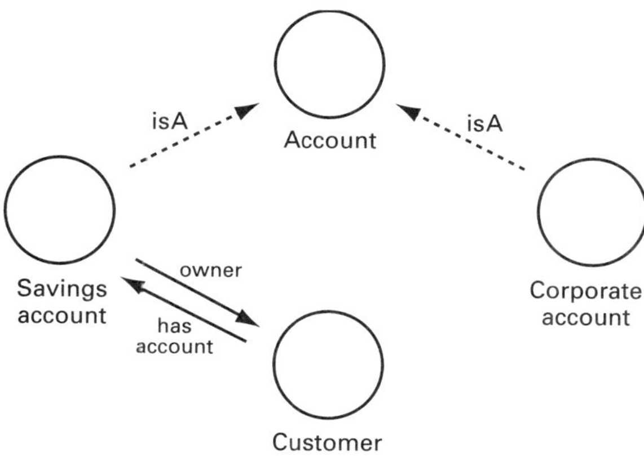

Figure 10.7 A schematic conceptual diagram modeling some entities and their associations.

users and the system goes through interface objects, even for nonhu-
man users. Examples of interface objects are a terminal and a communication protocol.

All use cases that a user needs for communication with a specific
interface object are connected to this interface object via *communication associations*. Therefore several use cases can be reached via one
interface object. However, one use case may communicate with outside the system via more than one interface object. Also, several users
may communicate with the system by use of the same interface
object. Two interface objects can have a communication association.

The interface objects serve as a translator of stimuli that are sent
from users to the use cases and vice versa, so the stimuli will be
transformed to something that the receiver can understand. The
demands on this transformation can be found in the *presentation
objects* and define the communication between the outside and inside
of the system. The presentation objects can be specified by finite
automations which define the possible states of the communication,
and a set of pictures and shows how information is to be presented for
the user at each state. One important property of defining the user
interface separately from the deeper structure of the system is that if
the system is moved to another outer environment, only the interface
objects have to be changed.

Services

A conceptual model consisting of use cases, entities, and interface
objects is a complete functional specification of a system in a semiformal form. The collective behavior of the system has been described in

such a manner that both the customer and the designer can be satisfied. The system is presented to the customer in terms of use cases that correspond to the different manners in which the system will be used. Those are entities which correspond to the objects in the customer's world and finally in terms of interface objects that define the customer's view of the system from the outside.

Through the entities and the interface objects, designers have obtained a source for structuring their model of the system into suitable modules. By letting each entity and each interface object correspond to a block, a system is obtained which seamlessly reflects its surroundings. Changes in the surroundings are frequently local in existing, real objects and will then also be local in the system. Unfortunately the use cases are not easy to modularize. A use case cuts right through the system and normally means that many mutually dependent system functions are used. By looking at the modeling of service, the objects which are identified so far will be put together into packets containing objects that correspond functionally. These packets are called *services*.

Services have two important tasks during system development:

- Identification of the packets that contain behaviorally related functions

- Identification of different packets of functions that will be offered to buyers of the system. To each customer corresponds a specific set of such packets.

These two functions of services motivate an analysis activity, not a design activity. The services are identified by the use of use cases. The use cases that are related functionally are put together in a service. However, one important criterion is that the behavior encapsulated in the use cases must be put into service *uniquely*. This means the same piece of behavior must not be found at more than one place in the service model, not even as a part of larger use cases. Therefore, behavior that is common to two or more use cases is identified and separated from these use cases and constitutes a use case of its own. This new, abstract use case is inherited by the use cases that share it, and it is allocated to a service independently. When all the unique behavior in the use cases has been mapped into the services, then the rest of the identified objects, that is, the entities and the interface objects, will be distributed among the services. This will be done by the use of the criterion of functional dependency between objects.

The services are related to the use cases in the following manner:

- A use case employs a specific set of services.

- A service can participate in many use cases.

- The set of use cases for a specific customer determines the mixture of services to be ordered.

The conceptual model of the services is the input to the design activities and provides support in the selection of the architecture for the design.

System design

Input to design is the analysis model with four conceptual diagrams—use cases, entities, interface objects, and services. The analysis model will now be seamlessly mapped into a design model which includes the final implementation in the form of the program code. Design is partitioned into subprocesses as shown in Fig. 10.8. The system-level design transforms the entities and services to a model of the system

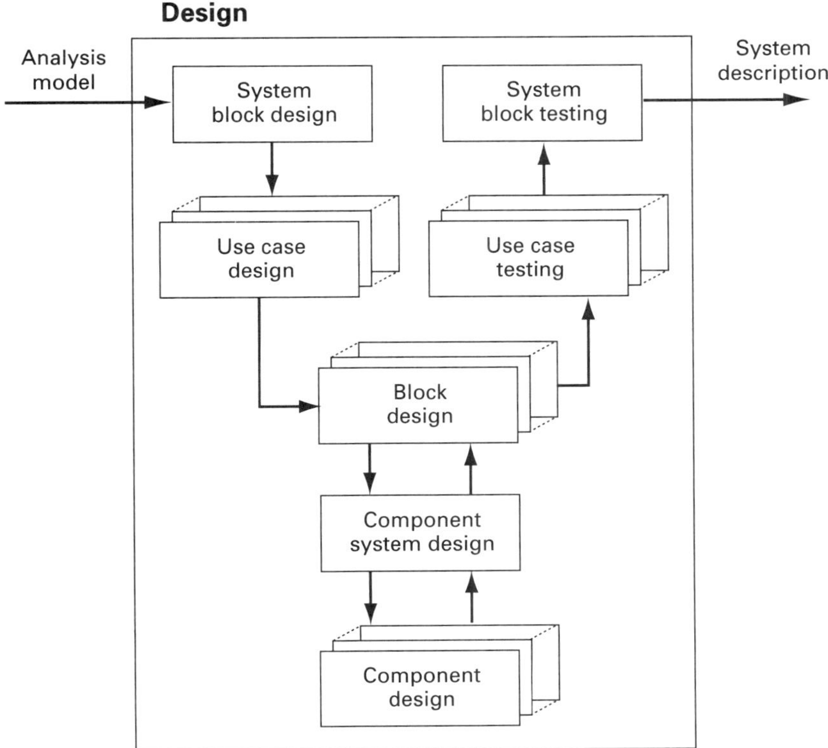

Figure 10.8 Design with its subprocesses.

TABLE 10.1   ObjectOry's Design Subprocesses

System block design
Use-case design
Block design
Component design
Use-case testing
System block testing

as a set of communicating physical blocks. Within this use, cases are transformed to test cases that will show how the use is implemented by the blocks. The block design breaks down each block into components, and components design either uses a library or specifies which modules are ready for programming. The subprocesses are listed in Table 10.1.

System block design is where the system structure is identified. The services and the objects in the services are used in the identification of the system blocks in a seamless fashion. A new model of the system is formed: The system is a set of communicating blocks.

Use-case design creates as many processes as there are use cases. The use cases are translated seamlessly to a new model which shows how each use case is implemented by means of the identified blocks.

In block design, one process is created for each block in the system.

Component system design is where the system components are identified. It is here that designers with experience in several applications participate. The component system design is responsible for the component library and consequently approves specifications and descriptions of new components. For very extensive system development activities, this process as well as the following process should be common to the design of several types of systems.

In component design, one process is created for each component in the library.

In use-case testing, the blocks that implement a use case are combined, and the use case is tested. Each use case is tested separately as a safeguard measure so that the system meets the requirements of the user. The use cases constitute the key aspect through the entire development activities.

In system block testing, integration tests make up the total set of use cases.

ObjectOry Methodology Discussion

The design model of a system is statically a set of interconnected blocks. These blocks communicate dynamically over well-defined

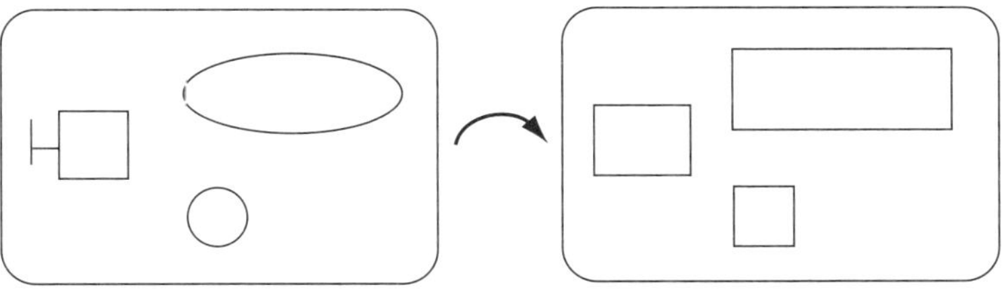

Figure 10.9 The services and objects contained in them correspond to blocks in the system block.

interfaces by sending some type of stimulus to one another. These stimuli can have different semantics that depend on how these blocks are implemented. The selection of a block is a compromise between the satisfaction of the requirements of a simple, ideal structure and the procurement of a system with good performance attributes. The ideal structure is achieved if each service is implemented as a block, a *function block,* and each object in all the services is implemented as an *object block.* In many cases it is possible that every object is translated and identified in the analysis directly into a block like this. When the block is structured, however, it is necessary to consider the available tools, such as language tools and the implementation environment. Other behavioral requirements such as response times, reliability, and efficiency will also influence the structure. In this manner a set of blocks is identified with each containing a set of object blocks which originate from the objects in the services, as shown in Fig. 10.9.

For large systems it is practical to group these blocks into large blocks called *subsystems.* A system block contains subsystems blocks, which in turn contain function blocks. At the lowest level in the block hierarchy, the object blocks exist.

Blocks are shown in a block diagram which presents the blocks and the communication paths between them, as shown in Fig. 10.10. The

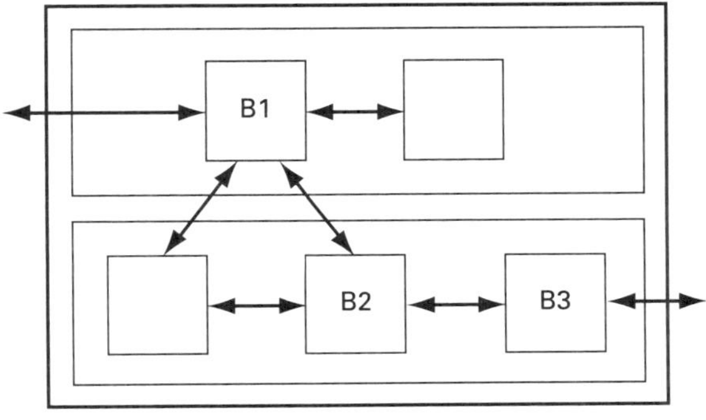

Figure 10.10 A schematic block diagram.

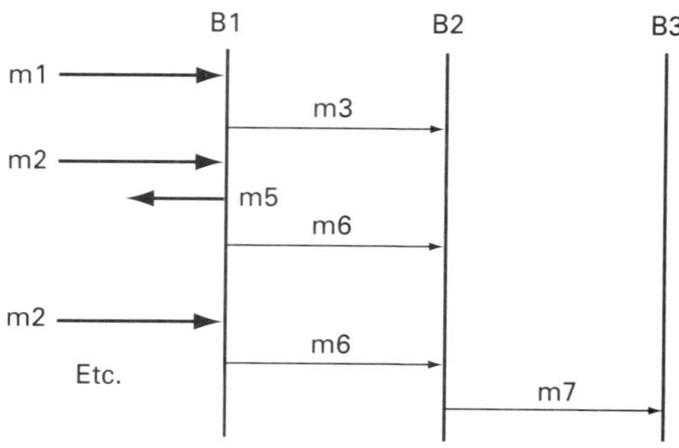

Figure 10.11   A schematic interaction diagram.

figure shows only the blocks that correspond to the object at the bottom of the isA structure. Blocks that correspond to objects higher up in this structure will instead be shown in an inheritance diagram. This diagram shows the isA associations between the blocks. The semantics in these associations are determined by the selected programming language.

Now the blocks have been identified, and the design work continues as each specified use case is implemented and described in terms of a subset of the blocks. This subset comprises the blocks that participate in the use case. This work is shown as an interaction diagram in Fig. 10.11, where the vertical time axis shows the interactions between the blocks in carrying out the use case. The exact semantics of the diagram are specified by the selected programming language. A skeleton of an interaction diagram with the permitted communication paths can be generated mechanically from the block diagram.

Blocks are application objects which are created in order that they may be combined with other blocks into a system. The blocks communicate with one another and fulfill the requested use cases. For example, a telephone system contains blocks which handle the communication with subscribers, blocks which handle the communication on junction lines that surround telephone exchanges, blocks which interconnect subscribers with other subscribers or lines, blocks which keep track of all the telephone calls, etc.

Blocks are reusable building blocks for customer adaptation of a specific application. There is an unambiguous relation between a service and a set of blocks. The blocks are equipment units that are in order and that assemble a system for a customer. Services are units that can be ordered. In Fig. 10.11, block B1 can receive two stimuli: m1 and m2. Other stimuli to block B1 may be extracted from other use-case interaction diagrams.

Blocks are implemented as classes in an object-oriented programming language. When one is designing a class that corresponds to a block, then properly interconnected components are used. The resulting source code of the block is tested by the designer and verified that it behaves as intended. If this is the case, then the block is output for use together with other blocks in use-case testing.

Components must be powerful, have simple, well-defined interfaces, be easy to learn and use, and have a wide area of use. In other words, components are highly reusable program elements. Some examples of components in the software field are the buffer, queue, list, and tree, which are suitable for use in normal programming and the implementation of algorithms. Other examples are the window, icon, and scroll area, which are suitable for the development of graphical human-machine interfaces. The components are defined on top of each other (or on top of the primitives); they are designed bottom-up.

During the implementation of a block the designer may recognize the need for a module that is judged for use in several other blocks. If the module is judged to be sufficiently useful for many other blocks, then the designer can propose that the identified module be standardized and classified as a component. Each component is implemented as a class in an object-oriented programming language.

ObjectOry has used different types of objects, listed in Table 10.2. These objects have a lot of different individual properties, but they also have many things in common. For example, there are instances of them. These instances belong to classes, and classes can inherit one another. All these common properties are found in a general type of object call Object, and all the object types inherit Object. The reason for all these different types of objects is that the criteria for identification of objects with different duties in the system are very different, as shown in Fig. 10.12.

Thus ObjectOry has combined a well-proved technique for large systems design called *block design* with conceptual modeling and object-oriented programming. These three techniques are very natural in unification since they rely on similar paradigms which aim at reusable software products, among other things.

TABLE 10.2   ObjectOry Object Types

Use cases
Entities
Interface objects
Services
Blocks
Components

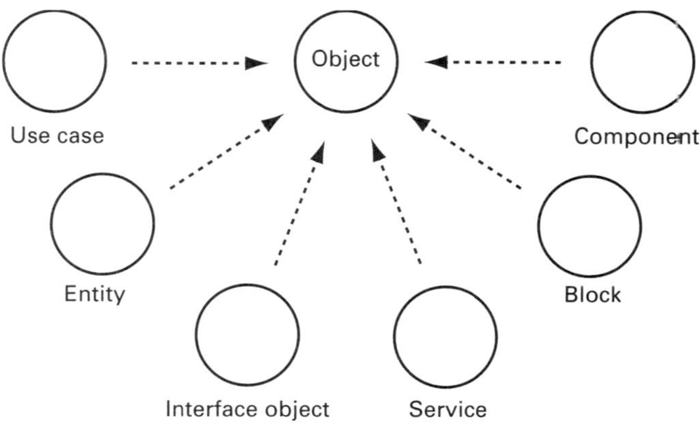

Figure 10.12   Common properties of the ObjectOry object types.

Advantages of ObjectOry

- Descriptions of system requirements in terms of real-world models are more easily understood by both analyst and client.

- Significant reduction of mistakes during requirements analysis reduces faults that are expensive to correct when detected later in the life cycle.

- Objects provide a natural way to model the description of concurrent activities.

- Encapsulation of data and operations in objects localizes the effects of change and hence reduces the cost of systems modification.

- Developers can understand the system quickly.

- Change in the development staff is easier because new staff can readily understand the design and purpose of the system.

- The major benefits of object-oriented concepts can be combined with languages that do not fully support these concepts, such as Ada or even Fortran and Cobol.

- When combined with the use of object-oriented programming languages, the maximum benefits of these languages are realized. (The ObjectOry methodology was developed by the Swedish company Objective Systems SF AB, Box 1128, S-164 22 KISTA, Sweden.)

Object-Oriented Structured Design

Object-Oriented Structured Design (OOSD) is a notation for the architectural design of software systems. It was developed by Anthony

Wasserman, Peter Pircher, and Bob Muller at Interactive Development Environment (IDE) and builds upon ideas from Constantine's structured design and Booch's object-oriented design. The OOSD synthesizes traditional, top-down design with modern concepts of object-oriented design to create a comprehensive approach for models of software designs.

OOSD goals

The major goal of OOSD is to support system partitioning into a software architecture. This provides a visual representation that shows the interfaces among design components. This supports automated generation of code for multiple programming languages, while remaining independent of any single language. Support of object-oriented concepts, classes, hierarchies, and inheritance is another goal of OOSD. This facilitates reuse of designs and design components. This method also provides a clear and simple notation that is suitable for automation and for easy communication among designers and reviewers.

OOSD concepts

OOSD is fundamental built on the following design concepts:

- Abstraction
- Modularity
- Concurrency

OOSD approach

The OOSD synthesizes top-down and bottom-up approaches to software design and various mixed approaches. The top-down design uses a process of functional decomposition to partition a system into modules. The structured design supports functional decomposition which uses structure charts as a design representation. A structure chart includes symbols for different module types and module connections, i.e., calls and parameters.

The object-oriented approaches are based on the identification of the classes of objects in a system. Classes are described in terms of behavior and structure, with each object modeling a real-world entity. For example, in a banking system there could be a class of checking accounts where each account would be an object. The object-oriented design proceeds by identifying classes that are appropriate for a given system. These classes are often derived from classes that have used previous designs and thereby support reuse. The object-oriented

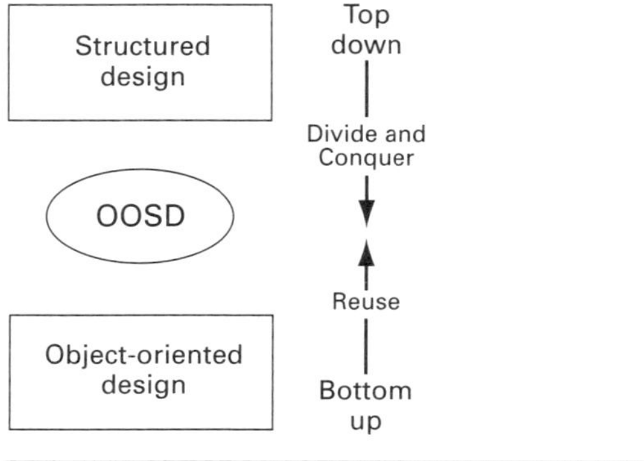

Figure 10.13 OOSD approach.

design is effectively a bottom-up design approach. The classes serve as building blocks in the overall design structure. Figure 10.13 illustrates the OOSD approach. The foundation of OOSD is structured design. It has been augmented by features for object orientation and concurrency. This approach permits designers to add to their experience with structured design (SD) and evolve toward OOSD.

OOSD notation

OOSD emphasizes a standard design notation that can be used and understood by all software designers, managers, and developers. The symbols used in OOSD also build on those from SD by adding the notation for exception handling, parallel processing, as well as the extension of Booch's OOD notation. The notation consists of the following parts, listed in Table 10.3.

Classes. Dynamic allocation and deallocation of storage is useful in many applications. In the definition of the class "storage" shown in Fig. 10.14, the operations are *allocate, free,* and *reset.* Each of these operations has a visible part and a hidden part. The visible part shows the interface to the operation, while the hidden part contains private information about the implementation details. Representation

TABLE 10.3   OOSD Notation Parts

Classes
Exceptions
Instantiation of objects
Generic classes
Instantiation of classes
Inheritance
Concurrency

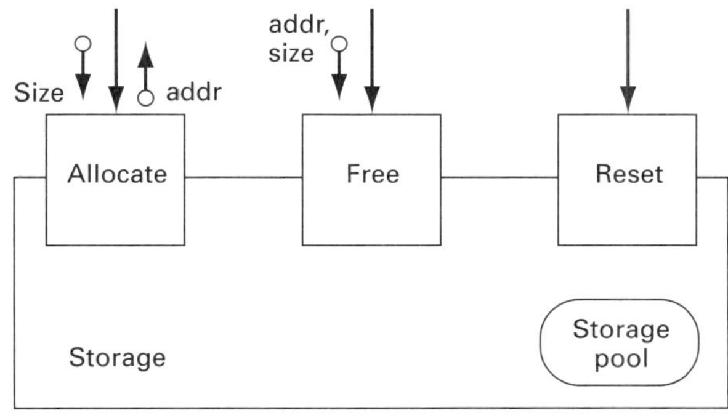

Figure 10.14   OOSD notation: dynamic allocation and deallocation of storage.

information is hidden in the data module *storage pool.* In Fig. 10.14, *allocate* accepts a single input data parameter, named *size,* and returns a single output data parameter, named *addr.* Both of these items are also used as inputs to the *free* operation.

Exceptions.   Operations on a class can raise exceptional conditions which indicate a failure of the operation. The exception handling features work as shown in Fig. 10.15. The defined operations are *push* and *pop,* and the defined exceptions are *over* and *under,* which are represented by the diamonds on the class definition for stack. The *push* operation, for example, accepts *item* as an input data parameter, accepts an object of the class (stack) as an input/output parameter, and can raise the *over* exception.

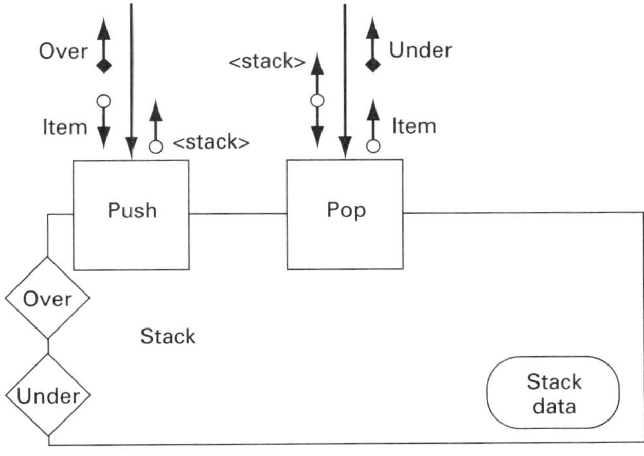

Figure 10.15   OOSD exceptions handling.

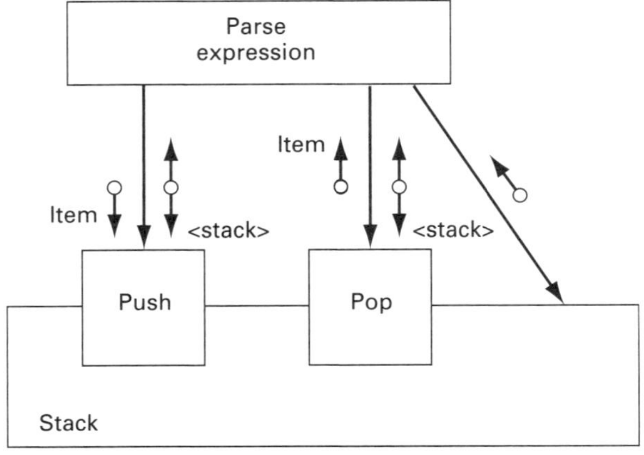

Figure 10.16 Instantiation of objects.

Instantiation of objects. Objects are defined as instances of a class and are normally defined in a module that uses the class. In Fig. 10.16, the module Parse Expression instantiates an object *evalstak* of the class *stack,* as shown by the return value on the thick arrow, which denotes instantiation or visibility. Multiple parameters can be used to show the instantiation of multiple objects.

Generic classes. A generic class definition is shown with a dashed box in Fig. 10.17. It has the same characteristics as a class definition with the added ability of denoting parameters. The generic class creates specific classes and provides value for the parameters. For example, the generic class *Table, size,* and *rectype* is composed of generic parameters that allow the creation of different classes of tables. The parameter *size* defines the size of the table, and the parameter *rectype* defines the type of records that comprise the table. The insert opera-

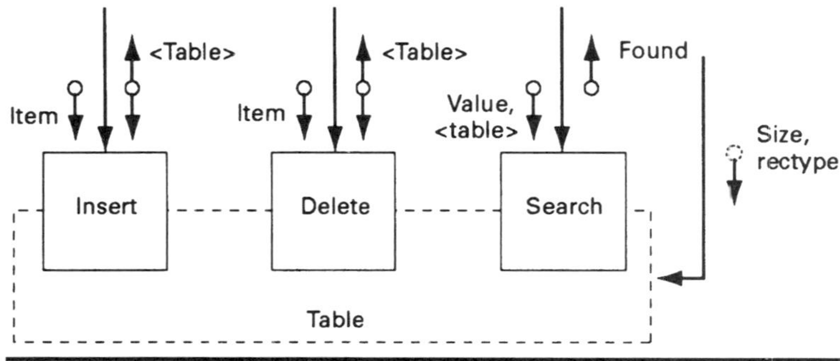

Figure 10.17 Generic classes.

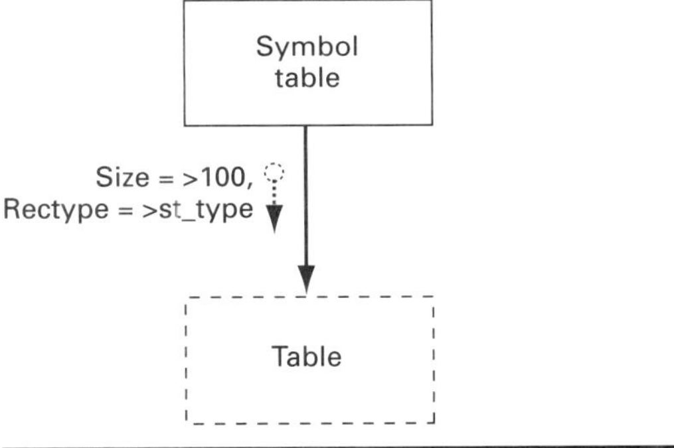

Figure 10.18　Instantiation of classes.

tion uses an input data parameter named *item* and an input/output data parameter of the class *Table*.

Instantiation of classes.　The generic class definition can be used in the instantiation of classes by providing values for the generic parameters. In Fig. 10.18, the class *Symbol Table* is derived from the generic class *Table* which could also be used for many other class definitions. The class *Symbol Table* inherits the operations *insert, delete,* and *search* from the class *Table,* so that they are defined on objects of the class *Symbol Table.*

Inheritance.　The object-oriented design requires a hierarchy of classes in which classes can inherit operations and structures from one another. For example, the definition of a class *polygon* can contain a subclass *rectangle,* which has in turn a subclass *square.* The class *polygon* has a superclass *shape.* A subclass inherits by default all the operations of its parent class, which is redefined. The subclass is extended with new operations or structure. Figure 10.19 shows that *polygon* is a subclass of *shape*; the dashed connection between the two lines indicates inheritance. The *area* operation is defined on the class *shape* and is automatically defined on the class *polygon,* which also contains the *sides* operation.

Concurrency.　OOSD provides support for the design of concurrent systems, as it is needed in real-time systems, transaction processing systems, and many other applications. The concurrency mechanism is very general and is based on Hoare's monitors. A monitor denoted by a parallelogram is similar to a class except that the monitor encapsulates data that are shared among various operations of the monitor. Figure 10.20 shows that in the buffering of data, one or more processes deposit data in a buffer (*put*), while one or more processes remove

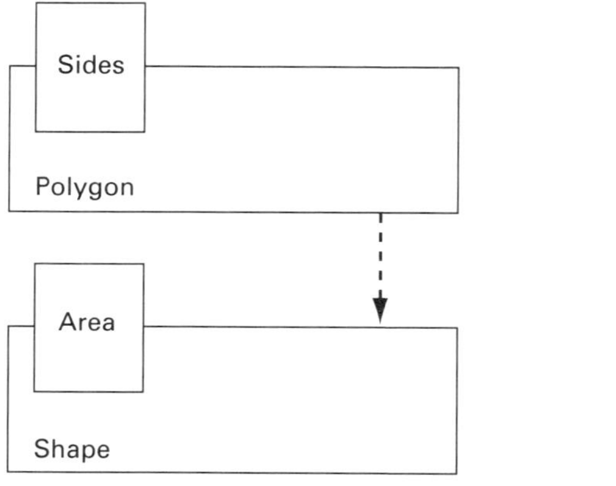

Figure 10.19 Inheritance.

data from the buffer (*get*). These operations require exclusive access to the shared data in *buffer data*. The need for shared access cannot be represented by a class, so a monitor is used to show this requirement.

OOSD benefits

The benefits of OOSD are that it can increase design quality, improve productivity, and create better communication among designers and reviewers. The method can be used for many different types of software designs and architectures and supports numerous programming languages. These include Ada and other object-oriented languages such as C++, Eiffel, and Smalltalk; as well as traditional programming languages such as Fortran and C.

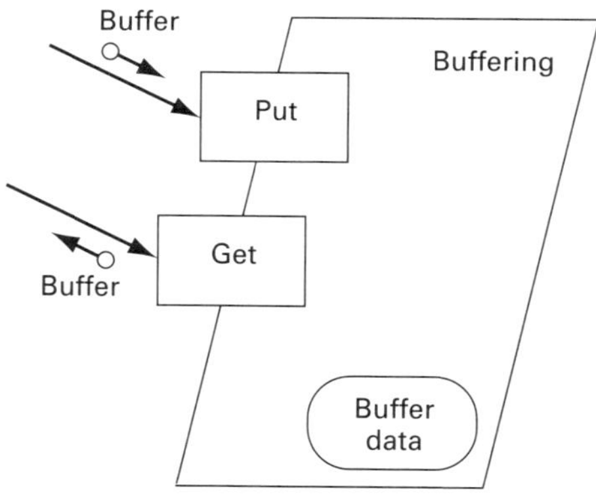

Figure 10.20 Concurrency.

The OOSD supports modern object-oriented approaches more effectively than other design notations and allows object-oriented design components to be gradually added to existing designs. The method also provides a well-defined visual interface to modules, classes, and monitors. This approach reduces design errors that are caused by improper interface specifications.

OOSD also supports reuse of designs, since the definition of classes and monitors is separated from the use. Thus a generic class definition, such as *Table,* can be used in the derivation of many class definitions for many systems and applications.

OOSD Application Example

An example of the design of automobile cruise control is discussed here at a very high level. The problem definition is as follows.

The cruise control system can operate only when the driver has started the engine successfully. When the driver activates the system, the system stores the current speed as the desired cruising speed and maintains that speed by monitoring actual speed, computing the required throttle position, and setting the throttle actuator to that value. While cruising, the driver can request the system to gradually accelerate, then stop acceleration and use the current speed as the new desired cruising speed; this is done with two buttons on the cruise control panel. Pressing the brake pedal stops the acceleration and suspends cruising; pressing the Resume button on the cruise control panel resumes cruising.

The driver may deactivate the system at any time by pressing the Off button on the cruise control panel. Turning off the engine also deactivates the cruise control; the hardware implements this by initiating a Deactivate event when the engine is turned off. If the driver wants to temporarily slow down, he or she can press the brake pedal; the driver can then instruct the system to resume cruising by pressing the Resume button.

Tire size and tire wear affect the speed measurements. Therefore, the system requires calibration of these measurements. When the cruise control is deactivated, the driver can start measuring a mile, then stop measuring a mile, both of which are buttons on the cruise control panel. The system will reset its internal speed conversion factor to reflect this calibration. To protect the driver, this feature is limited by factory-preset ranges so that only reasonable values for the conversion factor can be set by the driver.

Overall design of the cruise control software.   The overall object-oriented design strategy for the system, which is to be implemented in Ada, is to build active packages that monitor, actuate, and sense events and values in the hardware, then to interface these active packages to controlling procedures that implement the finite-state machines derivable from the requirements statement. The structure of the system hides all hardware interface details within logical packages that represent the specified features of the cruise control system. The structure also directly reflects the control structure required for each object.

The cruise controller. The Cruise_Controller diagram, shown in Fig. 10.21, show the top level of the cruise control design, which consists of the Cruise_Control procedure and the Cruise_Controller task that is lexically included within the procedure. The body of the procedure contains an entry call to enable entry of the controller task. That task monitors engine events and cruise control events, activating cruising or calibration as requested. The two procedures, activate_cruising and calibrate, are lexically included in the task, making them completely private. The task must have the engine and cruise control monitors visible. These monitors manage event handling for the appropriate set of events specified from the Events package. In this context, the task waits for an Engine_On event, then waits for any cruise_control event (indicated by passing Null_Event to the monitor wait_event interface). The task clears the events after processing them.

The activate_cruising procedure, shown in Fig. 10.22 is the largest component of the cruise control design and the most complex. This procedure monitors cruise control and brake pedal events in order to test for an acceleration or braking request and to wait for some cruise control request. This procedure controls the actual cruising behavior of the system by setting cruising speed, cruising, maintaining acceleration of cruising speed, resuming cruising after braking, and exiting or deactivating the cruise control when the driver turns off the engine or presses the Deactivate button.

The Speed package need only be visible to the set_speed_and_cruise procedure in this diagram. The cruise and maintain_acceleration procedures implement mutually exclusive processes and are developed further below.

The design logic for representing the relationship between setting speed, cruising, and resuming cruising requires division of the process into three procedures: cruise, set_speed_and_cruise, and resume_cruising. The last two procedures call the first; the difference is that set_speed_and_cruise sets the desired speed, which is declared within the activate_cruising procedure, while the resume_cruising procedure calls cruise without changing the desired speed. The choice

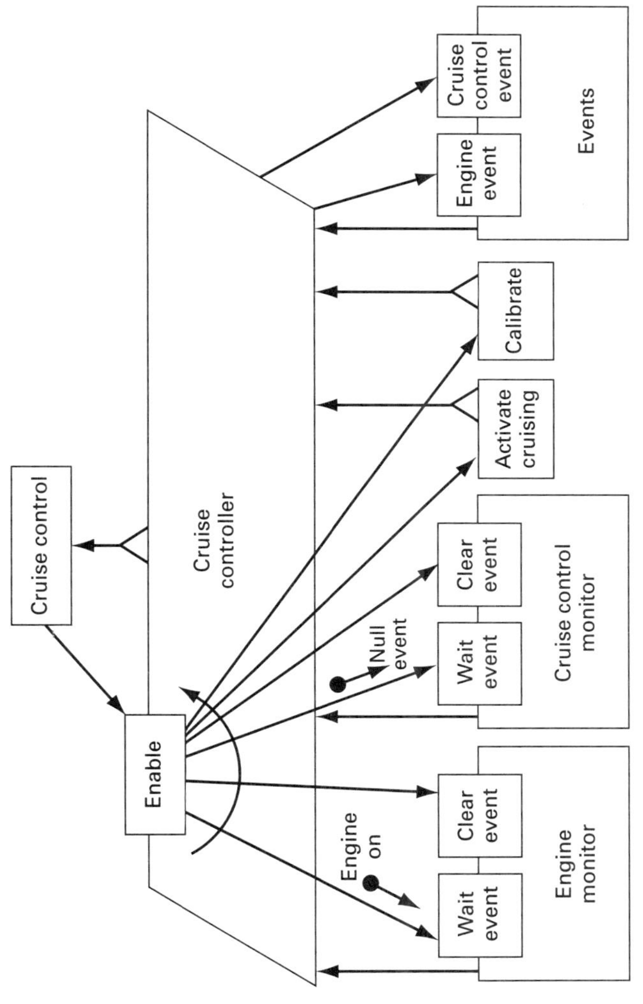

Figure 10.21 High-level architecture of the cruise control system.

171

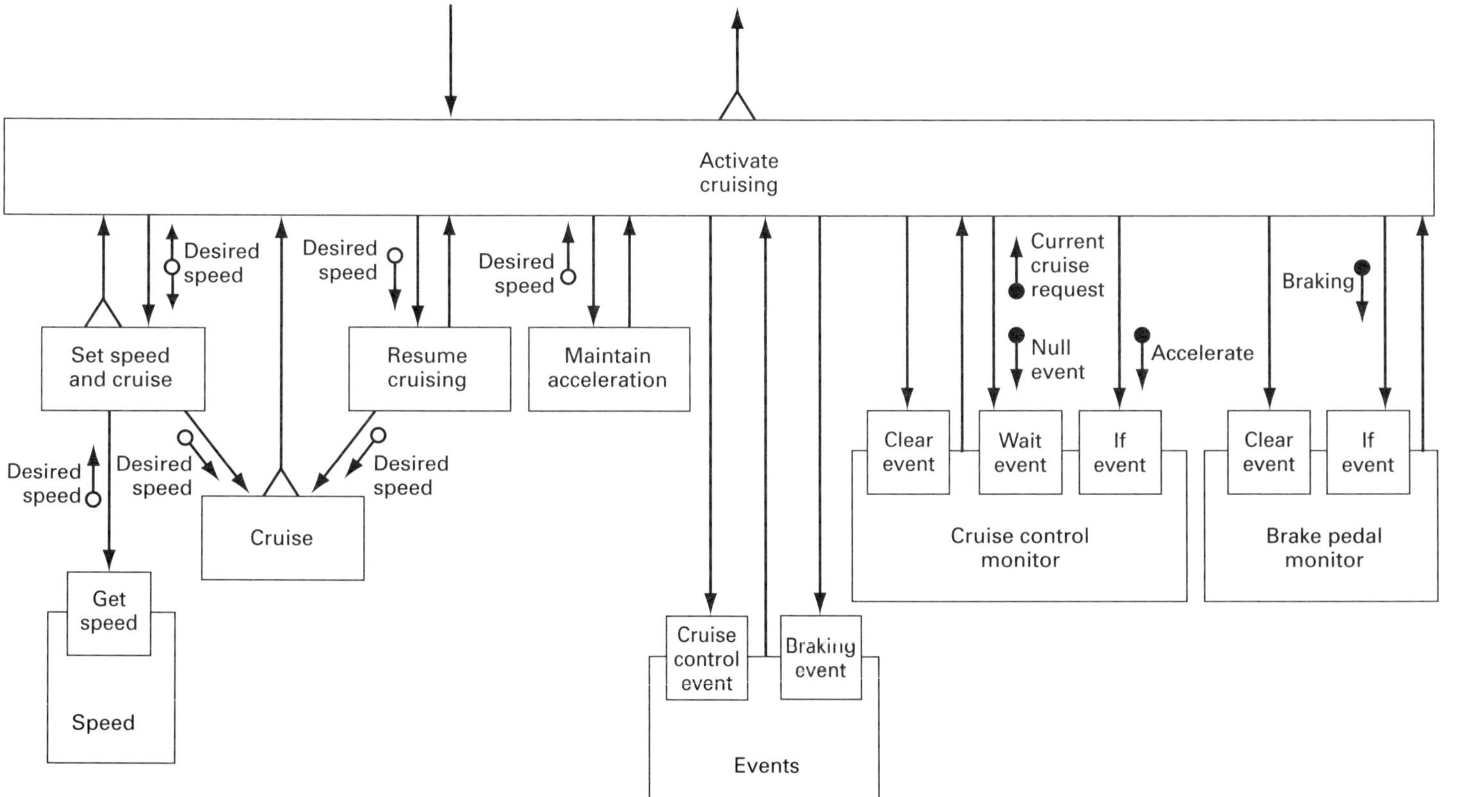

Figure 10.22 OOSD chart for activate-cruising package.

as to which routine to call depends on the flag value of the resume_ cruise_request variable, declared within the activate_cruising procedure. The decompositions for the calibrate, cruise, and maintain_ acceleration procedures are not shown.

Note that the rules for visibility in conjunction with lexical inclusion in Ada imply that all visibility really takes effect at the level of the top procedure in the inclusion hierarchy. In this case, all visibility is global to all the parts of the Cruise_Control procedure, despite the limited visibility shown in the diagrams. The design specifies lexical inclusion instead of breaking up the procedures into separate library units because the procedures have no meaning outside the Cruise Control system, cannot be reused, and should not be accessible to other procedures in order to guarantee effective concurrent processing. This does mean, however, that visibility relations are somewhat less useful in controlling reference errors within the Cruise_Controller task.

Events.   The Events package packages the various data types used to represent the several events that occur in the Cruise Control system. The Event type can represent any event in the system. The Braking_Event type can represent the Braking event. The Engine_ Event type can represent the starting and stopping of the engine. The Cruise_Control_Event type can represent any of the several starting and stopping of the engine. The Cruise_Control_Event type can represent any of the several Cruise Control events such as Activate, Stop Mile, or Accelerate. Any unit that must test a type or deal with an event must make this package visible. The Events package is shown in Fig. 10.23.

The monitor.   The Monitor is a generic package that represents an active package that monitors some type of event in the system. The type of event is a generic parameter, as is the interrupt that indicates the event occurrence and the object that represents the null event, which indicates that no event of the given type has occurred. The interrupt sets a value at a specific location in memory that indicates the event, which allows for multiple events at one interrupt.

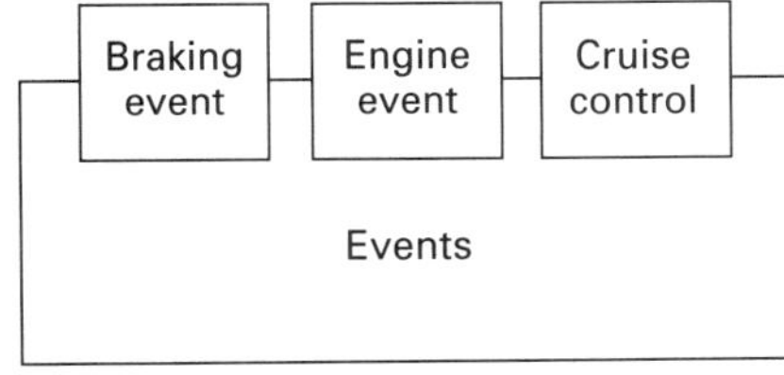

Figure 10.23   OOSD chart for events package.

A Monitor consists of two tasks, both of which handle the same asynchronous interrupt. The Monitor Task waits for the interrupt, then sets a data value in the Monitor package to hold the current event. The Monitor Task can also clear the event by setting the current event to the null event. The Wait Task waits for a specific event to occur. This enables a calling procedure to wait for a particular event, then to access the current event maintained by the Monitor Task when that event occurs.

The entries in the tasks are sequenced, as indicated by the numerals in the upper right-hand corner of the entry. In the Monitor Task, the monitor first receives an interrupt, then waits for a clear request before being able to receive another interrupt. In the Wait Task, the task first waits for a request to wait, then waits for the interrupt, looping until receiving the requested interrupt event.

The package must have the System package with its Address type made visible, as it uses a memory address to represent the interrupt parameter. No assumptions are made as to the nature of the Event type.

The interface for the Monitor package allows for several operations on the Monitor: getting an event (if one has occurred), testing for the occurrence of some event, testing for the occurrence of a particular event, clearing an event, and waiting for a particular (or any, if the parameter is the null_event) event.

The Monitor package illustrates the variable specification techniques used in OOSD. If a variable is global to several procedures, it can be shown as an explicit data module, as is current_event. If a variable is simply passed to another module or is returned from a module, it can be shown as a parameter on the call. Other variables that exist only locally and that are not passed to other modules are not shown. Such variables must be specified in annotations to the diagram or in the PDL associated with a module. The Monitor generic package is shown in Fig. 10.24.

The actuator.   The Actuator, shown in use in Fig. 10.25, is a generic package that represents an active package that actuates some hardware device external to the system. An Actuator gives the software system the ability to control the hardware. The type of actuator assumed here simply accepts a value at a given memory location and sets itself to that value. It is up to the software to set the value type to correspond correctly to the type of actuator. Thus, the generic package has two parameters, the Value type and the location address.

An Actuator consists of a single task that has a single entry, allowing the set_value interface to the package to activate the task, setting a particular value in memory. This in turn activates the actuator.

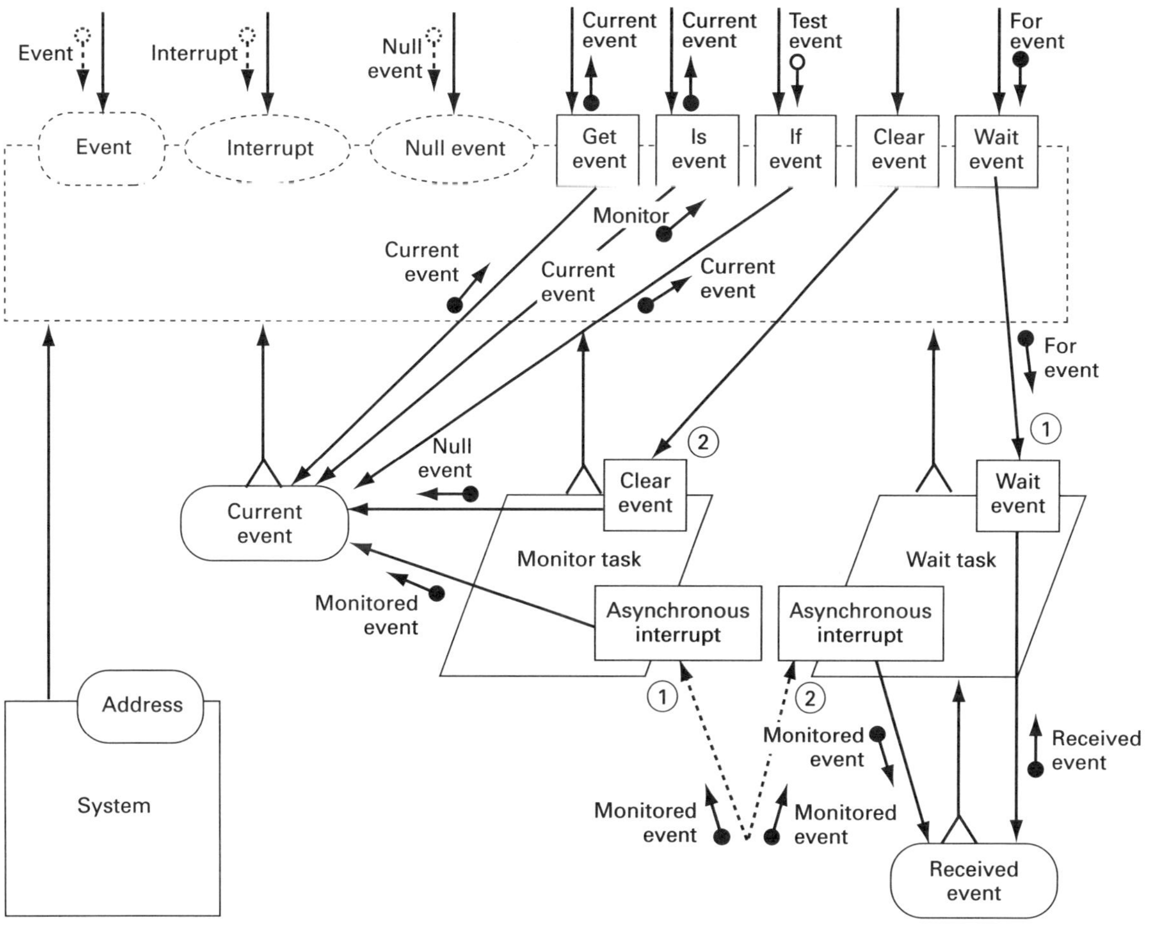

Figure 10.24   OOSD chart for the monitor generic package.

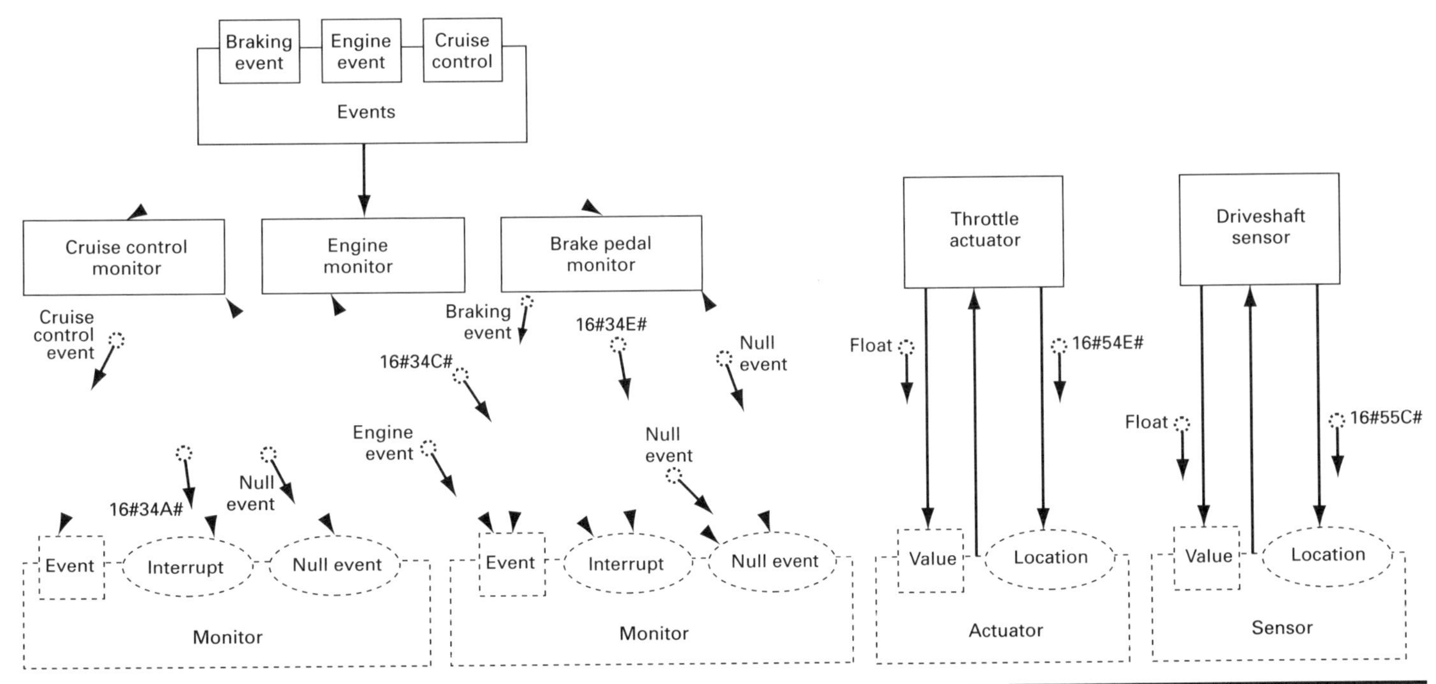

Figure 10.25 OOSD chart for auto parts package.

The sensor.   The Sensor, also shown in Fig. 10.25, is a generic package that provides an interface to a particular address in memory. This corresponds to an area maintained by an external hardware sensor that places a value into that area of memory, allowing the software system access to the value. This value is updated as often as the sensor hardware interrupts the system.

The package has two generic parameters, the Value type and the location address. The Value type allows the package to get access to any type of value stored by a sensor, the location address specifies the address of that value and allows the package to declare the reading variable at that address using a representation clause. Whenever a caller calls the read_value function, it reads the value currently stored in the reading variable, which is at the location specified by the location parameter.

The auto parts.   The Auto Parts diagram, in Fig. 10.25, shows the generic instantiations that represent the various Monitors, Actuators, and Sensors used in the Cruise Control system.

The three monitors (Cruise Control, Engine, and Brake Pedal) are instantiations of the Monitor package. Each of these monitors is instantiated with one of the three Event types (Cruise_Control_Event, Engine_Event, and Braking_Event, respectively) and with a specific address as the interrupt. The Throttle Actuator and the Driveshaft Sensor are instantiations of the Actuator and Sensor packages using the Float type to represent the value types and specific addresses to represent locations of the values.

The instantiation specifications appear as parameters to the calls from the packages to the generics. The generic Monitor appears twice in order to simplify the diagram, which would otherwise have too many lines crossing one another. Each instantiation must have its respective generic package visible, as indicated by the visibility connections.

The Monitor instantiations must have the Events package accessible, as specific event types are used in the instantiation.

The instantiations do not show the exported subprograms that are inherited from the generic package, and thus there is no need for the generic reference to include those either. When a procedure calls the instantiations, the subprograms will appear there.

The speed package.   The Speed package, shown in Fig. 10.26, implements various procedures and a task that enables the cruise control system to monitor the speed of the automobile continuously. This package allows the system to get the current speed, get the current acceleration, and set the rotation factor.

The Speedometer is an independent, or entryless, task that constantly reads the number of rotations from the Driveshaft Sensor and

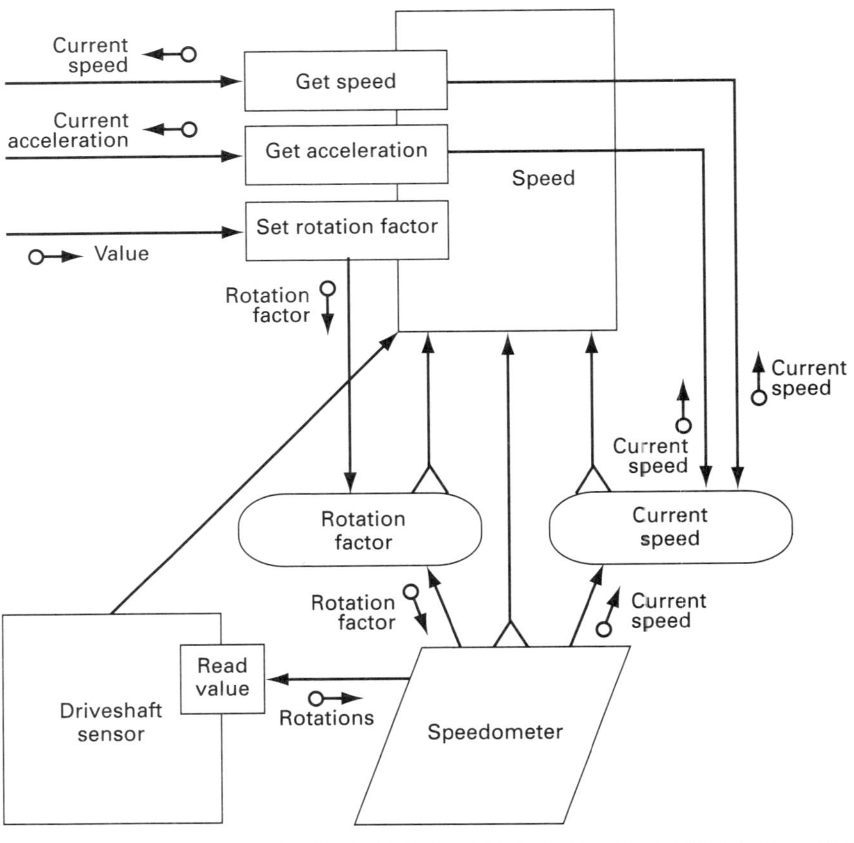

Figure 10.26   OOSD chart for the speed package.

computes from the rotations and the rotation factor the current speed, which it places in a variable that is global to the package. When a caller calls the get_speed function, it returns the value that is currently in the variable. When a caller calls the get_acceleration function, the function calls the current speed twice to compute the rate of change of speed. When a caller calls the set_rotation_factor procedure, it puts the value passed into the internally global rotation factor variable, after checking to make sure the value is between the factory-preset minimum and maximum values.

This package hides the implementation details surrounding speed from the rest of the system. This package could also be used in other areas of the automobile to implement a speedometer display or to run the odometer.

Object-Oriented Design Methods and CASE Tools

This chapter describes object-oriented design (OOD) methods and CASE tools. The OOD methods focus upon the design and implementation aspects of the software process. Grady Booch is the developer of this method. OOD addresses these activities: preliminary design, simulation, prototyping, detailed design, coding, testing, and software maintenance phases. An example of Palladio software is discussed to enhance the OOD process.

This chapter also describes the CASE tools for the object-oriented methods ObjectTeam by CADRE and ObjectMaker by Mark $\vee$ Systems.

Object-Oriented Design by Palladio Software

Object-oriented design by Palladio uses the Booch method. OOD is an enabling technology for software development. OOD allows the developer to apply object-oriented software engineering principles in design and development of the software. OOD creates software modules that can be reused and easily maintained.

The object-oriented software design activity includes three elements: notation, process, and tools. The notation allows the model to be expressed clearly to others to adequately represent all abstractions. The process is the flow of activities and results in the construction of the model. The tools enforce rules, reduce errors, and improve efficiency.

OOD Models

There are multiple views in an OOD: the logical view and the physical view. The logical view shows the key abstractions and mechanisms that indicate relationships, semantics of classes, and objects. The logical view also specifies the template for class construction. The physical view specifies which modules will contain class definitions and variable declarations. The physical view allocates execution threads to processes on physical processor (mechanism).

Object System/Designer is the trademark of Palladio software. Using Windows 3.0, the Booch notation and method can be drawn. Object System/Designer is suited for developers striving to model small and large object-oriented software systems. The easy-to-master operator interface allows users to quickly create and edit diagrams. Full printing functions allow software developers to communicate their ideas easily to team members and customers and/or users.

Figure 11.1 illustrates a view of the logical class mode showing the key classes and their relationships. The relationship can be labeled, annotated with cardinality, and qualified for visibility. Each class can be expanded to an associated state diagram. The class categories expand to another class diagram, allowing for a hierarchy of class diagrams and classes.

Multiple object diagrams may be created for each design file. All visibility annotation is supported as shown in Fig. 11.2. The use of the right mouse button can place the visibility of the right object. Object nesting can be accomplished automatically by drag and drop with the help of the icon.

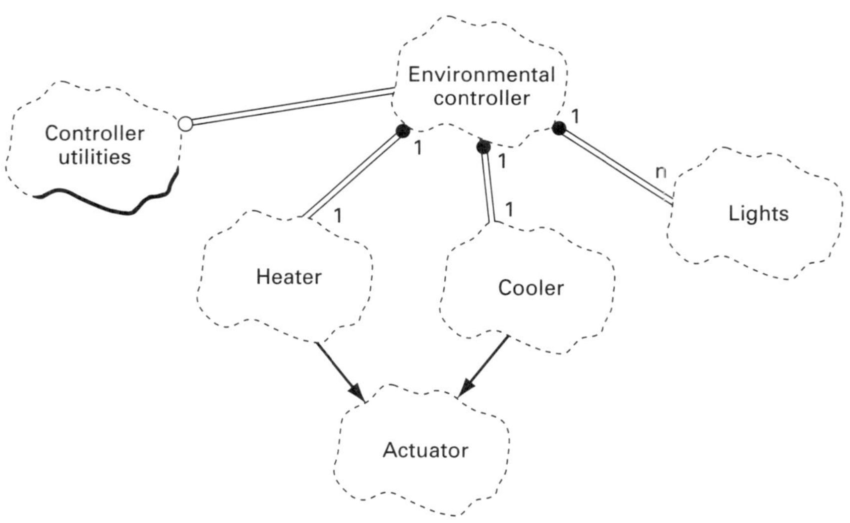

Figure 11.1   Class diagram.

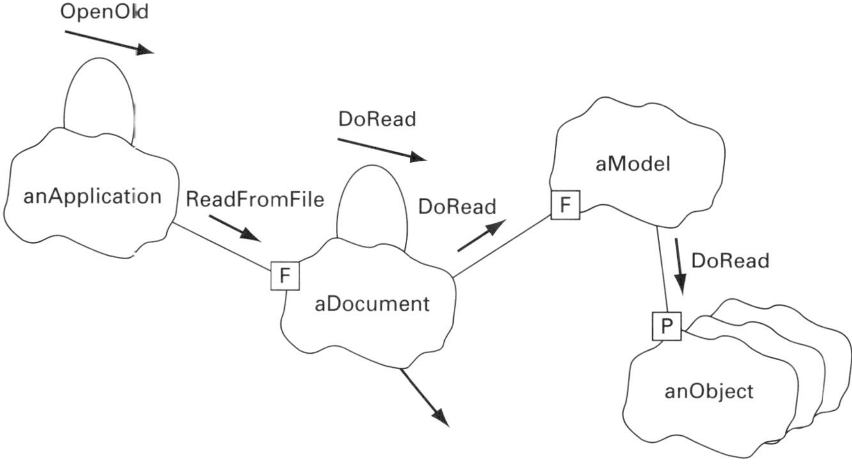

Figure 11.2 Object diagram.

Each class has an associated state diagram, as shown in Fig. 11.3. Transition arrows are positioned automatically. Click and type to add/edit transition labels. Figure 11.3 shows normal, start, and end states.

All icons in Fig. 11.4 have an associated template. Edit the template by double-clicking on the icon. Figure 11.5 illustrates devices and processors in the system as part of the physical design.

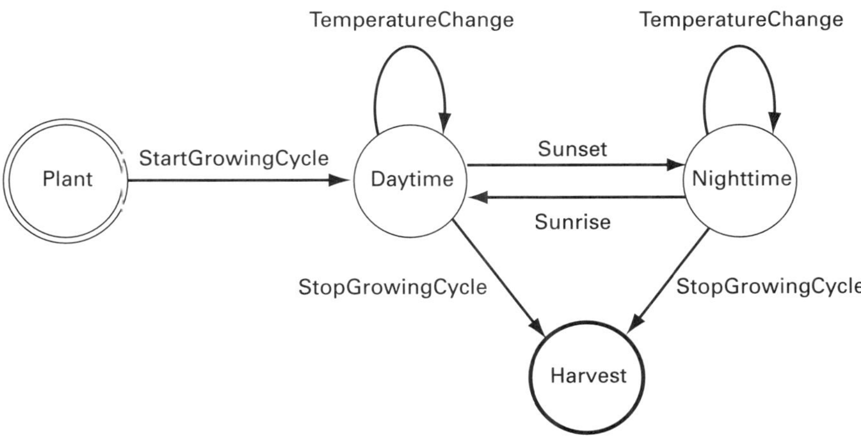

Figure 11.3 State diagram.

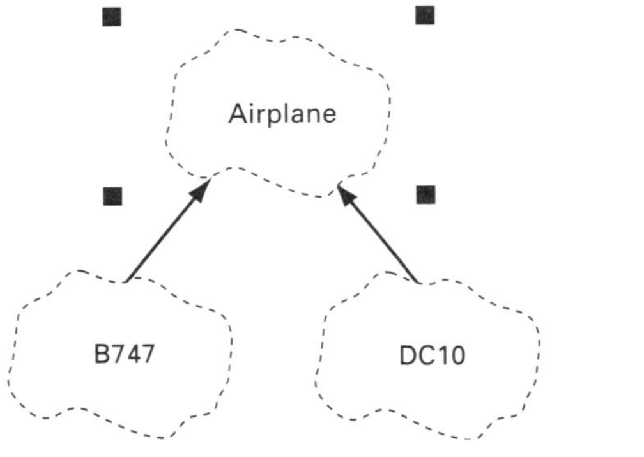

Figure 11.4 Template.

ObjectTeam

ObjectTeam is a suite of object-oriented software development tools providing automation for object-oriented methods. The ObjectTeam tools assist in achieving shorter development life cycles and in improving software quality, which will further reduce maintenance costs. The ObjectTeam tools also lower the object-oriented project costs, enhance software reuse, and shorten time for completion of the project. The ObjectTeam tools support the object-oriented methods of Rumbaugh and of Shlaer and Mellor. These methods allow developers to raise the level of abstraction, focus on critical aspects of the application, help team members collaborate on designs, and have better communication with users and customers.

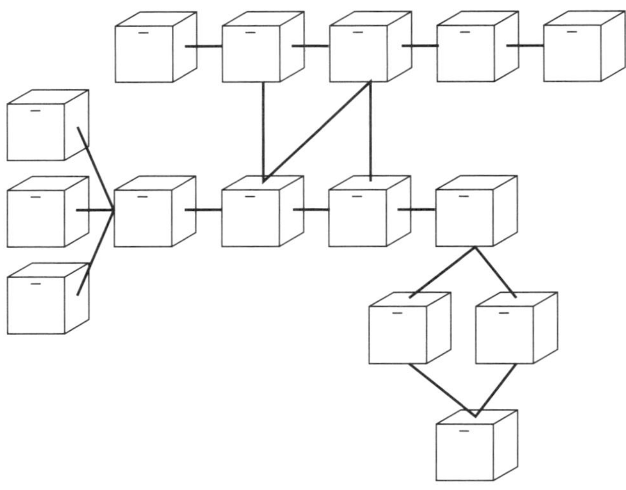

Figure 11.5 Process diagram.

The ObjectTeam tools make the critical difference in object-oriented analysis and design. The object-oriented application models that are created with the help of these tools are stored for reuse. Thus software developer productivity is enhanced through automatic code and document generation. Higher quality is ensured through comprehensive correctness checking provided by the ObjectTeam tools.

ObjectTeam for Rumbaugh Methodology

ObjectTeam for Rumbaugh is called the *Object Modeling Technique* (OMT) and provides a well-defined object-oriented software development process. A key feature of this technique is its use of a common application model and notation for object-oriented modeling, design, and implementation. ObjectTeam for Rumbaugh consists of Paradigm Plus/Cadre Edition, which provides automation of the Rumbaugh technique that includes Object, Dynamic, and Functional Models. Through its common, multiuser object repository, ObjectTeam for Rumbaugh supports an iterative approach by allowing objects to be stored and accessed throughout the development life cycle. ObjectTeam for Rumbaugh also enables developers to reuse C++ class libraries and to generate design in C++, Ada, SQL, and OODBMS implementation languages.

Paradigm Plus/Cadre Edition is an object-oriented application development tool for automating software construction using the Rumbaugh object-oriented method. Supplying an integrated set of development tools for object-oriented analysis and object-oriented design, Paradigm Plus/Cadre Edition also supports code generation for software development in the C++ and Ada languages. Paradigm Plus/Cadre Edition promotes reuse by providing utilities for reverse engineering C or C++ code into its common Object Repository.

Paradigm Plus/Cadre Edition also provides database definition construction support for ANSI SQL and Oracle 7.0 relational databases, as well as object-oriented databases from Versant, ObjectStore, Objectivity/DB, ONTOS ODBMS, and Raima Object Manager. A wide choice of platforms, networks, and customization options help developers ensure that the product fits comfortably into their existing development environment.

Figure 11.6 shows the Paradigm Plus/Cadre Edition supporting OMT, developed by Dr. James Rumbaugh. Using OMT, software engineers develop object models and object-oriented software designs that are implemented in OO programming languages. OMT supports expressive notations for defining problems and requirements and for producing OO designs using a common notation throughout the

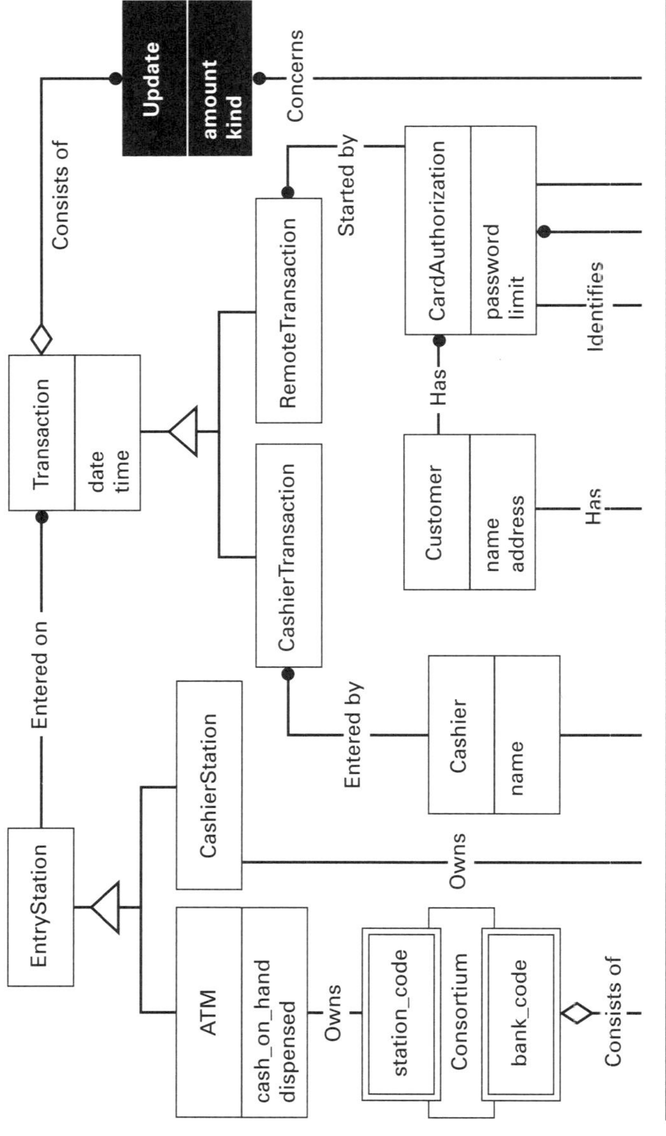

Figure 11.6 Object diagram (OMT).

analysis, design, and implementation life cycle. Paradigm Plus/Cadre Edition supports the following OMT diagrams:

- Object diagrams
- State diagrams
- Data flow diagrams
- Event trace diagrams

Paradigm Plus/Cadre Edition also provides consistency and completeness checking reports for the OMT diagrams. Completeness checking uses the BASIC Script Language and can be modified by the users. The BASIC Script Language is a featured language that is used to customize the behavior, interaction, and output from the Paradigm Plus/Cadre Edition Object Repository. Within Paradigm Plus/Cadre Edition, this language provides completeness checking, reports, and code generation, among other facilities.

The scripts are a powerful means for developers to extend the product's features to meet specific project needs. The BASIC Script Language is a full implementation of the BASIC programming language and includes the access to all data Object Repository, typed variables, file input and output, flow of control, an extensive function library, and access to the operating system shell.

Code construction from the specification level (class/typed/package/ object definition) is supported for the Object Model in the C++, Ada, SQL, and OO databases. Code construction includes the following language constructs, where applicable:

- Class definition
- Data member
- Function prototypes
- Single and multiple inheritance
- Polymorphic operations
- Public, private, and protected attributes
- Constructor and destructor functions
- Package specification and body

All code and data definition construction is performed in the BASIC Script Language. The source code for each BASIC Script is supplied with Paradigm Plus/Cadre Edition, allowing users to customize outputs to suit their specific needs and preference.

Paradigm Plus/Cadre Edition is designed with an open architecture based on a common Object Repository. Through the Basic Script Language and industry standard export formats, developers have open access to every stored object and relationship. Paradigm Plus/Cadre Edition easily interoperates with third-party development tools and external dictionaries, providing complete support for cut and paste of ASCII text bit maps, import and export of ASCII and *Comma Separated Value* (CSV) text, export of PostScript files, and custom output using the Basic Script Language. In addition, the product makes use of the native window/operating system drivers whenever possible. Paradigm Plus/Cadre Edition can be integrated with commercially available version control and configuration management systems. A snapshot of the entire Object Repository consists of a limited number of files.

Paradigm Plus/Cadre Edition offers many different tools to capture, view, edit, and navigate. These include

- Diagram Editor produces graphical diagrams and models for the OMT method as well as user-defined diagrams.

- Matrix Window Editor views and edits the classes versus attributes stored in the Object Repository, using a convenient cross-referenced matrix format.

- Repository Browser views and edits every object and relationship stored in the Object Repository.

- Dialog Boxes is used to enter and edit various properties associated with classes, objects, etc.

The on-line help facility is a standard hypertext system and includes index (feature-specific), commands (functionality-specific), and Rumbaugh (method-specific). Paradigm Plus/Cadre Edition allows the user to create and attach drawings composed of text and graphical primitives (lines, circles, polygons, rectangles, etc.) to a diagram symbol. Modifications made to a diagram are automatically reflected in the underlying Object Repository as well as any "views" (diagrams, browsers, matrices) that are open at the time. Users can link multiple diagrams in a model into an arbitrary network of diagrams; and every symbol in a diagram can be "exploded" into one or more subdiagrams. This capability can be used to create diagram levels.

Nodes and connecting arcs in diagrams are repositioned automatically. An alignment toolbox allows diagram items to be aligned, spaced evenly, etc. In addition, an *automatic diagram* feature allows users to click on an object and generate a Rumbaugh specific diagram showing the selected object and its relationships to other objects.

Paradigm Plus/Cadre Edition allows the user to create ad hoc reports through the use of the BASIC Script Language. The standard reports provided include statistics, object model, dynamic model, functional model, object summary, object traceability, diagram summary, diagram traceability, data dictionary, audit trail/user log-in, design check, and consistency check. Paradigm Plus/Cadre Edition stores all information about a development project in an active common Object Repository, which is designed to be the foundation for OO application development. Developers interact with the Object Repository, using the diagram editor, repository browser, and matrix window to create, view, and modify the data types stored in the Object Repository. The power of the Object Repository is evident in that when a change is made to an object or relationship in one place, that change is automatically reflected everywhere else it appears. Developers generate source code and documentation or reports directly from the Object Repository. Also, using the BASIC Script Language, developers have an easy means for the Object Repository to interact with user-written programs that produce custom outputs.

ObjectTeam for Shlaer/Mellor Method

ObjectTeam for the Shlaer/Mellor methodology provides a formal development approach that emphasizes completeness and correctness throughout the software development life cycle. A key to the methodology is its ability to support large projects by allowing developers to partition complex problems into smaller, more manageable components. ObjectTeam for Shlaer/Mellor, consisting of Teamwork/OOA and Teamwork/OOD, provides support for all the graphical and textual descriptions associated with the Shlaer/Mellor methodology, including semantic support for Domains, Subsystems, and the OODLE notation for object-oriented design, as shown in Fig. 11.7. The tools feature documentation generation as well as code generation for C++ and Ada, and they provide support for multiple user development teams. ObjectTeam is a product of Cadre Technologies Inc.

Teamwork/OOA is based on the Shlaer/Mellor method and is a graphical modeling environment, uniquely designed to help systems analysts capture and refine high-quality object-oriented software specifications. This tool reduces system complexity by allowing analysts to graphically describe a system from many perspectives, including

- Object information models—to show the objects and their relationships

- Object communication models—to show the messages between the objects

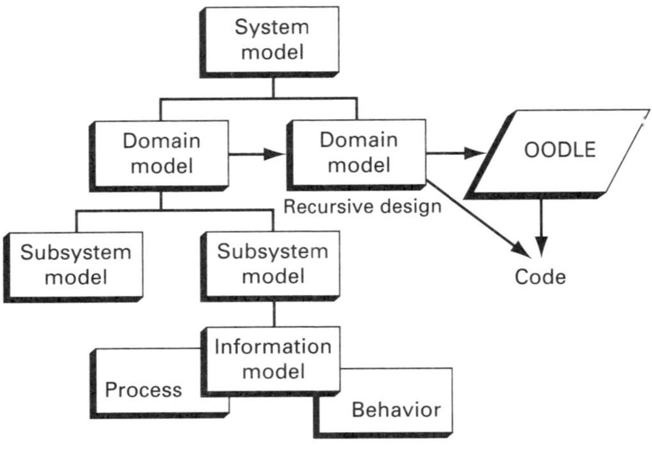

Figure 11.7   OOD (Shlaer/Mellor).

- State models—to show the behavior of objects

- Process models—to show the processing that each object performs

Each of these perspectives is described through a set of supporting diagrams and reports, improving communication between development team members and users and helping to ensure that the resulting system fully meets its requirements.

One characteristic of the Shlaer/Mellor method is its ability to divide a problem into separate domains and partition each domain into smaller subsystems. This tool provides the ability to model the domains of an application using the domain charts, and to specify bridge descriptions. This serves as the basis for the recursive design approach to software development. This method's support for partitioning a project into smaller Subsystems, with checking support for interfaces between subsystems, allows a project to be worked on in parallel.

Teamwork/OOA enhances large-scale development through its built-in configuration management facilities and multiuser architecture. Teamwork/OOA provides multiuser access that allows developers to share a group of work products and then merge their changes without overwrites.

Teamwork/OOD is a graphical tool set that helps software developers design and engineer efficient and reusable object-oriented code. By allowing developers to work at a graphical, higher level of abstraction, Teamwork/OOD simplifies object-oriented software development and helps to ensure its successful implementation. This improves productivity by automating the time-consuming manual steps involved in OOD and by automatically generating C++ code as well as systems documentation. This method also improves software quality by checking designs for completeness and accuracy.

Based on the Shlaer/Mellor object-oriented design language environment (OODLE) notation, Teamwork/OOD lets developers create and view their designs from four different perspectives:

- Class diagrams show the external views of individual classes.

- Inheritance diagrams show the inheritance relationships between classes.

- Dependency diagrams show the client/server and friend relationships between classes.

- Class structure charts show the internal structure of the code within classes.

These four views allow developers to represent the fundamental concepts of OOD, including encapsulation of data, inheritance, polymorphism, and data typing.

ObjectMaker

The Mark $\vee$ Systems product for object-oriented methods consists of ObjectMaker, ProcessMaker, and MethodMaker. The Mark $\vee$ product supports many object-oriented methods, such as Darts; Bailin; Berard; Booch; Buhr; Chen; Coad and Yourdon; Colbert; Constantine; Demarco; Embly, Kurtz, and Woodfield; Firesmith; Fusion; Gane and Sarson; Harel; Hatley and Pirbhai; Martin and Odell; ObjectOry; Page-Jones; Rumbaugh; Shlaer and Mellor; Ward and Mellor; SPS; Wirfs and Brock; Yourdon; DFD; DOD-STD-2167A; F-Nets; Petri Nets; R-Nets; Semantic Nets; and Block diagrams.

ObjectMaker provides rule-driven and repository-based CASE support for software and process modeling. This includes requirements analysis, top-level design, detailed design, and enterprise, work flow, and process modeling. *Rule-driven* means that all tool behavior is pre- and post-conditioned by predicate logic rules. This provides flexibility and the power to support a wide range of methods and to readily modify methods to meet specific process and problem domain requirements.

ObjectMaker produces object-oriented code, and it can be easily customized by the user to suit her or his own object-oriented method. ObjectMaker can be used from the initial generation of proposals through requirements analysis to code generation and maintenance.

It includes a data repository that maintains the intricate semantic relationships between symbols and diagrams and the project dictionary. Document and diagram data can be output to a number of popular publishing software packages including Frame, Interleaf, Pagemaker, Ventura Publishing, Microsoft Word, and WordPerfect.

The automatic code generation facility maintains consistency between the code templates, the design diagrams, and their naming conventions. Code generation modules are for Ada and C++. The actual percentage of automatically generated code is high—up to 100 percent—but will vary depending on the level of detail in the source diagrams and repository.

ProcessMaker

ProcessMaker is a specialized drawing tool which is coupled to an underlying semantics repository and code and text generators. This develops a graphical representation of a process. ProcessMaker checks the syntax of diagrams as they are entered. Information from the diagrams plus additional information entered into ProcessMaker is captured in a structured (Entity Relationship Attribute) database, allowing further consistency and completeness checks as defined by certain methods. Report tables are provided to enable process definitions to be viewed from yet another angle—Who is responsible for which tasks, or what tasks can follow this one?

MethodMaker

MethodMaker is the extension of ObjectMaker which allows rapid development of new method notations. MethodMaker allows the user to modify and extend existing ObjectMaker method support to meet project and organizational requirements. MethodMaker utilizes two notations—Menu Definition and Icon Definition—which allows users to diagram their method's unique structure by specifying icon types, user-interface views, and constraints between the icons. From these diagrams, MethodMaker automatically implements ObjectMaker tool support for the method notation.

Object-Oriented Software Implementation

"The cautious seldom err."

ARISTOTLE

12

Object-Oriented Programming Languages

The object-oriented software development method is receiving wide acceptance as a standard technology within the software industry. The new technology changes the nature of software analysis and design as an industrial process. Software products can be developed in a way similar to hardware products. Object-oriented programming is a change from writing instructions to interconnecting reusable software components. In the future, a system engineer or domain engineer will be equipped with components catalogs. The components with which he or she interconnects can be reached for higher-level products—application products or other, more specialized components. This process will result in high productivity, low software development cost, short schedule, and quality products. The object-oriented developed software will be easier to maintain.

One widely accepted view of our computing future is that we will eventually become a community with a few producers (object implementors) supplying many consumers (object users). The consumers will be programmers and power users who will build applications by drawing from a stock of interoperable objects before writing custom code or building custom objects to fill in functionality gaps [DBMS, June 1995]. This chapter offers an overview of object-oriented programming (OOP) languages.

Object-Oriented Programming

Object-oriented programming is defined as structured and designed around objects. OOP includes encapsulation (the class concept), extensibility (inheritance by prefixing), and reusability (specialization and dynamic binding). In OOP, the class serves as the abstraction mechanism whereby concepts are formalized. Classes resemble an abstract data type in that they contain both data and the code that manipulates the data. Also the classes can be multiple instantiations of objects that can be used to build data structures. Furthermore, an existing class can be extended or specialized with the help of a prefixing mechanism, where a subclass inherits attributes from its parent class. This facilitates the development of reusable software [Lund]. OOP is considered to be the future in the computer industry for software development. OOP is an ideal design for next-generation programming techniques.

OOP requires programmers to learn new object-oriented languages which hold totally a new approach. The object-oriented approach needs proper planning and design to achieve maximum benefits, especially from reusable objects [DBMS, August 1994].

OOP Languages

The main features of an object-oriented programming language are interfacing, programming by extension, programming libraries, and parallel and real-time processing. Interfacing means that the language must talk with other languages. These days, there is hardly any system which is stand-alone. A system will interface with other external systems. Programming by extension is closely allied to reusability. A program can be extended without any modification to existing components. The programming by extension does not disturb existing software and hence eliminates the risk of introducing errors. This avoids recompilation costs. The programming libraries bring important benefits by extending the strong typing across the boundaries between separately compiled units. The parallel and real-time processing supports time-critical real-time as well as distributed applications.

The object-oriented thinking started with Simula 67 and SmallTalk efforts in the 1960s. Some of the other major object-oriented languages are object-oriented COBOL, Ada 95, and C++.

Simula

Object-oriented programming was first discussed in Norway in the early 1970s in connection with the Simula language. Developed to help model and simulate real-world processes, Simula is unique because, instead of defining data and procedures, programmers define modules that model the real-world objects that they are trying to simulate. Simula is the first object-oriented language to introduce classes and objects, inheritance, and dynamic binding of procedures. Simula has a full compile-time type-checking facility. There is a choice between static and dynamic binding of procedures. The language contains information hiding through attribute protection, sequential and direct access files, formatted or unformatted, process based on non-preemptive scheduling, and process-oriented simulation features. One goal in the design of Simula has been to enable the compiler to detect as many errors as possible. For instance, type-and-parameter checking is performed during the compilation. This is true even for dynamically bound procedures and for classes and procedures defined in externally compiled source modules. At present Simula includes attribute protection, dynamically bound procedures, text handling capabilities, and standardized file I/O with choice of sequential or direct access files. Simula is used for discrete simulation. In Simula, unused memory space is automatically reclaimed by a garbage collector [Lund Simula System].

SmallTalk

SmallTalk is a pure object-oriented language. It was designed around an object-oriented framework. SmallTalk really is small. The language provides window-based graphical user interfaces (GUIs). The programming in SmallTalk depends upon a large class library and the interactive programming environment. The language features are different from those of most other object-oriented languages.

There is no compiler, linker, or dedicated editor in this language. Instead, there are browsers, workspaces, inspectors, walkbacks, and transcript windows operating under a single GUI. The browsers are multipaned windows that display the interrelationship of the elements of SmallTalk. System, class, method, message, and file browsers are each aimed at presenting a specific view of the SmallTalk environment. All but the file browsers allow one to edit the code. The workspaces provide the playgrounds of SmallTalk. They are free-form editing spaces or scratch pads linked to the compiler and are used for everything from testing code fragments to viewing and editing text files. The transcript workspace is generally reserved for messages generated by the system and is a convenient space to send debug messages. The walkbacks, inspectors, and debuggers are the heart of SmallTalk's debugging facilities. Walkbacks are displayed when SmallTalk detects an error or a breakpoint. The debugger offers many tools for detecting and correcting code errors. An inspector provides an X-ray view of an object, allowing the user to examine and modify it [Herndon].

There are no header files, function prototypes, static members, or in-line functions in this language. Instead, the environment is structured to manage the SmallTalk source code and declarations. The language includes objects, classes, methods (member functions), variables (global and local), function overloading, and inheritance. The classes and methods of SmallTalk are not just a class library but are an integral part of the environment that makes up the language. Everything interacts with everything else in SmallTalk.

Ada 95

Ada 95 is an object-oriented language. It is practically the standard of the international computer industry. It is approved by all the international organizations, such as the American National Standards Institute (ANSI) and the International Organization for Standardization (ISO). Ada 95 is a revised version of Ada, updating the 1983 ANSI Ada standard [ANSI 83] and the equivalent 1987 ISO standard [ISO 87] in accordance with ANSI and ISO procedures. Ada 95 is an evolution of Ada 83 and keeps all the compatibility of the Ada 83. This enhancement increases the flexibility and reliability of Ada and introduces more object-oriented features. Ada 95 is more applicable to wider domains. Ada 95 includes more features of object-oriented programming, programming in the large, and real-time and parallel programming. Ada 95's major features are as follows:

1. Interfacing with external systems is accomplished by provision of features such as representation clauses and pragmas. There was a general need for a more flexible approach, allowing, for instance, the secure manipulation of references and passing of procedures as parameters. An example arises when one is interfacing into the GUI where it is often necessary to pass a procedure as a parameter for callback. For example,

```
procedure Call_Word_Processor is...
procedure Ring_Bell is...
type Action_Call is access procedure;
type Button_Type is
  record
    X_Pos:Integer;
    Y_Pos:Integer;
    Action_When_Left_Button_Pushed:Action_Call;
    Action_When_Right_Button_Pushed:Action_Call;
  end;
Button_1:Button_Type: = (100,50,Call_Word_Processor,Ring_Bell);
                  -(X, Y ,    Left Button  ,    Right Button)
Draw_and_Register_Button(Button_1);
```

2. Programming by extension is closely allied to reusability. Although Ada's package and generic capability are an excellent foun-

dation, nevertheless experience with the object-oriented paradigm in other languages has shown the advantages of being able to extend a program without any modification to existing proven components. Not only does this avoid disturbing existing software, thus eliminating the risk of introducing errors, but also it reduces recompilation costs. For example,

```
Tagged Type
type Point is tagged
  record
    X,Y: Real : =  0.0
  end record;
type Painted_Point is new Point with
  record
    Paint:Color : =  White;
  end record;
      --Components X and Y are inherited
Another Tagged type
type Rectangle is tagged
  record
    Length : Float : =  0.0;
    Width : Float : =  0.0;
  end record;
function Perimeter (R :in Rectangle) return Float is
begin
  return 2.0 * (R.Length + R.Width);
end Perimeter;
Tagged Types - Inheritance
type Cubcid is new Rectangle with
  record
    Height:Float : =  0.0;
  end record;
```

Discussion: Here Cuboid inherits Perimeter from Rectangle, since Perimeter is a primitive operation. To prevent this, you need to override the operation. One way to do this is to write a new Perimeter. A better way is to base the new Perimeter on the parent class operation as follows.

```
Now Tagged Types - Inheritance and View Conversion
type Cuboid is new Rectangle with
  record
    Height : Float : =  0.0;
  end record;
function Perimeter (C:in Cuboid) return Float is
begin
  return Perimeter (Rectangle(C))*2 + (4*C.Height);
end Perimeter;
```

3. Program libraries bring important benefits by extending the strong typing across the boundaries between separately compiled units. However, the flat nature of the Ada 83 library resulted in problems of visibility control; for example, it prevented two library pack-

ages from sharing a full view of a private type. A common consequence of the flat structure was that packages became large and monolithic. This hindered understanding and increased the cost of recompilation. A more flexible and hierarchical structure was necessary. Here are examples:

```
Hierarchical Libraries:
package Complex_Numbers is
  type Complex is private;
  function "+" (Left, Right:Complex) return Complex;
  ... - similarly "-", "*", and "/"
  function Cartesian_To_Complex(Real,Imag:Float)return Complex;
  function Real_Part(X:Complex)return Float;
  function Imag_Part(X:Complex)return Float;
private
...
end Complex_Numbers;
```

Discussion: If you want to add more features to the package (say, polar notation), you must do so in a manner that minimizes side effects. Users who are already "with" the package should not have to recompile, nor should they find additions to their "name space." The solution is to create a package of Complex_Number, but a separate package in its own right. This is referred to as a *child* package.

```
package Complex_Numbers.Polar is
  procedure Polar_To_Complex(R,Theta:Float)return Complex;
  function "abs"(Right:Complex)return Float;
  function Arg(X:Complex)return Float;
end Complex_Numbers.Polar;
```

4. *Tasking.* The Ada rendezvous paradigm is a useful model for abstract description of many tasking problems. But experience has shown that a more monitorlike approach was also desirable for common shared-data-access applications. Furthermore, the Ada priority model needed revision in order to enable users to take advantage of the greater understanding of scheduling theory which had emerged since Ada 83 was defined. Here is an example of protected types.

Discussion: Protected types provide a low-level, lightweight, data-oriented synchronization mechanism whose key features are as follows:

- A protected object has hidden components; these components are intended to be shared among multiple tasks.
- The protected operations of the protected object provide synchronized access to the components.
- Protected types have three kinds of protected operations: protected functions, protected procedures, and entries.

A protected object provides coordinated access to shared data, through calls on its visible protected operations, which can be protected subprograms or protected entries. Protected procedures provide mutually exclusive read/write access to the data of a protected object. Protected functions provide concurrent read-only access to the data. Protected entries also provide exclusive read/write access to the data and additionally specify a barrier (a boolean) expression. This barrier must be true prior to the protected entry call proceeding.

```
package Mailbox_Pkg is
  type Parcels_Count is range 0..Mbox_Size;
  type Parcels_Index is range 1..Mbox_Size;
  type Parcel_Array is array(Parcel_Index)of Parcels
  protected type Mailbox is
    -- put a data element into the buffer
    entry Send(Item:Parcels);
    -- retrieve a data element from the buffer
    entry Receive(Item:out Parcels);
    procedure Clear;
    function Size return integer;
  private
    Count        :Parcels_count: = 0;
    Out_Index  :Parcels_Index: = 1;
    In_Index    :Parcels_Index: = 1;
    Data          :Parcels_Array;
  end Mailbox;
end Mailbox_Pkg;


package body Mailbox_Pkg is
  protected body Mailbox is
    entry Send (Item:Parcels) when Count < Mbox_Size is
-- block until room
    begin
      Data(In_Index): = Item;
      In_Index: = In_Index mod Mbox_Size  + 1;
      Count: =  Count  + 1;
    end Send;
    entry Receive (Item:out Parcels) when Count > 0 is
-- block until non-empty
    begin
      Item: =  Data(Out_Index);
      Out_Index: =  Out_Index mod Mbox_Size + 1;
      Count : =  Count-1;
    end Receive;
    procedure Clear is
    begin
      Count : =  0;
      Out_Index : =  1;
      In_Index : =  1;
-- only one user in Clear at a time
    end;
    function Size return integer is
    begin
      return Count;
-- multiple users can read size
    end;
    end Mailbox;
end Mailbox_Pkg;
```

[Source: Dr. David Cook]

Highlights of Ada 95

The highlights of Ada 95 are its inherent reliability and its ability to provide abstraction through the package and private type. Like Ada 83, Ada 95 includes strong typing. Most of the errors are detected at compile time, and of those remaining many are detected by runtime constraints.

Ada 83 does not often interface with non-Ada systems. Moreover, the type model coupled with the flat library mechanism can cause significant costs through the need for apparently unnecessary recompilation. Ada 95's goal is to give the language a more open and extensible feel without losing the inherent integrity and efficiency of Ada 83, that is, to keep the software engineering but allow greater flexibility. An overview of Ada 83 is given in the next chapter. The additions to Ada 95 which contribute to this more flexible feel are the extended or tagged types, the hierarchical library, and the greater ability to manipulate pointers or references.

As a consequence, Ada 95 incorporates the benefits of object-oriented languages without incurring the pervasive overhead of languages such as SmallTalk and C++. Ada 95 remains a very strong typed language but provides the prime benefits of all key aspects of the object-oriented paradigm.

Another area of major change in Ada 95 is in the tasking model, where the introduction of protected types allows a more efficient implementation of standard problems of shared data access. This brings the benefits of speed provided by low-level primitives such as semaphores without the risks incurred by the use of such unstructured primitives. Moreover, the clearly data-oriented view brought by the protected types fits in naturally with the general spirit of the object-oriented paradigm. Other improvements in the tasking model allow a more flexible response to interrupts and other changes of state.

Ada 95's major improvements

Ada 95 consists of seven annexes: systems programming, real time, distributed systems, language interfaces, information systems, safety and security, and numerics. The systems programming covers a number of low-level features such as in-line machine instructions, interrupt handling, shared variable access, and task identification. The real-time annex addresses various scheduling and priority issues including setting priorities dynamically, scheduling algorithms, and entry queue protocols. It also includes detailed requirements on the abort statement for single-and multiple-processor systems and a monotonic time package.

The distributed systems annex defines two forms of partitions and interpartition communication, using statically and dynamically bound, remote subprogram calls. The language interfaces define additional facilities for communication with programs in other languages. The information systems annex defines a number of packages providing detailed facilities for manipulating decimal values and conversion to external format using picture strings. This annex also defines a comprehensive package for string manipulation. The safety and security annex addresses restrictions on the use of the language and requirements of compilation systems for programs to be used in safety-critical applications. The numerics annex addresses the special needs of the numeric community. One significant change is the basis for model numbers. Ada 95's major improvements are programming by extension, classwide programming, abstract types and subprograms, summary of type extension, dynamic selection, other access types, hierarchical libraries, private child units, protected types, task scheduling and timing, and generic parameters. [Source: Ada 9X Project Report, Copyright 1993 Intermetrics, Inc.]

C++

C++ is an object-oriented language, one popular among programmers. Actually C++ is a hybrid language, an object-oriented extension to C. And C++ consists of many low-level features of C language. A developer in C++ needs to know both hardware and operating system environments. The learning curve for C++ is higher than for other object-oriented languages such as SmallTalk. We will discuss C++ in the next chapter.

Object COBOL

Object COBOL is scalable and portable, looks a lot like COBOL, and allows people to gradually move into the object paradigm [Software Magazine]. That is why the American National Standard Institute's Object-Oriented COBOL Task Group is working to remodel COBOL as an OOP language calling COBOL Object Oriented Language (COOL). Over time, legacy application code could be retooled into objects, probably with assistance from artificial intelligence based conversion products [Datamation]. The X3J4 Technical Committee, a subgroup of The American National Standards Institute (Ansi), is actively working on a standard for object Cobol [*Software Magazine*, April 1995].

Distributed Object Environment

The *distributed object environment* (DOE) builds enterprise-scale solutions of application development by allowing the replacement of monolithic applications with sets of smaller software components connected by an infrastructure. This paradigm is also referred to as *software right-sizing* by SunSoft. DOE allows programmers to build applications by assembling components. Developers can reuse, or purchase, existing components which adhere to standard interfaces and manipulate them with high-level tools. SunSoft has worked with the standard bodies, chiefly the Object Management Group (OMG), to ensure that third-party solutions are available for the vertical market. DOE takes into account that components will be built in different programming languages, by different vendors, running in a heterogeneous computing environment; yet it emphasizes that these components must integrate seamlessly to produce business solutions.

DOE is the culmination of object-oriented programming by SunSoft. Software modules, called *objects,* encapsulate both data and behavior and are described exclusively by the interface they present to the requestor of their services. Thus, requestors need not know how an object performs a particular service, allowing for multiple implementations to coexist in a given environment. Therefore DOE recognizes that objects may also be distributed throughout the enterprise, over the network, all over the world.

In 1988, Sun Microsystems began the Spring research project to build an object-oriented environment for distributed applications. The following year, the Object Management Group (OMG) was formed, with Sun as one of its founders. The aim of the OMG is to standardize distributed object technology. Sun coauthored the first standard, Common Object Request Broker Architecture (CORBA) specification, which was adopted by Sun as part of the Spring project. CORBA specifies how client and server objects communicate over the network, with server objects describing the services they provide (i.e., their interface), with the Interface Definition Language (OMGIDL). This language is independent of the programming language used to implement the object's services. OMGIDL is "compiled" into a programming language to access the service or be accessed via the Object Request Broker (ORB). The client does not need to know where the server is, accessing its services via an object reference that contains enough information to locate the object. This location transparency is key to developing scalable, enterprisewide applications [*Application Development Trend,* September 1994].

The Microsoft contribution to this view of computing with shared objects, or component objects, is *Object Linking and Embedding* (OLE). The OLE provides a language-independent binary standard for object sharing [DBMS, June 1995]. Automation OLE allows an application or OLE object to communicate with another OLE object. An automation server is an OLE object that listens for automation commands. The Common Object Model (COM) is Microsoft's underlying model for OLE. An open architecture for cross-platform development of client/server applications, COM provides a standard so that separately developed and maintained objects can interact across process, processor, or network boundaries. In OLE, the object builder is called the Object Factory. It creates an instance of an object [*Datamation,* May 1995]. OLE is compliant with CORBA. The COM is the joint effort of Digital Equipment Corporation and Microsoft Corporation.

Ada—An Overview

This chapter presents an overview of Ada. Ada is the result of an effort by the U.S. Department of Defense to control the increasing costs of its software engineering, development, and maintenance. The U.S. Army, Air Force, and Navy each began to look for its own standard language. Ada was selected after a lengthy process, and the Ada language reference manual was adopted as Military Standard 1815. A revised manual was published in July 1982 under the designations *Draft Revised Military Standard 1815A* and *Draft Proposed ANSI Standard Document for Editorial Review.*

Ada is an object-oriented language with the limitation that it supports objects and classes but limited inheritance. Ada is a computer language created to fit the environment of the U.S. Department of Defense (DOD). It includes specific features to discipline the guidance of software engineering. Ada provides many important features that are used to develop a reliable, long-lasting systems software. To discuss in detail everything about Ada is beyond the scope of this book.

Ada's Construct

Ada construct is the package with the collection of encapsulated resources that are used by other packages. These resources consist of data and programming units that operate on those data. The construct of Ada consists of networks of packages with multiple abstraction levels based on packaging, nesting, and rendezvous relationships. The main program in Ada consists of a procedure with no parameter, as shown:

```
procedure NAME is
-- Declarations
begin
-- STATEMENTS
end NAME;
```

Ada's Main Features

Ada main features are data typing, packages, subprograms, exception handling, generics, and tasking. These are presented in Fig. 13.1. The *Language Reference Manual* (LRM) will be referred to many times to introduce information about valuable packages, such as Text_IO.

Data Typing

Ada type is a set of values and/or a set of operations applicable to the values. Ada is a strongly typed language. This provides the basis for

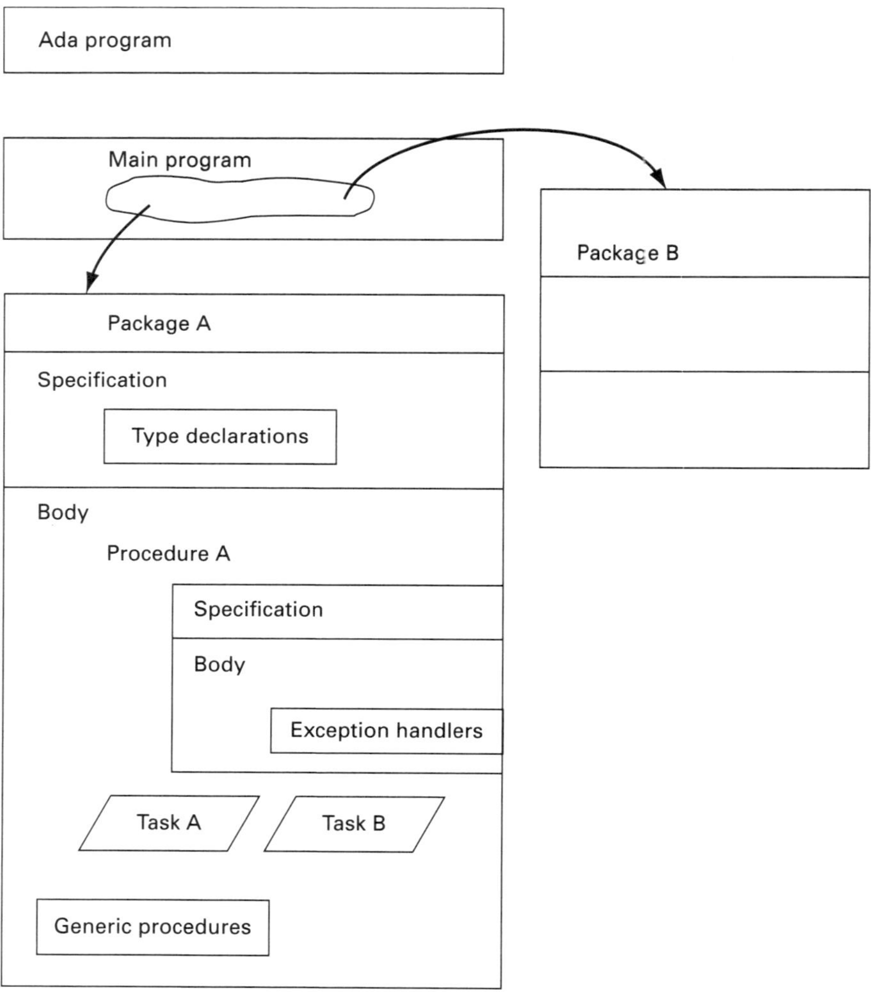

Figure 13.1   Overview of a typical Ada program.

protecting objects within the system software product. Ada supports and encourages data abstraction, user-defined data types, and maintainable, readable names for objects and types. Some examples of Ada objects and types are detailed below:

```
type ROCKET_TYPE is (MANY DIFFERENT TYPES)
DESTINATION : ROCKET_TYPE : =  NOTKNOWN
```

Strong data typing is the explicit definition and enforcement of the characteristics of data objects. Objects of a given type can either take on values defined for that type or undergo operations defined for that type. Ada has the facility at compilation to check data-typing errors [Courtesy: Meridian Ada Compiler].

Data Type Classes

Ada data type classes are *scalar, composite, access, private,* and *task* types.

Scalar

The scalar types are values that have no components. These types are numerics (integer, float) and enumeration.

Numerics

Integer. Integer types are as follows:

Set of values	..., − 3, − 2, − 1, 0, 1, 2, 3, ...
Attributes	First, Last, Pred, Succ
Examples:	Integer'First
	Integer'Last
	Integer'Pred (3) = 2
	Integer'Succ (4) = 5

Declaration examples:

```
Item          : integer              -- initial value undefined
Smallest      : integer : = Integer'First;
Sum           : integer : = 0;
Limit         : constant integer : = 1_000; -- one thousand
```

User-defined integer types

```
type temp_type is range -10..200;
type grade_type is range 0..100;
Temperature: temp_type : = 75;
Grade       : grade_type;
```

Examples:

```
Grade: =  70;  -- valid
Temperature : =  Temperature + 8;      -- valid
Grade: =  Temperature; -- invalid
```

Mod and rem operations.   Mod and rem operators return the remainder of the integer division between their operands. Rem returns the true remainder when operands are negative. For example,

$$15 \bmod 3 = 0 \qquad 15 \operatorname{rem} 3 = 0$$

$$15 \bmod 7 = 5 \qquad 12 \operatorname{rem} 7 = 5$$

$$7 \bmod 12 = 7 \qquad 12 \operatorname{rem} (-7) = 5$$

$$-12 \operatorname{rem} (-7) = -5$$

The sign of the remainder is equal to the sign of the dividend.

Float.   Float represents a set of real numbers in the range of

```
Float'First .. Float'Last
```

This set is implementation-dependent. Real numbers in Ada are represented as numbers with a decimal point. The decimal point must be surrounded by at least a single digit, for example,

$$4.0$$

Only objects of the same type may be mixed. Any other mixture of types will not be valid. For example,

```
Distance : =  Length;    -- is not valid
```

Any numeric type can be converted to any other numeric type. For example,

```
Target_type_name (expression_to_convert)
Float(6) is same as 6.0
Integer (2.4) is same as 2
Distance : =  Meters_Type (Length);
```

Enumeration type.   This is a data type for which the values are defined by the software engineer. For example,

```
type Day_Type is (Sun, Mon, Tue, Wed, Thr, Fri, Sat);
type Color_Type is (White, Blue, Red, Green, Black);
```

Object declarations:

```
Today    : Day_Type;
Color    : Color_Type;
```

Correct assignments:

```
Today    : = Wed;
Color    : = Blue;
```

Operations:

```
assignment    : =
relational    = / = > <…
membership    is not in
```

Attributes

```
Day_Type'First            --Sun
Day_Type'Last             --Sat
Day_Type'Succ (Thr)       --Fri
Day_Type'Succ (Today)     --is Wed if Today is Tue
Day_Type'PRED (Tue)       --Mon
```

Composite

Composite types represent data types which contain more than one component. The composite types are values with components, and these are *arrays* and *records*.

Arrays. Array types describe collections of components of the same type. Individual components are selected by discrete index. Array indices must be of type discrete, that is, integer, or enumeration, or character type. Constrained array types are arrays with known boundaries at compilation time. The unconstrained array types are arrays whose boundaries are not specified at compilation time. For example, these are constrained array types:

```
type List_type is array (1..3) of integer;
A: List_type;
```

Unconstrained array types. When a package supplies an array structure as a resource, the boundaries of the array should be left unspecified. Then different users can create arrays of different sizes to meet their particular needs, for example,

```
type List_type is array (integer range <>) of integer;
```

Records. Records are a collection of components of possibly different types. Each component is denoted by a component name. A *static* record is one whose structure is fixed at compilation time. A *discriminated* record is one whose structure is dependent on the value of a discriminant.

Ada also provides the ability to define your own data types. These data types are very useful for validating user input commands. A type can be defined so that a limited range of input will be accepted. This improves the security of the system software by making the software more understandable and reliable.

Access

The *access* types are values that provide access to other objects. When a simple data object such as an integer or a record is declared, the storage space for that object is allocated. The allocation and the size of this storage space remain fixed for the lifetime of the object. Such an object is called *static*. For most applications, static data objects are satisfactory. However, in some situations, the number of data objects is not known in advance. In some other applications, many objects might have a very short life. Therefore, an alternative to static data objects is needed so that storage can be allocated dynamically at runtime. Dynamically allocated objects are referenced indirectly by an access type. For example,

```
type Integer_Pointer is access integer;
P,Q : Integer_Pointer;
-- P and Q are pointer variables. They will point to integers at
   runtime
-- P and Q contain null at this point
```

Private

The *private* types are values that are not known to users. Only the set of operations is known to users. The task types are values that are individual tasks. Private data types in general enforce abstraction, hide low-level information, and protect structures from erroneous use.

Ada Packages

Ada packages are the unique feature and the basic building block of programs. These consist of a collection of logically related entities. These entities are types, objects, subprograms, tasks, generic units, and even other packages. These entities are the result of object-oriented requirements analysis and design. Resembling a system common area library, an Ada package consists of the package specification and the package body.

The *package specification* determines exactly what the package's resources are. These resources are available to the remainder of the system and are visible to a user. The package is said to export these resources and contains the visible interface to the rest of the system software. The package specification, through declarations and comments, must give users everything they need to know in order to use the types, objects, and operations in a given package. The outline of a package specification is as follows:

```
package PACKAGE_NAME is
    --
    --
    --WHAT IS PROVIDED
    --
    --
end PACKAGE_NAME;
```

Below is an example of a package specification:

```
package ROBOT_MOVEMENT is
    type SPEED is range       0..500;
    type DISTANCE is range    0..800;
    type DEGREE is range      0..359;
    procedure  GO_FORWARD
                (HOW_FAST:IN SPEED;
                HOW_FAR:IN DISTANCE);
    procedure  REVERSE
                (HOW_FAST:IN SPEED;
                HOW_FAR:IN DISTANCE);
    procedure  TURN (HOW_MUCH:IN DEGREES);
end ROBOT_MOVEMENT;
```

The *package body* contains the implementation of those resources that have been declared in the package specification. It contains the logical instructions of what the program unit is supposed to do. This is the private portion of the package body, and it may not be referenced outside the package. The concept of the package explains how information hiding can be accomplished. This information hiding ensures that the user cannot change the package according to whim. This is a design constraint. The software engineer can change the body to make it more efficient without affecting the user's view of the package.

Any local entities declared within the package body are visible only in that package body, that is, types, objects, subprograms, packages, etc. Since the specification and body may be compiled separately, it is easier to develop the specification first during OOD and to write the package body during the implementation (coding). If the package specification and package body are compiled separately, Ada makes it imperative that the package specification be compiled first, because it contains symbol tables, subprogram interfaces, and entity definitions. Once the package is developed, the user will get the specification source and object code, but only the object code of the body.

An outline of a package body follows:

```
package body PACKAGE_NAME is
      --
      -- HOW IT IS IMPLEMENTED
      --
end PACKAGE_NAME;
```

Here is an example of a package body:

```
-- DEFINE LOCAL DECLARATIONS
-- DEFINE IMPLEMENTATION OF SUBPROGRAMS
-- DEFINE IN SPECIFICATION
package body ROBOT_MOVEMENT is
      -- LOCAL DECLARATIONS
      procedure RESET_SYSTEM is
      begin
            --IMPLEMENTATION
      end RESET_SYSTEM;
      procedure GO_FORWARD...is...
      procedure reverse...is...
      procedure TURN...is...
end ROBOT_MOVEMENT;
```

Subprograms

Subprograms are the basic nonconcurrent executable units of Ada programs. A subprogram can be called by simply specifying its name and supplying the parameters, if any. There are two forms of subprograms—procedures and functions. These two units are meant to perform a single operation.

Procedure

A procedure is a sequence of statements that perform a high-level operation. A procedure defines the action to be performed. It contains a local declarative part. Procedures help in segregating large programs into modules, components, and units that are easier to write and read.
    Take this example:

```
procedure IDENTIFIER_NAME (formal parameter) is
```

The IDENTIFIER_NAME is the name that you, the software engineer, assign to the procedure. The procedure specification defines the name of the procedure and the parameters to be passed, as shown in this example:

```
procedure ADD    (FIRST: in INTEGER;
                 SECOND: in INTEGER;
                 RESULT: out INTEGER);
```

Here FIRST is the formal parameter name, **in** indicates the parameter mode, and INTEGER is the parameter type. Each procedure should be named according to the operation that it performs. Procedure format is shown as follows:

```
procedure NAME (FORML PARAMETERS) is      -- specification
     -Declarative part                    -- body starts
begin
     -Executable part
end NAME;                                  -- body ends
```

Here is an example of a procedure specification:

```
procedure    GET_NAME (NAME: out STRING);
             GET_NAME (PERSONAL_NAME);
```

The body of a procedure consists of the following:

- Specification which defines the procedure name and formal parameters
- Declarations which declare types and objects as necessary
- Executable statements which detail the procedure

For example, we write a procedure to calculate the area of a rectangle:

```
procedure area_of_rectangle (length, width: integer) is
     Area: integer
begin
     Area: = length*width;
     ...
-- Instructions to print result are missing
     ...
end area_of_rectangle;
```

Formal parameters are the arguments or variables needed in order for the procedure to execute. Actual parameters are the means by which the calling unit supplies necessary information and communicates with the called procedure. Formal parameters are identified by parameter specifications.

```
identifier_list: mode type_mark
```

Here identifier_list is simply the name given to the object or formal parameter, type_mark defines the parameter to be of a certain type, and each formal parameter is a specified mode. The mode denotes that the associated actual parameter supplies a value for the formal parameter, or the formal parameter supplies a value to the actual parameter, or both.

The allowable modes are as follows:

in denotes "read." This is also the default value in a procedure.

out denotes "write."

in out denotes "read/write."

```
           in
caller  ——> called unit
         in out
caller  <——> called unit
          out
caller  <—— called unit
```

Ada specifies these modes for all formal parameters in subprograms. These modes represent the flow of data between a subprogram and the caller program. Each mode also specifies the type of operations that can be applied to the parameters inside the subprogram. If the mode is omitted, then it is taken to be **in.**

For example, compute a worker's payroll:

```
with Text_IO, Integer_Text_IO, Float_Text_IO;
use  Text_IO, Integer_Text_IO, Float_Text_IO;
procedure Worker_Payroll is
     Worker_ID                              : integer;
     Hours_worked, pay_rate, net_pay        : float;
     Marital_status                         : character;

procedure get_worker_data (ID             : out integer;
                           hours, rate    : out float;
                           status         : out character);

begin
     put ("Enter worker ID, hours, rate, marital status:");
     get (ID);
     get (hours);
     get (rate);
     get (status);
end get_worker_data;

procedure calculate_net_pay (hours, rate  : in float;
                             status        : in character;
                             net_pay       : out float) is
     deductions : float;
begin
     if status = `single' then
       deductions : = 70.00;
     else
       deductions : = 50.00;
     end if;
       net_pay : = (hours * rate) - (deductions);
```

```
   end calculate_net_pay;

begin -- worker_payroll
     get_worker_data (worker_ID, hours_worked, pay_rate,
                      marital_status);
     Compute_net_pay           (hours_worked,    pay_rate,
                      marital_status, net_pay);
     put ("Worker ID:    ");   put (worker_ID);        new_line;
     put ("Hours worked:");    put (hours_worked);     new_line;
     put ("Hourly rate: ");    put (pay_rate);         new_line;
     put ("Marital status:");  put (Marital_status);   new_line;
     put ("Net pay:       ")   put (net_pay);          new_line;
end worker_payroll;
```

Function

Function is a subprogram. Function, like procedures, allows us to declare entities we want known only to the function within a declarative region. A function can return a single value to the calling program. The single value does not mean a single entity. The single value can be a record structure or composite values. The body of a function consists of the following:

- Specification which defines the function name and formal parameters

- Declarations which declare types and objects

- Executable statements which detail execution of the function operation

For example,

```
functionIDENTIFIER_NAME (Formal_parameters) return
     DATA_TYPE:
```

Here, IDENTIFIER_NAME is the name assigned to the function by the software engineer. The name of the function should describe the value returned by the function. The function format is

```
function NAME (Formal Parameters) return TYPE_NAME is
```

The function format starts with an Ada reserved word, then function name, optional formal parameters, then another Ada reserved word *return,* and finally the type of the value returned by the function. If the function body immediately follows this specification, the specification ends with the Ada reserved word *is*; otherwise, the function declaration ends with a semicolon.

As an example, find the area of a circle.

```
function area_of_circle (radius: float) return float is
     Pi   : constant float : = 3.14;
```

```
       area : float;
begin
       area : =  Pi * (radius **2);
       return area;
end area_of_circle;
```

A Case Study

You have just attended an Ada conference in Washington, DC. You
opted to drive from Oklahoma. You know the distance between the
two places because you checked the mileage on your odometer at the
start. You have used a certain number of gallons of gas to cover the
distance. You are submitting the bill to be reimbursed by the main
office. The accounting staff at the office are fussy. They want to provide a report showing your beginning mileage, ending mileage, and
gallons used. They also want to calculate the number of miles per gal-
lon (MPG) your car averaged. They can only understand Ada. Your
best option is to write a stand-alone procedure using Text_IO. They
are really fun people to work with, as they want your figures to be
accurate to the hundredths.

Here is one possible solution:

```
-- SYSTEM_ID                      :...
-- SOFTWARE ENGINEER              : JAG SODHI
-- MODULE NAME                    : MPG.ADA
-- MODULE PURPOSE                 : CALCULATE MILES PER GALLON
                                    UPTO HUNDREDTH
-- WRITTEN BY                     : JAG SODHI
-- DATE WRITTEN                   : DEC 1987
-- UPDATE BY                      : JAG SODHI
-- UPDATE DATE                    : JAN 1988
-- ENVIRONMENT                    : USING TEXT_IO.INSTANTIATED FLOAT_IO.
-- INPUT                          : USER INPUT, VALUES - FLOAT
-- OUTPUT                         : DISPLAY FLOAT VALUES
--
--

with Text_IO; use Text_IO; -- "with" makes Text_IO available
-- "use" makes everything visible in Text_IO
procedure MPG_ADA is
      package MPG_IO is new FLOAT_IO (float);
      -- Generic template is stamped instantiated for type float
      -- MPG_IO is our definition
        use MPG_IO;
             begin_mile:float; -- ":" declares statement
             end_mile: float;
             gas_used: float;
             miles_per_gallon: float;
        --
        -- so far declare statements have been written
        --
        -- now begin writing executable statements
        begin - my_procedure, initiate a block of instructions
        --
             new_line (10);--start of the printing line
```

```
        put("Please enter the beginning mileage:");
        get(begin_mile);
        put("please enter the ending mileage:");--display
        get(end_mile);
        put("please enter gallon used:");
        get(gas_used);
        miles_per_gallon: = ((end_mile)-
                                (begin_mile))/(gas_used);
--  ": = " assign values
        put("MPG = ");
        put(miles_per_gallon,5,2,0);
    --now width 5, right adjusted
    end; - identifies end of control structure
```

An alternative, better-structured approach is as follows:

```
with Text_IO; use Text_IO;
procedure my_proc is
     begin_miles, end_miles, gals, mpg: float;
procedure Get_Input is
begin
     put("Enter beginning miles");
     get(begin_miles);
     get(end_miles);
     get(gals);
end Get_Input;
--

     procedure Calc_Result is
     begin
     mpg: =  (end_miles - begin_miles)/gals;
end Calc_Result;
--

procedure Display is
begin
     put("mpg = ");
     put(mpg);
end Display;
--

begin -my_proc
     Get_Input;
     Calc_Result;
     Display;
end my_proc;
```

Conditional Statements

The following paragraphs describe and show the use of some of the important constructions in Ada.

IF .. THEN.. ELSE.

Square brackets [ ] enclose an optional item that may occur no more than once. An **if** statement selects for execution one or none of the enclosed sequences of statements, depending on the value of one or more corresponding conditions.

```
— condition optional is within [ ]
if [condition]
      then
      statement(s);
endif;
```

Example:

```
if price > 50.00
      then
      discount : =  0.10;
endif;
```

An if...then...else statement allows you to select one of two possibilities:

```
if condition then
      statement(s);
else
      statement(s);
endif;
```

Example:

```
if time = 1630 then
      shut_down_computer;
      Go_home;
else
      Keep_working;
endif;
```

Another form of **if** statement is

```
if..then..elsif..then..else..
```

It allows one to select from several alternatives.

```
if condition_1 then
      statement(s);
elsif condition_2 then
      statement(s);
else -- optional
      statement(s);
endif;
```

Example:

```
if score > =  90 then
      Grade : =  'A';
elsif
      Score > =  70 then
      Grade : =  'B';
elsif
      Score > =  60 then
```

```
      Grade : =  'C';
else
      Grade : = 'F';
endif;
```

Loops

A loop statement specifies the repeated execution of a sequence of statements. There are three basic loop structures in Ada—infinite loops, while loops, and for loops.

Here is an example of infinite loops:

```
loop                      loop
    :                             inhale;
    :                             exhale;
    :
end loop;                 end loop;
```

Here is an example of **while** loops:

```
while condition
loop                      N : =  1;
    :                     while N < =  30
                              loop
    :                             put(N);
                                  N : =  N + 1;
end loop;                 end loop;
```

The **while** loop is used to indicate that the repetition of the loop should stop when a given condition changes.

Here is an example of **for** loops:

```
for ID in loop_range   sum : =  0;
    loop               for M in 1..20
    :                      loop
                               sum : =  sum + M;
    end loop;          end loop;
```

For loop parameters should not be declared.

Exit statement

The **exit** statement provides a mechanism to interrupt the loop iteration. At the exit statement, control is passed to outside the loop block. Here is an example:

```
loop
    Pump_gas;
    if car_tank_full then
            exit;
    endif;
end loop;
pay_for_the_gas;
```

Any statement can be used within the loop. Another form of selection is a *case* statement. For example,

```
case delete is
when 1 = >
      statement(s);
      ..
      ..
when 2 = >
      statement(s);
      ..
      ..
when 3|4|7 = >
      null;
when others = >
      statement(s);
end case;
end loop;
```

When clauses may appear zero or more times in the **case** statement. And **when others** clauses may appear only once in the **case** statement, immediately preceding the **end case.**

The if, case, and loop statements above should always be terminated by the appropriate end statement (endif, end case, end loop). The next word should be placed on the next line for visibility. Uniform indention spaces between the **then** and **end_if** statements should be maintained for readability. The key word **else** should be in line with the other key words, again for readability.

Exception Handling

Ada provides a feature called exception handling to catch errors during component or unit execution. This feature is easy to put into practice and results in software products that are very readable and reliable. Real time systems often must be designed as systems which never halt. This requires the ability to handle error situations which, although rare, are quite likely to arise given enough time. The following are examples of exceptions internal to Ada:

- Constraints_error
- Numeric_error
- Program_error
- Storage_error
- Tasking_error
- Disk_read_error
- Data_entry_error

Exceptions are raised as a result of runtime errors. When an error occurs, the exception at the current level is raised, and if it is not supported at the current level, then an exception is raised at the next higher level until it is processed by an exception handler. Here is an example:

```
with Text_IO; use Text_IO;
procedure main is
      package F_IO is new float_IO;
      use F_IO;
      X: float : =  -5.0;
-- establish X as a float value which we are going to get
begin
      main_loop : while X/ =  0.0 loop
                Block 1 : (declare)
--

                begin
                        get (X);
                        put (X);
                Exception
                when DATA_ERROR  = > put ("Please reenter…");
                end Block 1;
      end loop main_loop;
end main;
```

A mechanism to fix runtime errors, an exception handler must always be implemented inside a block. A block is a sequence of statements between **begin** and **end.** When an exception occurs in a given sequence of statements, their execution will be abandoned. Control is then passed to an exception handler within the same block, but will never return to the point where the exception was raised.

The user-defined exceptions can also be declared in a package specification. The package body then may raise the exception and leave the handling up to the package user. The package user can handle the exception in the same manner as mentioned above. For example,

```
procedure user_exception is
      water_temp        : integer;
      temp_too_hot      : exception;
begin
      ..
      if water_temp > 400 then
              raise temp_too_hot;
      endif;
      ..
      ..
exception
      when temp_too_hot  = > put("Temperature too hot");
      when others  = > put (All other exceptions handled");
end user_exception;
```

Generics

Generics are procedures or packages written independent of type. These are templates of Ada program elements. Several instances of a generic package can be created by simply instantiating with different data types. A generic cannot be called but can be instantiated. Generics provide reusable software in Ada. Data objects are used to define the template and instance as follows:

- To define the template, use a type declaration.

- To define an instance, use an object declaration.

Generic program units can be defined as follows:

- To define the template, use a generic declaration.

- To define an instance, use a generic instantiation.

The productivity benefits of generics are excellent. Generics provide factorization, reduce the size of a program text, yield more compact code, and remove duplication of source code. Generics also have a positive effect on system software reliability, modularity, and understandability. Generics provide an excellent method for software reuse. Reliability is enhanced through the use of generics because a previously verified software component or unit is less likely to contain coding errors. Generics increase maintainability, readability, and efficiency of software engineering. Generics reduce software engineering development and maintenance time and costs. The following is an example of a generic program unit:

```
Generic
      type TB_RANGE_TYPE is range < >;
      type NUMBERS is range < >;
package TB_TABLE_HANDLER is
            procedure Add ( );
              .
              .
private
      TB_TABLE: array(TB_RANGE_TYPE) of NUMBERS;
end TB_TABLE_HANDLER;
```

Tasks

Tasks are the programs, modules, components, or units that may operate in parallel; that is, they can be executed concurrently. A task consists of a specification and a body.

Task specification includes entries that define the communication paths available to other tasks. The communication mechanism between tasks is called a *rendezvous*. Tasks have entries that are called by other tasks. The entries are specified in the task specifications. Tasks have procedurelike interfaces to users, as in this example:

```
        TASK-NAME
ENTRY_1  [ADDRESS_1]
         ...
ENTRY_N  [ADDRESS_N]
```

Here is a sample Ada program that shows the use of tasks:

```
with Text_IO; use Text_IO;
procedure Passive_UPS is
--
task UPS is -passive task
      Entry Accept_Package;
      Entry Send_Package;
end UPS;
--
task body UPS is
begin
      locp
      accept Accept_Package;
              put_line ("UPS is ready to accept a package from the
                      sender");
              accept Send_Package;
              put_line ("UPS is ready to send a package to the
                      receiver");
end UPS;
--
task sender; - active task
--
task body sender is
begin
      loop
              UPS.Accept_Package;
end sender;
--
task receiver; --active task
task body receiver is
begin
      loop
              UPS.Send_Package;
      end loop;
end receiver;
--
begin
      null;
end Passive_UPS;
```

When the program is executed, the following will be displayed:

UPS is ready to accept a package from the sender

UPS is ready to send a package to the receiver

UPS is ready to accept a package from the sender

UPS is ready to send a package to the receiver

UPS is ready to accept a package from the sender

UPS is ready to send a package to the receiver

Ada Code Generation Example

Ada provides the facility for the separation of specification and implementation. However, there is a one-to-one correspondence between a specification and its implementation (if one exists). This example presents an implementation scheme which provides multiple representations of an object. It is possible to choose an implementation from the available implementations. The user of the specification need not be concerned with the details of implementation.

A programming paradigm such as object-oriented programming which permits separation of specification and implementation provides several advantages. Specification provides an abstraction from computation which allows the use of complex objects without having to be concerned with their implementation. The user of a specification is spared the implementation details. The burden of the appropriate choice of data structures is handled in the implementation and can be postponed as long as necessary. However, once the implementation chooses a data structure, the user has no other choice. Modern programming languages incorporate this concept in their design and provide adequate facilities for separation of specification and implementation. In particular, Ada supports this separation of specification and implementation in generics, packages, tasks, etc. The implementation bundles together data structures and the operations on the data structures. The specification provides the view of an object and a set of operations on it. Put another way, the specification provides the view of an abstract data type. There is a one-to-one correspondence between the specification and implementation. The user of the specification has no control over the choice of data structures and algorithms used in the implementation.

In some applications, efficiency might depend on the choice of data structures and algorithms. In such cases, the facility to select an implementation will be useful. As an example, consider a linear programming problem. The types of efficient representations are different for large sparse matrices and small matrices. The particular choice will depend on the application. So, ideally, one would like to have a linear programming package with the flexibility to choose efficient representation. The issue, then, is to provide specifications of abstract data types together with the capability to choose appropriate implementation. Such specification should not diminish the advantages of the separation of specification and implementation. This example is concerned with an Ada solution to multiple representations of abstract data types and the means to choose an implementation. The user of the specification still need not be concerned with implementation details. The next section provides a definition of abstract data type, an example of the problem, and an Ada solution. The complete Ada program and output from a trial run are given in the appendix. Some side effects of the solution are discussed.

Abstract data type

An *abstract data type* (ADT) consists of a set of objects and a set of operations characterizing the behavior of the objects. The set of objects can be defined using relations of the operations. The specification of the ADT provides the name of the ADT and the names of the operations. The details of the operations are hidden in the implementation. An implementation of an ADT is called a *realization* of the ADT. An ADT can have more than one realization. An example is given in the next section.

Let us examine the ADT *stack* and two of its possible implementations. The ADT stack is defined by a set of functions and a set of defining relations. The implementations using an array and a linked list are examined.

```
abstype STACK is
     functions :
        FUSH     :     STACK x OBJECT --> STACK
          POP    :     STACK --> STACK
          TOP    :     STACK --> OBJECT

      relations:
          POP    ( PUSH) = id
          FUSH     ( POP, TOP ) = id if STACK is not
                                    EMPTY
end STACK
```

The implementations must obey the defining relationships of the ADT. Two implementation schemes are shown below:

```
array-implementation is
/* using scalar I and array A */
I <-- 0;
PUSH:
      I <-- I + 1; A[I] <-- X; /* X is an object */
  POP:
      I <-- I-1;
  TOP:
      value of A[I];
end array-implementation;
```

and linked-list-implementation is

```
/* using HEAD as pointer to the top of the list, and a structure
   LIST with two components INFO and LINK */
HEAD <—— NULL;
PUSH:
     TEMP <—— new LIST        /* TEMP is a temporary pointer to a
                                 cell */
     TEMP.INFO <—— X; TEMP.LINK <—— HEAD;
            HEAD <—— TEMP:
  Pop:
     HEAD <—— HEAD.LINK;
  TOP:
     value of HEAD.INFO;
end linked-list-implementation;
```

In the above implementation schemes, the data structures array, the linked list, and both persistent scalar variables I and HEAD are internal to the implementation. The operations PUSH, POP, and TOP are the only names visible to outside users. It is easy to verify that both implementation schemes satisfy the defining equations. It is also obvious that the implementations of functions are directly related to the data structure chosen for the implementation. When an implementation is abstracted, information is lost. In order to be able to choose a specific implementation, relevant information must be preserved by the abstraction. So, in this example we examine an abstraction process which preserves the relevant information.

Realization as a type

An ADT can be implemented using several data structures. We call an implementation of an ADT t a *realization* of t. A realization essentially is a data structure.

A data structure consists of three components:

- A set of function definitions
- A storage structure
- A set of algorithms, one for each function

For our discussion, an algorithm is identified with its function name. Therefore, we can view a data structure as a pair (S,F) where S represents a storage structure and F represents a set of functions. An equivalence class structure can be imposed on a set of data structures. Let D be a set of data structures. Two data structures $d_1 = (S_1, F_1)$ and $d_2 = (S_2, F_2)$ in D are *equivalent* if d_1 and d_2 are realizations for the same set of ADTs. If D consists of exactly one equivalence class and if the equivalence is imposed by an ADT t, then D is called a *realization class* for t. In other words, every member of D will be an implementation of the ADT t. The set D contains more information (e.g., storage structure) than the ADT t itself. If the information hidden in D is available to the user of t, then that user will be able to choose the appropriate realization based on the application from D. This can be achieved by viewing D as a type. We call this type *realization*. Using D and t, we can define a new type which allows one to select a realization for an ADT. This new type is called *rabstype* where, as an ADT, it is called *abstype*. The formal definitions are given below:

1. TYPE is realization

   VALUES are in D

   OPERATION is selection: $D{\rightarrow}d$, where d is a member of D.

2. TYPE is rabstype

   VALUES are in $t \times D$.

   OPERATION is binding: $(t,d){\rightarrow}t,d$ where t,d refers to an instance of t with realization d.

An Ada package specification for the ADT stack is given in the next section. The operations, selection, and binding defined above will correspond to an instantiation of a generic package. The type rabstype is implemented as a generic package specification.

Ada implementation

To implement the above concepts in Ada, the realization type should be visible through the specification. The following package specification provides a specification:

```
package STACK_IMPLEMENTATION_LIST is
     type LIST_OF_STACK_IMP_TYPE is
             (ARRAY_IMP, LINKED_LIST_IMP);
     generic
             STACK_IMP : LIST_OF_STACK_IMP_TYPE;
     package STACK is
             procedure PUSH (OBJECT : INTEGER);
             procedure POP;
             function TOP return INTEGER;
     end STACK;
end STACK_IMPLEMENTATION_LIST;
```

The list of available implementations is made visible as the values associated to the enumeration type LIST_OF_STACK_IMP_TYPE. The choice of an implementation is the same as instantiation of the generic package STACK using the appropriate value. For the complete implementation and a test run, the reader is referred to the appendix. Some of the advantages and disadvantages related to this approach are discussed in the next section.

<table>
<tr><td>Object names</td></tr>
<tr><td>Function names</td></tr>
</table>

Figure 13.2 Specification Window.

Side effects of the approach

The method illustrated by the specification in the previous section can be used to construct interfaces to reusable software. The specification can be viewed as a window as shown in Fig. 13.2.

Object names refer to implementation type, and the function names refer to a function or a procedure. For example, assume that there are several procedures which implement sorting algorithms such as bubble sort, quick sort, etc. Then the function name can be *sort,* and object names can be *bubble, quick,* etc. The advantage is that the user of the specification needs to be concerned only with the algorithm type and the name of the function. The user need not know which packages to use or what specific name to use. The disadvantage, however, is the inefficiency associated with generic instantiation. The runtime inefficiency probably can be removed by appropriate substitutions at compile time if such capability exists.

Appendix

```
-- This package provides the list of available implementations of
the abstract data type STACK.
package STACK_IMPLEMENTATION_LIST is
type LIST_OF_STACK_IMP_TYPE is (ARRAY_IMP,LINKED_LIST_IMP);
     --List of implementations.
generic
     STACK_IMP : LIST_OF_STACK_IMP_TYPE; - Implementation type to
be chosen.
-- Abstract data type follows:
package STACK is
     procedure PUSH (OBJECT:INTEGER);
     procedure POP;
     function TOP return INTEGER;
end STACK:
end STACK_IMPLEMENTATION_LIST:

-- This package body contains all implementations including the
subprograms associated to abstract data type STACK.
with TEXT_IO; use TEXT_IO;
package body STACK_IMPLEMENTATION_LIST is
     package INT_IO is new INTEGER_IO(INTEGER);
     use INT_IO;
     type ARRAY_TYPE is array (1..100) of INTEGER;   -- storage
                                   for array implementation.
     type NODE;
     type LINK is access NODE;
```

```
    type NODE is      -- storage for linked list implementation.
           record
                   VALUE : INTEGER;
                   NEXT : LINK;
           end record;
    STACK_ARRAY     : ARRAY_TYPE;
    STACK_TOP       : INTEGER : =  0;        -- stack top for array
    LINK_TOP: LINK : =  null;         -- stack top for linked list
-- Array implementation of PUSH.
    procedure ARRAY_PUSH (OBJECT:INTEGER) is
    begin
           STACK_TOP : =  STACK_TOP + 1;
           STACK_ARRAY (STACK_TOP) : =  OBJECT;
-- Messages to verify the actions.
           PUT("ARRAY IMPLEMENTATION OF PUSH IS USED AND VALUE
                                         PUSHED IS");
           PUT(OBJECT);
           NEW_LINE:
    end ARRAY_PUSH;
-- Linked list implementation of PUSH.
    procedure LINK_PUSH (OBJECT : INTEGER) is
           TEMP : LINK;
    begin
           TEMP : =  new NODE;
           TEMP.VALUE : =  OBJECT;
           TEMP.NEXT : =  LINK_TOP;
           LINK_TOP : =  TEMP;
-- Messages to verify the actions.
           PUT("LINK IMPLEMENTATION OF PUSH IS USED AND VALUE
                                         PUSHED IS");
           PUT(OBJECT);
           NEW_LINE;
    end LINK_PUSH;

--Array implementation of POP.
    procedure ARRAY_POP is
    begin
           STACK_TOP : =  STACK_TOP - 1;
-- Messages to verify the actions.
           PUT("ARRAY IMPLEMENTATION OF STACK IS USED AND VALUE
                                         POPPED IS");
           PUT(STACK_ARRAY(STACK_TOP + 1));
           NEW_LINE;
    end ARRAY_POP;

-- Linked list implementation of POP.
    procedure LINK_POP is
    begin
-- Messages to verify the actions.
           PUT("LINK IMPLEMENTATION OF STACK IS USED AND VALUE
                                         POPPED IS");
           PUT(LINK_TOP.VALUE);
           NEW_LINE;
           LINK_TOP : =  LINK_TOP.NEXT;
    end LINK_POP;
-- Array implementation of the function TOP.
    function ARRAY_TOP return INTEGER is
    begin
-- Messages to verify the actions.
           PUT("ARRAY IMPLEMENTATION OF STACK IS USED AND VALUE
                                         OF TOP IS");
           PUT(STACK_ARRAY(STACK_TOP));
```

```
                    NEW_LINE;
                    return STACK_ARRAY(STACK_TOP);
            end ARRAY_TOP;
-- Linked list implementation of the function TOP.
            function LINK_LIST_TOP return INTEGER is
            begin
-- Messages to verify the actions.
                    PUT("LINK IMPLEMENTATION OF STACK IS USED AND VALUE
                                                OF TOP IS");
                    PUT(LINK_TOP.VALUE);
                    NEW_LINE;
                    return LINK_TOP.VALUE;
            end LINK_LIST_TOP;
-- The implementation of the abstract data type STACK. It uses one
-- of the abovedefined implementations.
            package body STACK is
                    procedure PUSH (OBJECT : INTEGER) is
                    begin
                            if STACK_IMP = ARRAY_IMP then
                                    ARRAY_PUSH(OBJECT);
                            elsif STACK_IMP = LINKED_LIST_IMP then
                                    LINK_PUSH(OBJECT);
                            else
                                    null;
                            end if;
                    end PUSH;
                    procedure POP is
                    begin
                            if STACK_IMP = ARRAY_IMP then
                                    ARRAY_POP;
                            elsif STACK_IMP = LINKED_LIST_IMP then
                                    LINK_POP;
                            else
                                    null;
                            end if;
                    end POP;
                    function TOP return INTEGER is
                    begin
                            if STACK_IMP = ARRAY_IMP then
                                    return ARRAY_TOP;
                            elsif STACK_IMP = LINKED_LIST_IMP then
                                    return LINK_LIST_TOP;
                            else
                                    return -1000;
                            end if;
                    end TOP;
            end STACK;
end STACK_IMPLEMENTATION_LIST;


-- This is a main program to test the package STACK which is a
                                        generic package
-- which implements the abstract data type STACK. It is possible to
-- select theimplementation one likes from among the available
implementations. This
-- program tests the generic package STACK by instantiating with
the two
-- possible values.
-- Since its purpose is to verify the relevant packages, there are
no means
-- of handling exceptions.
with TEXT_IO; use TEXT_IO;
```

```
with STACK_IMPLEMENTATION_LIST;
use STACK_IMPLEMENTATION_LIST;
procedure STACK_CHECK is
      package INT_IO is new INTEGER_IO(INTEGER);
      use INT_IO;
begin
-- Test array implementation of STACK.
      declare
              package STACK_PACKAGE is new STACK(ARRAY_IMP);
              use STACK_PACKAGE;
              X,Y:INTEGER;
      begin
              for     I in 1..5 loop
                      PUT("INTEGER TO BE PUSHED :");
                      GET(X);
                      NEW_LINE;
                      PUSH(X);
                      Y : =  TOP;
              end     loop;
              for     I in 1..4 loop
                      POP;
                      Y : =  TOP;
                      PUT("NEW TOP IS :");
                      PUT(Y);
                      NEW_LINE;
              end     loop;
      end;
-- Test linked list implementation of STACK.
      declare
              package STACK_PACKAGE is new STACK(LINKED_LIST_IMP);
              use STACK_PACKAGE;
              X, Y: INTEGER;
      begin
              for     I in 1..5 loop
                      PUT("INTEGER TO BE PUSHED :");
                      GET(X);
                      NEW_LINE;
                      PUSH(X);
                      Y : =  TOP;
              end     loop;
              for     I in 1..4 loop
                      POP;
                      Y : =  TOP;
                      PUT("NEW TOP IS :");
                      PUT(Y);
                      NEW_LINE;
              end     loop;
end;
```

Sample Output

```
INTEGER TO BE PUSHED :
ARRAY IMPLEMENTATION OF PUSH IS USED AND VALUE PUSHED IS     100
ARRAY IMPLEMENTATION OF STACK IS USED AND VALUE OF TOP IS     100
INTEGER TO BE PUSHED :
ARRAY IMPLEMENTATION OF PUSH IS USED AND VALUE PUSHED IS     200
ARRAY IMPLEMENTATION OF STACK IS USED AND VALUE OF TOP IS     200
INTEGER TO BE PUSHED :
ARRAY IMPLEMENTATION OF PUSH IS USED AND VALUE PUSHED IS     300
ARRAY IMPLEMENTATION OF STACK IS USED AND VALUE OF TOP IS     300
INTEGER TO BE PUSHED :
```

```
ARRAY IMPLEMENTATION OF PUSH IS USED AND VALUE PUSHED IS        400
ARRAY IMPLEMENTATION OF STACK IS USED AND VALUE OF TOP IS        400
INTEGER TO BE PUSHED :
ARRAY IMPLEMENTATION OF PUSH IS USED AND VALUE PUSHED IS        500
ARRAY IMPLEMENTATION OF STACK IS USED AND VALUE OF TOP IS        500
ARRAY IMPLEMENTATION OF STACK IS USED AND VALUE POPPED IS       500
ARRAY IMPLEMENTATION OF STACK IS USED AND VALUE OF TOP IS        400
NEW TOP IS :          400
ARRAY IMPLEMENTATION OF STACK IS USED AND VALUE POPPED IS       400
ARRAY IMPLEMENTATION OF STACK IS USED AND VALUE OF TOP IS        300
NEW TOP IS :          300
ARRAY IMPLEMENTATION OF STACK IS USED AND VALUE POPPED IS       300
ARRAY IMPLEMENTATION OF STACK IS USED AND VALUE OF TOP IS        200
NEW TOP IS :          200
ARRAY IMPLEMENTATION OF STACK IS USED AND VALUE POPPED IS       200
ARRAY IMPLEMENTATION OF STACK IS USED AND VALUE OF TOP IS        100
NEW TOP IS :          100
INTEGER TO BE PUSHED :
LINK IMPLEMENTATION OF PUSH IS USED AND VALUE PUSHED IS         600
LINK IMPLEMENTATION OF STACK IS USED AND VALUE OF TOP IS         600
INTEGER TO BE PUSHED :
LINK IMPLEMENTATION OF PUSH IS USED AND VALUE PUSHED IS         700
LINK IMPLEMENTATION OF STACK IS USED AND VALUE OF TOP IS         700
INTEGER TO BE PUSHED :
LINK IMPLEMENTATION OF PUSH IS USED AND VALUE PUSHED IS         800
LINK IMPLEMENTATION OF STACK IS USED AND VALUE OF TOP IS         800
INTEGER TO BE PUSHED :
LINK IMPLEMENTATION OF PUSH IS USED AND VALUE PUSHED IS         900
LINK IMPLEMENTATION OF STACK IS USED AND VALUE OF TOP IS         900
INTEGER TO BE PUSHED :
LINK IMPLEMENTATION OF PUSH IS USED AND VALUE PUSHED IS        1000
LINK IMPLEMENTATION OF STACK IS USED AND VALUE OF TOP IS        1000
LINK IMPLEMENTATION OF STACK IS USED AND VALUE POPPED IS       1000
LINK IMPLEMENTATION OF STACK IS USED AND VALUE OF TOP IS         900
NEW TOP IS :          900
LINK IMPLEMENTATION OF STACK IS USED AND VALUE POPPED IS        900
LINK IMPLEMENTATION OF STACK IS USED AND VALUE OF TOP IS         800
NEW TOP IS :          800
LINK IMPLEMENTATION OF STACK IS USED AND VALUE POPPED IS        800
LINK IMPLEMENTATION OF STACK IS USED AND VALUE OF TOP IS         700
NEW TOP IS :          700
LINK IMPLEMENTATION OF STACK IS USED AND VALUE POPPED IS        700
LINK IMPLEMENTATION OF STACK IS USED AND VALUE OF TOP IS         600
NEW TOP IS :          600
```

C++ An Overview

C++ is an object-oriented programming (OOP) language that was developed to make software programs modular where the focus of a program will be structured around data instead of the application, such as with procedural languages. This chapter presents an overview of the C++ computer software language and some of its key features, which help to distinguish it from procedural languages. For a more rigorous approach to understanding C++ syntax, the interested reader is referred to C++ textbooks and tutorials written by authors such as Bjarne Stroustrup, Ira Pohl, and Apple Computers Inc. In this chapter, C++ syntax is identified by *italic* type.

Introduction

The C++ program language was developed at AT&T Bell Laboratories by Bjarne Stroustrup during the early 1980s and was released in 1985. The C programming language was chosen as the base language for C++ due to C's versatility, highly portable code, and because the C language was considered low-level enough to be useful as a systems programming language that fit into the UNIX programming environment. In 1980, features such as classes were added to C; the resulting language was called *C with Classes*. During the early 1980s, C with Classes was redesigned and extended; the major additions were the ability to redefine functions in derived classes and the ability to overload the basic operators of the language. Thus, C++ can be considered to have evolved from C language. As a result, some features between C and C++ remain similar; for example, neither C nor C++ allow loops to step through enumerated types. Version 2.0 of C++ was released in 1990, once additions were made to C++ to improve support for large-scale library building, which include multiple inheritance, abstract classes, and linkage to other languages.

C++ is a programming language that is applied to model real-world problems by expressing components of the problem as classes of objects that have inherited properties. C++ objects serve to partition a program into smaller, more manageable units, resulting in programs that are modular and easier to update or maintain. Other benefits of modular programs are reliability, correctness, and consistency in projectwide standards. These features allow C++ to be regulated better than procedural languages. However, the object-oriented paradigm is more than just objects. This discussion focuses on some of the unique features of the language, such as classes, data hiding, polymorphism, software reuse, object-oriented analysis and design (as applied to C++), and inheritance.

A fundamental difference between C++ and procedural languages is the use of classes, which provide the means for implementing user-defined data types, associated functions, and operators that comprise objects.

C++ programs take advantage of client-server and peer-peer relationships. In a client-server relationship, the client is aware of the server; however, the server is not aware of the client. However, in a peer-peer relationship, objects are aware of one another. For this discussion, a client-server environment will be applied, where the client is the user of an application and the server *is* the application.

Class

A C++ class type is similar to a record type or struct in C language; it contains behaviors (which are global to the program) and data items. Behaviors can be added to a class at any time. For example, consider creating a class called *automobile*. It is accepted practice to use nouns for class names that are descriptive of the function of its objects. The class contains a set of behaviors and an internal state; for example, some behaviors are instructions, such as start, stop, or turn right and left. Behaviors in a class are actions which are common to objects of that class. Once the class has been instantiated, more behaviors can be modified, deleted, or added at any time.

When a class is instantiated in C++, it is defined as a base class. If the base class that has been defined is generic, such as automobile, then a class of class automobiles may be instantiated. If a class or a number of classes are derived from a base class, then the subclasses are derived classes. The base class can be used as a common interface to its derived class. Public and protected behavior and internal states are common to the base class as well as the derived classes. An example of a derived class of automobile would be class *motorcycle*. A motorcycle is propelled by a gas-powered engine, has tires, and has other similar features. An advantage of using this sort of class hierarchy is that the software can be reused.

A base class can be created from a number of derived classes that share a common set of behaviors, which is referred to as *abstraction*. An abstract class also provides a public interface for its subclass; otherwise, it will not be instantiated. For example, assume that a class is instantiated, where the class is a base class and is named *automobile*. A subclass of the class *automobile* can be instantiated and is named *motorcycle*. This is a reasonable subclass to the automobile base class since both are mechanized forms of transportation. As a result of both classes sharing common behaviors, a single interface can be applied. Some benefits of using a common interface are that less coding is required and, at the test stage, less testing is required. The end result is a program that is modular and contains software code that is reusable. A member function implements the classes' behavior.

The base class *automobile* encapsulates common behaviors and internal states of all its derived classes, such as *motorcycle*. In the *automobile* base class, common internal state members are declared whereas the derived class *motorcycle* declares any new internal state (for example, remaining stationary for a motorcycle will require different actions than it will for an automobile).

A problem with programs written using procedural languages is that as they grow very large, with hundreds or thousands of function names, so it becomes very difficult to keep them mentally clumped into groups. By using base and derived classes, a hierarchy is formed, which allows for easier maintainability and potential reuse.

An advantage of partitioning a large project into a software program with classes is that classes can enforce the semantics of each system interface better than procedural languages; and this reduces the number of bugs in software code.

Objects

The client-server environment, in C++, lets a client send messages to instruct the application to perform certain tasks. Objects perform specific tasks; in other words, an applications response to a message is the behavior that modules of the program express. A module is referred to as an *object*. A C++ object is a language structure that ties data with the functions operating on those data. In a broader sense, objects have an entity which possesses a set of attributes and behaviors that describe its nature and functionality. An object or a set of the same type of objects is defined in a class. Once constructed, objects are used in place of lines of code for commands or actions, simplifying programming and customization of programs.

A class contains an internal state and behavior of an object or multiple numbers of similar objects. Each object of a particular class shares the same behaviors, which are considered global (in C++ it is referred to as *public*), where all behaviors are made available to other classes in the program.

A class data item is the internal state of the object, for example, engine size, or number of tires on the automobile (four for cars, sometimes eight for trucks with larger load capacity). However, the internal-state items are the same even though the values are different.

A class consists of an arbitrary number of objects, where each object is an instance of the class and shares similar behaviors. For example, the base class *automobile* can have an instance such as a sedan, or the class *automobile* can have many other instances such as station wagon, pickup truck, and sports car. These objects are similar since they share common behaviors and data. C++ specifies names and types of data comprising the internal state of a object of a class, which is similar to a record type, in Pascal, or Struct, in C language. An example of two objects that have a similar internal state is a truck and car object, where each has an engine, tires, and a steering wheel. They also perform the same functions, in the sense that they start, brake, and stop. However, each is clearly unique since their engine sizes, the possible number of tires each may have, and steering wheel sizes may be different. A motorcycle, even though its behaviors are the same for the same message, could not be an object of the class *automobile* because the number of tires it has is not four.

A C++ object is a module of computer software code that consists of attributes (internal state) and behaviors which describe its nature and function. The behavior, of an object, is the response to a message from a client and is normally *public*—it can be accessed from anywhere within the program. The object's internal state describes the object and is normally defined as *private*—it cannot be accessed from anywhere else in the program except its *class*. The internal state consists of the attributes of the object *car* such as steering wheel, tires, and engine which allow the car to perform multiple functions. These features are important for the car to operate but are not of concern to a client; therefore, these internal-state items can be specified as *private*. The car's behavior is a response to a message from a client, such as start, stop, or brake.

Data Hiding

Data hiding is a feature of C++ where access privileges of class data members are limited. Some ways of hiding data can be accomplished by limiting the visibility of data members, limiting relationships with other objects, and limiting knowledge of types and classes. Hiding unnecessary details makes the software code modular, focuses on the behavior of objects, and makes the software more reusable.

C++ classes often have hidden fields, which the implementation part of the program needs in order to distinguish derived types from base types. Hidden fields are also needed if a base class is virtual, making the fields harder to map to existing data structures. For example, a client is not required to know how a car object functions in order to operate it, only that a steering wheel will turn the car and the brake pedal will cause the car to stop. It is not important at that time for the client to be made aware of what causes the wheels to turn or the car to come to a stop; only the expected public behavior is important. As a result, the internal state of car object, such as engine, steering column, and tires, can be specified as *private,* or *protected,* and thus would be hidden from the rest of the program. The advantage of hiding data is the potential reduction of debugging and easier maintenance.

Polymorphism

In C++, polymorphism is evident when one message is sent to several objects, but each object responds differently due to different internal states of each object. This also applies to the derived classes of a base class, again due to the particular nuances of each individual class. Even though the behavior of each object will be different, objects of a base class and its derived class or classes can share a common interface. For example, the automobile class and a motorcycle subclass can share a common interface, because each has many of the same behaviors (the same message to turn can be sent to both objects, as can the message to stop). Even when differences exist in their behaviors, the motorcycle derived class can override the base class, thus allowing for a single interface to be applied. For example, once both objects respond to the stop message, each will behave differently—the car will remain stationary as long as the client depresses the brake pedal, but once a motorcycle stops, the client must keep the cycle from falling over by using both legs.

Inheritance

A feature of C++ language is its facility for inheritance of attributes by an object to or from a parent object or object class. Inheritance is an extension to the data type that allows for the creation of objects which inherit the behaviors of previously defined classes and provides a mechanism for deriving new classes by adding features to an existing base class. Class hierarchy can be constructed, where derived classes inherit features from a base class. Derived class can be thought of as a child to the parent (or base) class where some behaviors are inherited from the parent. The inheritance feature enables a programmer to reuse an existing class and modify it if necessary. In essence, most of a class may be reused, with any enhancements being made in the derived class.

C++ supports both single and multiple inheritance; single inheritance occurs when an object inherits from a single parent, and multiple inheritance occurs when a derived class inherits behaviors from multiple numbers of base classes. For example, a motor home inherits behaviors from the base class *automobile* as well as some behaviors from (a newly instantiated) base class named *house*. This feature of C++ reduces maintenance efforts, since refinements in the *base class* automatically become available to the inheriting class.

Inheritance is also closely related to the idea of polymorphism—it allows objects of a derived class to be used in any context where an object of its base class is expected. Inheritance promotes code reuse and allows existing modules to be customized for new applications and maintainability. Inheritance promotes code reuse by allowing derived classes to use code defined in base classes.

Object-Oriented Analysis and Design

Object-oriented analysis (OOA) of a problem consists of defining the task, which the system should perform, by categorizing the problem into real-world objects and their behaviors. *Object-oriented design* (OOD) of a solution by applying the C++ language is not a linear task, in the sense that a design step may not necessarily be complete before another step is modified; also the design is not necessarily a single-iteration process. For instance, the system requirements are defined, the requirements are distributed into objects of classes, and the design is optimized by applying inheritance and software reuse. Then instead of optimizing the system, the object requirements may need to be modified, taking into account information hiding. The end result is that modifications and enhancements occur on several fronts, at the same time. The end result, however, should be a design where data, types, and classes are kept as private as possible.

Sample Program

The following sample program was originally published in *Ada and C++*. It applies polygons as objects for the purpose of demonstrating the advantage of using an object-oriented development environment when writing code that is reused. This program uses heap storage for objects; the heap is temporary storage. This part of the code does the following:

1. Creation and deletion of temporary objects.

2. Traversal of pointer reference among temporary objects.

```cpp
// header file for appendix A: appA.h
#include <stream.h> // name may be different on some systems
#include <string.h>

typedef int Coord; // coordinates represented as integers

class Point { // a point in two-dimensional space
  public:
  Coord x, y; // X & Y coordinates
  Point (  { x = y = 0; }
  Point ( Coord newX, Coord newY) { x = newX; y = newY; }
  void show () {
    cout << x << "," << y;
  }
};

class Box {
  public:
    Point 11, ur; // lower left & upper right corners

  Box () { }
  Box ( Point p1, Point p2) { 11 = p1; ur = p2; }
  void show () {
    cout << "with lower left at ";
    11.show ();
    cout << " and upper right at ";
    ur.show ();
    cout << "\n";
  }
};

class shape {
  public:
  Box bBcx; // bounding box of shape
  Shape *nextShape // next shape on the same layer

  Shape () { }
  Shape ( Point p1, Point p2) : bBox ( p1, p2) { }
  virtual void show () {
    cout << " a shape ";
    bBox.show ();
  }
};

class Rectangle : public Shape {
  public:
    Rectangle () { }
    Rectangle ( Point p1, Point p2) : ( p1, p2) { }
    virtual void show () {
      cout << " a rectangle, which is ";
      shape :: show ();
  }
};
```

```cpp
class Layer {
  public:
    shape * firstShape; // first shape on layer
    char layerName [32];
  Layer ( char *name) { // only constructor
    strcpy ( layerName, name );
    firstShape = NULL;
  }
void delFirstShape () { // delete first shape in this layer
  Shape *toDelete = firstShape;
  if ( toDelete != NULL ) {
    firstShape = toDelete->nextShape;
    delete toDelete;
  }
}
void show () { // show all shapes in the layer
  shape *current = firstshape;
  cout << "\nlayer " << layerName << " contains:\n";
  while ( current != NULL ) {
    current-> show ();
    current = current->nextShape;
  }
}
}; // end of Layer definition

  // main program for appendix A: appA.C

#include "appA.h"
main () {
  Layer *metal;
  shape *pShape;

  // **** phase 1: create a layer ****
  // create instance of a layer
  metal = new layer (" metal ");

  // add two rectangles and generic shape to the layer
  pShape = new Rectangle ( Point (0,0), Point (10,10) );
  metal-> addShape (pShape); // update linked list
  pShape = new Shape ( Point (10,10), Point (20,20) );
  metal-> addshape (pShape);
  pShape = new Rectangle ( Point (10,20), Point (73,88) );
  metal-> addshape (pShape);
    // show all shapes in the layer
  metal-> show ();

    // **** phase 2: modify layer
    // remove first shape from layer then show result
  metal-> delFirstShape ();
  metal-> show ();
}
```

Building and Running the Application

The following command will allow the system to compile the code
written above.

```
CC appA.C
```

You may wish to name the resultant program file *appA* for consistency. In any case, run the program and save the output. For example, you might use

```
appA > appA.output
```

You are saving the output only so that you can compare it with the results of building and running the application giving in the "Converted C++ Program" appendix and the "Conversion Using Container Objects" appendix, so you may choose to print it instead.

Some of the key syntax features are explained, following the program. Features of this program include the following:

A C++ class provides a mechanism for decomposing a large system into modules that are categorized by general behaviors and attributes, also referred to as the *internal state* of a class.

Classes have members that are functions, which are either *public, protected* or *private* to other classes in the program. This restriction prevents unanticipated modifications to the data structure. It also comprises the type, name, and parameters of a class's behavior. A member function is a definition of the function and procedure which implement the public behaviors of a class. A member function that provides public access to *private* internal-state variables (data members) of a class is referred to as an *assessor.*

Objects and object variables (constructors) cannot exist until after a class has been defined. A constructor, provided by the software engineer, initializes a variable instance of its class and is an object that is invoked, by the compiler, anytime an instance of its associated class is created. A destructor deallocates a variable of its class. If an object has been allocated dynamically, then its associated memory can be deallocated by a destructor. This is done by implicitly invoking the destructor upon block exit for any class variables declared inside the block.

Class variables of this program, such as metal and pShape, are the data to be manipulated by the operations by a class.

metal: A variable to store a reference to an instance for the class Layer

pShape: A variable to store a reference to an instance for the class Shape

In the above code the variables, metal and pShape, are declared before they can be used. However, they do not need to be at the head of a block; they can be mixed in with executable statements. The advantage of this feature is that variable declarations are closer to where they are executed.

Multiple numbers of objects with similar internal states and behaviors can exist within a single *class* by assembling objects and linking them together with *data paths,* a term that refers to software code which links one object to another. For example, objects that are similar to a four-door sedan, such as a two-door sedan or a sports car, can be thought of as instances of the same class.

Objects are created and deleted by using constructors and destructors. A *constructor* is a member function whose name is the same as the class name and that initializes a variable of a class; the variable is an object. A *destructor* deletes (deallocates) the variable. In order to use an object, a variable must be declared, the object must be created and initialized, and then a message must be sent to the object to use the object. A variable, for an object in C++, is declared as a pointer-based struct, in C language. Once an object has been created by use of a constructor, the variable can be *overloaded,* which is the process of giving several meanings to an operator or a function. The flexibility of using objects that are capable of responding to a message in several different ways offers a reduction in writing software code. For example, each of the three types of cars listed above will respond to a message such as *accelerate* in a different way. The sports car will accelerate faster than either of the sedans. Overloading an operator allows the program objects to also respond in such a manner.

In C++, objects are related if one passes a message to another or if one passes addresses as parameters or stores the address in a data member or in a variable. For example, two cars are related if one is towing another since the car towing must send messages to the car being towed.

Stack-based objects are automatically removed from memory whereas pointer-based objects must be deleted by applying a destructor. An object can dispose of itself; or if the object is only called by another object, then the owner object should delete the object.

Overloading is a technique of giving many meanings to an operator or a function where the type of argument used by the operator or function determines the meaning. The meaning selected depends on the type of argument used by the operator function. By using properly coded C++ routines and overloading, the same equation can be implemented almost exactly as it is written. Storage obtained by *new* is persistent and not automatically returned on block exit. When storage return is desired, a destructor function must be included in the class. A destructor is written as an ordinary member function whose name is the same as the class name and is preceded by the tilde symbol. Typically, a destructor uses the unary operator *delete,* another addition to the language, to automatically deallocate storage associated with a pointer expression. In the above program, input and output (I/O) statements are made using libraries, which is more flexible than procedural languages since libraries can be extended to other applications.

Objects cf type *private* of different classes and types cannot access the same field types. A C++ constructor defines the initial internal state of the object and is a member function that is called when an object is created. It does not return anything; thus it should not have a return type. A constructor name is the same as the class name. Constructors are called in the order in which they were created and are frequently overloaded. However, if a derived class does not have a data member, then a constructor does not need to be declared; since the constructor of the base class is constructed before the derived class, the public behaviors and internal state will be automatically inherited from the base class. In general, public behaviors of a subclass (derived class) can be created by use of inheritance, defining a new behavior in the subclass, modifying (overriding) inherited behaviors.

C++ uses libraries for basic input/output; specifically, the C++ header file *stream.h* overloads the operators (<< and >>) to act as I/O functions.

Internal-state items can be declared *private* where privacy allows part of the implementation of a class type to be hidden. *Public* members are available to any function within the scope of the class, whereas *private* members are available for use only by other member functions of the class; it may be a good idea to limit the public interface of a class. A member function can also be declared *protected*; this makes a data member available to the subclass only. Public and protected member functions are inherited by a derived class. Private member functions are unknown to other objects whereas public and protected member functions are accessible from derived objects.

In C++, variables must be declared before they are used. However, a variable does not need to be at the head of a block; for example, a declaration can occur after an executable statement. One advantage to doing this is that the variable is closer to where it is used.

Only *public* and *virtual* type member functions can be polymorphic.

A feature of C++ is that the return types of member functions can be declared *virtual,* where virtual functions are initially defined in the base class.

In C++, member functions can be overloaded. This is where the two functions have the same name but different parameter lists.

A limit to using the override feature in C++ is that a member function that is to be overridden must be known in advance.

Another important concept in OOP is the promotion of code reuse through the *inheritance* mechanism. This is the mechanism by which a new class is *derived* from the existing *base* class.

Inherited behaviors can be modified or eliminated, using the overriding feature in C++. A derived class inherits the description of the base class. It can then be altered by adding members, overloading existing member functions, and modifying access privileges.

Explanation of terms that are used in the program:

::	A scope resolution operator that is used to assign a member function to a class.
virtual	Informs the compiler that classes derived from this class *may* override the member function.
Public	Indicates the visibility of the members that follow it. Without this keyword the members and data are private to the class. Public members are available to any function within the scope of the class declaration.
Private	Members are available for use only by other member functions of the class. Privacy allows part of the implementation of a class type to be hidden.
stream.h	A header which introduces I/O facilities for C++. The stream I/O in C++ can discriminate among a variety of simple values without needing additional formatting information. C++ uses header files (filename.h) for consistency.
Cout	Standard output.
Point, Box	Two class names. Classes are defined in the header file.
new	A unary operator that takes as an argument a data type that can include an array size. It allocates from free storage the appropriate amount of memory to store this type and returns the pointer value that addresses this memory.
/ /	Used for a comment line.
const	A declaration which cannot be changed or cannot take on a new value somewhere else in a program. It replaces some uses of the preprocessor command *define* to create named literals. C++ permits expressions in the constant declarations themselves, so no initialization is required. In C++, constants are automatically considered global unless they are declared otherwise. As a result, the header file needs to be included only once.
CIN	The input stream variable is the standard keyword used in C++, and the symbol $>>$ is the standard input operator in C++. The input operator assigns values from the input stream to a variable.
inline	The keyword specifies that a function is to be compiled, if possible as a macro. The *inline* is a feature in C++ that allows it to use other languages in several ways.

Function   Declarations define and declare functions which are at the head of *main*. They inform the compiler of the type and number of arguments to expect for each externally specified function. The list of arguments can optionally include variable names. C++ does not have keywords distinguishing between function and procedure.

Identifier   Identifiers reflect their use in a program; in this way, they serve as documentation, making the program more readable. C++ normally assumes a 4-byte integer value, except on some machines.

Software Reuse

Software reuse allows new applications to be developed with a minimum amount of writing of new computer software code. But to justify reusing software, it must cost less than developing new code, to meet a specific need.

The benefit of not writing new code is that the problems of bugs and maintenance do not occur. To make the general practice of reuse of software successful, it is necessary to make the discovery of a pre-existing software component to fill a specific need cost less than developing the component anew. Without the reuse feature, each minor variation in the program would require code replication.

Libraries allow codes to be reused and enhance portability. An advantage of using a modular programming language such as C++ is that classes can be stored in a library—even a class which was originally applied to a different program. The benefit of using libraries is that they can be customized to different machines and are easily extended to new applications.

Object-oriented programs can be reused and extended and are modular. Extendibility allows for a software program to be changed over its lifetime and allows it to perform new tasks, which allows the system to evolve.

Reusability allows applications to be assembled by applying preconstructed program modules (objects). C++ allows a transition from an application-centered to a data-centered framework. If the scope of the program requires modification, then new coding is kept to a minimum, if software reuse is maximized, since the program is broken into modules where variables are mostly local rather than global.

C++ offers advantages over procedural languages; for example, as procedural languages become large, with hundreds of function names, they become harder to keep mnemonic. Thus, C++ is efficient for solving complex problems by applying objects and distributed processing methods. Also, procedural languages will become cumbersome in terms of keeping them clumped into groups.

The types of parameters are listed inside the header parentheses. By explicitly listing the type and number of arguments, strong type checking and assignment-compatible conversions are possible in C++. Weak type checking in traditional C kept it from being widely taught at an introductory level. Since C++ applies modular programming techniques, it is efficient to implement CAD/CAM, object-oriented database, and graphics applications, and to reengineer a significant number of C programs. C++ is a dynamic language that has evolved, and continues to evolve; but a problem with C++ is that there is no standard as yet. Different vendors of C++ offer different attributes, which make their versions unique. This makes learning the language more difficult than it would be if it were standardized.

Acronyms

ACAP	Analyst capability
ACVC	Ada compiler validation capability
ADL	Ada design language
ADS	Aion development system
AEXP	Application experience
AI	Artificial intelligence
ANSI	American National Standards Institute
APSE	Ada programming support environment
CASE	Computer-aided software engineering
CCSOM	Computer center software operational manual
CDR	Critical design review
CDRL	Contract data requirements list
CFD	Control flow diagram
CISAM	Computer instruction set architecture manual
CLIN	Contract line item number
CM	Configuration management
CMM	Capability maturity model
COCOMO	Constructive cost model
CORBA	Common object request broker architecture
COTS	Commercial, off-the-shelf
CPM	Critical path method
CPU	Central processing unit
CSC	Computer software component
CSCI	Computer software configuration item
CSDM	Computer software development methodology
CSOM	Computer system operator manual
CSU	Computer software unit
DBDD	Database design document
DBMS	Database management system
DD	Data dictionary
DDL	Data definition language
DFD	Data flow diagram

DID	Data item description
DML	Data manipulation language
DOD	Department of Defense
DOE	Distributed object environment
DSD	Data structure diagram
EC	Estimated cost
ELOC	Estimated line of code
ER	Entity relationship
EST	Eastern standard time
EV	Earned value
FCA	Functional configuration audit
FQT	Formal qualification testing
FSE	Forward software engineering
GFS	Government-furnished software
GUI	Graphic-user interface
HMI	Human-machine interface
HOOD	Hierarchical object-oriented design
HPO	High-performance option
HWCI	Hardware configuration item
ICAM	Integrated computer-aided manufacturing
ICT	Intelligent CASE tool
IDD	Interface design document
IDEF	*ICAM def*inition
IEEE	Institute of Electrical and Electronics Engineers
I/O	Input/output
IORL	Input/output requirements language
IORTD	Input/output relationships and timing diagram
IRD	International resources dictionary
IRP	Iterative refinement process
IRS	Interface requirements specification
ISO	International organization for standardization
IV&V	Independent verification and validation
JSD	Jackson system development
JSP	Jackson structured programming
KBMS	Knowledge base management system
KBS	Knowledge base system
LOE	Labor of efforts
LRM	Language reference manual
MAGEC	Mask and application generator and environment controller
MANPRINT	Manpower and personnel integration
MODSIM	Modular simulation language
MRE	Magnitude of relative error
NATO	North Atlantic Treaty Organization
NDS	Nondevelopment software
OAM	Object analysis model
OBM	Object behavior model

OCD	Operational concept document
OIM	Object information model
OLE	Object linking and embedding
OMG	Object management group
OML	Object management library
OO	Object-oriented
OOD	Object-oriented design
OODB	Object-oriented database
OODBMS	Object-oriented database management system
OODM	Object-oriented design method
OOM	Object-oriented methodology
OOP	Object-oriented programming
OOSD	Object-oriented structured design
OPM	Object process model
OSF	Open software foundation
OSI	Open system interconnection
PC	Personal computer
PCA	Physical configuration audit
PCAP	Programmer capability
PDL	Program design language
PDR	Preliminary design review
PERT	Program evaluation and review technique
PPD	Predefined process diagram
PSA	Program statement analyzer
PSL	Program statement language
P-Spec	Process specification
PST	Pacific standard time
QA	Quality assurance
QAS	Quality assurance section
RDM	Requirements definition model
RE	Re-software engineering
RELY	Required software reliability
ReuSE	Reusability search expert
RFP	Request for proposal
ROM	Read-only memory
RM	Refinement method
RSE	Reverse software engineering
RSI	Report specification interface
RSL	Requirements statement language
RSO	Reusable software objects
RT	Requirements tracer
RTE	Runtime environment
RTL	Runtime library
RUSE	Required reusability
SA	Structured analysis
SADT	Structured analysis and design technique

SBD	Schematic block diagram
SCR	Software cost reduction
SD	Structured design
SDD	Software design document
SDF	Software development file
SDL	Software development library
SDP	Software development plan
SDR	System design review
SECP	Software engineering conversion plan
SED	Software engineering design
SEDD	System engineering design document
SEDP	Software engineering development plan
SEI	Software engineering institute
SEMP	Software engineering maintenance plan
SERA	Software engineering requirements analysis
SIOM	Software input/output manual
SIP	Software installation plan
SOW	Statement of work
Spec	Specification
SPM	Software programmer's manual
SPS	Software product specification
SQL	Software query language
SREM	Software requirements engineering methodology
SRR	System requirements review
SRS	Software requirements specification
SSA	Structured system analysis
SSD	Strategies for system development
SSDD	System/segment design document
SSP	Software support plan
SSR	Software specification review
SSS	System/segment specification
STD	State transition diagram
STP	Software through pictures
STR	Software test report
STT	State transition table
SUM	Software user's manual
TAGS	Technology for the automated generation of systems
TRR	Test readiness review
UC	User cases
UCRA	User-centered requirements analysis
UI	User interface
VDD	Version description document
VDM	Vienna development methodology
VEXP	Virtual machine experience
VMVT	Virtual machine volatility target
WBS	Work breakdown structure

References

Abbott, R. J.: *An Integrated Approach to Software Development,* Wiley, New York, 1986.

Association for Computing Machinery (ACM), Communications, May 1991, August 1991, March 1992, June 1992, September 1992, September 1993.

Association for Computing Machinery (ACM), SIGSOFT Software Engineering Notes, December 1990, May 1990, September 1990, January 1991, April 1991, April 1992, July, 1992.

Association for Computing Machinery (ACM), Software Engineering Notes, January 1993.

Ada Quality and Style: Guidelines for Professional Programmers, Software Productivity Consortium, VA, 1995.

Agresti, W. W.: *Tutorial: New Paradigms for Software Development,* Computer Society Press, Los Angeles, 1986.

AI Expert, Miller Freeman publication, Aug. 1990.

Air Force, Deputy Assistant Secretary Office, *Ada and C++: A Business Case Analysis,* 1991.

Allworth, S. T., and R. N. Zobel: *Introduction to Real-Time Software Design,* Springer-Verlag, New York, 1987.

ANSI/MIL-STD-1815A, *Reference Manual for the Ada Programming Language,* American National Standards Institute, February 17, 1983, Washington, D.C.

Apple Computer, Inc., *Introduction to Object-Oriented Programming.*

"Application Development Trends", Sept. 1994. An SPG Publication.

Ardis, Mark, A., and Berztiss, Alfs T.: *Formal Verification of Programs,* SEI Curriculum Modules, 1988, Pittsburgh, PA.

Balzer, R.: "A 15 Year Perspective on Automatic Programming," *IEEE Transaction on Software Engineering.* SE-11(1): 157–167, Nov. 1985. Balzer, R., T. Cheathm, and C. Green: "Software Technology in the 1990s: Using a New Paradigm," *Computer,* 16(11): 39–46, Nov. 1983.

Bauer, F. L.: "Programming as an Evolutionary Process," *Proceedings of 2d International Conference on Software Engineering,* IEEE Computer Society, January 1976, pp. 222–234.

Berard, V. Edward: *Essays on Object-Oriented Software Engineering,* vol. 1, Prentice-Hall, Englewood Cliffs, NJ, 1993.

Bergland, G. D., and R. D. Gordon: *Software Design Strategies,* IEEE Computer Society Press, Washington, 1981.

Birrell, N. D., and M. A. Ould: *A Practical Handbook for Software Development,* Cambridge University Press, New York, 1985.

Bjorner, D., and C. B. Jones: *Formal Specifications and Software Development,* Prentice-Hall, Englewood Cliffs, NJ, 1982.

Blank, J., and M. J. Krijger: *Software Engineering: Methods and Techniques,* Wiley-Interscience, New York, 1983.

Boehm, B.: "Software Engineering," *IEEE Trans. Computers,* C-25(12): 1226–1241, Dec. 1976.

Boehm, B.: *Software Engineering Economics,* Prentice-Hall, Englewood Cliffs, NJ, 1981.

Boehm, B.: "A Spiral Model of Software Development and Enhancement," *IEEE Computer,* 21(5), May 1988.

Bohm, C., and G. Jacopini: "Flow Diagrams, Turing Machines and Languages with only Two Formation Rules," *Communications of the ACM,* 9(4), May 1966.

Booch, G.: *Software Engineering with Ada,* Benjamin/Cummings Publishing, Menlo Park, CA, 1982.

Booch, G.: "Object-Oriented Development," *IEEE Transactions on Software Engineering,* SE-12(2): 211–221, Feb. 1986.

Booch, G.: *Object-Oriented Analysis and Design with Applications,* Addison-Wesley, Reading, MA, 1994.

Brackett, John W.: *Software Requirements,* SEI Curriculum Module SEI-CM-19-1.0, Dec. 1988, Software Engineering Institute, Pittsburgh, PA.

Bridge, Dec. 1992, SEI, Carnegie-Mellon University, PA.

Budde, R., K. Kuhlenkamp, L. Mathiassen, and H. Zullighoven: *Approaches to Prototyping,* Springer-Verlag, New York, 1984.

Budgen, David, and Richard Sincovec: *Introduction to Software Design,* SEI Curriculum Module SEI-CM-2-1.2 (Preliminary), July 1987.

Buhr, R. J. A.: *System Design with Ada,* Prentice-Hall, Englewood Cliffs, NJ, 1984.

Cameron, John: *JSP & JSD: The Jackson Approach to Software Development,* IEEE Computer Society Press, Washington, 1989.

Cardelli, L., and A. Wegner: "On Understanding Types, Data Abstraction, and Polymorphism," *Computing Surveys,* 17(4), Dec. 1985.

Carmichael, A.: *Object Development Methods,* SIGS Publication, New York, 1994.

Case, A.: *Team System Analysis,* Prentice-Hall, Englewood Cliffs, NJ.

Chen, P. P.: "The Entity-Relationship Model—Toward a Unified View of Data," *ACM Transactions on Database Systems,* 1: 9–36, Mar. 1976.

Clement, P. C., R. A. Parker, D. L.Parnas, J. E. Shore, and K. H. Brit: *A Standard Organization for Specifying Abstract Interfaces,* Naval Research Laboratory, Washington.

Coad, Peter, et al.: *Object Models: Strategies, Patterns & Applications,* Prentice-Hall, Englewood Cliffs, NJ, 1994.

Coad, Peter, and J. Nocola: *Object-Oriented Programming,* Prentice-Hall, Englewood Cliffs, NJ, 1993.

Coad, Peter, and Edward Yourdon: *Object-Oriented Analysis,* Prentice-Hall, Englewood Cliffs, NJ, 1990.

Coleman, Derek, et al.: *Object-Oriented Development: The Fusion Method,* Prentice-Hall, Englewood Cliffs, NJ, 1994.

Collofello, James S.: *The Software Technical Review Process,* SEI Curriculum Module SEI-CM-3-1.2 (preliminary), July 1987.

Collofello, James S.: *Introduction to Software Verification and Validation,* SEI Curriculum Module, 1988.

Communications Week, July 1992.

Computer Design, a Pennwell publication, June 1989, May 1991, Apr. 1993, Aug. 1993.

Computerworld, May 1992.

Connor, M. F.: "Structured Analysis and Design Technique (SADT) Introduction," *Engineering Management Conference Record,* IEEE, May 1980, pp. 138–143.

Cook, Capt. David: *Object Oriented Development and Object Oriented Programming in Ada and Ada 9X,* U.S. Air Force Academy, Colorado Springs, CO, 1992.

Cross, N.: *Development in Design Methodology,* Wiley, New York, 1984.

CrossTalk, The Journal of Defense Software Engineering, published by the Software Technology Support Center, Aug. and Oct. 1992.

Datamation, a Cahners publication, Oct. 1992.

Davis, C. G., S. Jajodia, P. A. Ng, and R. T. Yeh: *Entity-Relationship Approach to Software Engineering,* North-Holland, New York, 1983.

DBMS Client/Server Computing, an M&T publication, Jan. 1993.
DBMS Client/Server Computing, an M&T publication, August 1994.
DBMS Client/Server Computing, an M&T publication, June 1995.
DEC Professional, Aug. 1991, Sept. 1991, Apr. 1992.
Defense Electronics, a Cardiff Publishing Co., Feb. 1993.
DeMarco, T.: *Structured Analysis and System Specification,* Prentice-Hall, Englewood Cliffs, NJ, 1979.
Dijkstra, E. W., F. Dahl, and C. A. R. Hoare: *Structured Programming,* Academic Press, New York, 1972.
DOD Ada Joint Office, "Ada Methodologies: Concepts and Requirements" (Methodman Doctrine), Nov. 1982.
DOD, Deputy Assistant Secretary of the Air Force, *Ada and C++: A Business Case Analysis,* 1991.
DOD, MIL-STD-SDD (498), Draft, Military Standard for Software Development and Documentation, Dec. 1992.
Domain Engineering Guidebook, Software Productivity Consortium, VA, 1992.
Druffel, L.: "Software Technology for Adaptable, Reliable Systems—Program Strategy," *SIGSOFT Software Engineering Notes,* 8, April 1983.
Embedded Systems, a Miller Freeman publication, Apr. 1991, Mar. 1992.
Fairly, R.: *Software Engineering Concepts,* McGraw-Hill, New York, 1985.
Federal Computer Week, Aug. 1992, Aug. 1993.
Firth, Robert, Bill Wood, Rich Pethia, Lauren Roberts, Vickey Mosley, and Tom Doice: *A Classification Scheme for Software Development Methods,* Tech. Rep., Software Engineering Institute, Carnegie-Mellon University, Nov. 1987, Pittsburgh, PA.
Fox, J. M.: *Software and Its Development,* Prentice-Hall, Englewood Cliffs, NJ, 1982.
Freeman, Peter, and Anthony Wasserman: *Tutorial on Software Design Techniques,* IEEE Computer Society, Washington, 1983.
Gane, C., and T. Sarson: "Structured Systems Analysis: Tools and Techniques," *Computer,* July 1977.
Gommaa, H.: "Software Development of Real-Time Systems," *Communications of the ACM,* 29: 657–668, July 1986.
Goodenough, John B., and Mark W. Borger: *Ada Usage/Performance Specification,* SEI, ACM Ada Letters, Fall 1990.
Government Computer News, Aug., Oct., and Nov. 1992.
Gries, D.: "A Note on a Standard Strategy for Development Loop Invariants and Loops," *Science of Computer Programming,* 2, 1982.
Harel, D., A. Pnueli, and R. Sherman: "On the Formal Semantics of Statecharts," *Proceedings of the 2d IEEE Symposium on Logic in Computer Science,* Ithaca, NY, June 22–24, 1987, IEEE Press, New York, 1987.
Harel D.: *STATEMATE: A Working Environment for the Development of Complex Reactive Systems,* IEEE Press, New York, 1988, pp. 396–406.
Hatley, D., and Pirbhai, I.: *Strategies for Real-Time System Specifications,* Dorset House, New York, 1987.
Heitz, M.: *HOOD: Hierarchical Object Oriented Design for Development of Large Technical and Realtime Software,* CISI Ingenierie, Direction Midi Pyrenees, Nov. 1987.
Henderson-Sellers, B., and J. M. Edwards: *Object-Oriented Knowledge,* vol. 2: *The Working Object,* Prentice-Hall, Englewood Cliffs, NJ, 1994.
Hoare, C. A. R.: "An Overview of Some Formal Methods for Program Design," *Computer,* Sept. 1987.
Hori, S.: *CAM-I Long Range Planning, Final Report for 1972,* Illinois Institute of Technology Research, Chicago, 1972.
HP Professional, Nov. 1990.
Humphrey, S. Watts: *CASE Planning and the Software Process,* Tech. Rep., CMU/SEI-89-TR-26, SEI, Pittsburgh, PA.
Husa, J. D.: "Stimulating Software Engineering Process—A Report of the Software Engineering Planning Group," *ACM SIGSOFT Software Engineering Notes,* 8(2), Apr. 1983.

Hutt, A.: *Object Analysis and Design: Description of Methods,* Irwin Professional Publishing, Burr Ridge, IL, 1994.
IEEE, *Computer,* Feb. 1991, Aug. 1992, Dec. 1992, and June 1993.
IEEE, *Expert,* Fall 1989.
IEEE, *Software,* Nov. 1990, Jan. 1991, Sept. 1993.
IEEE: *Software Engineering Standards,* 3d ed., New York, 1989.
IEEE, *Spectrum,* Oct. 1990, Jan. 1991, July 1992, Sept. 1992, and annual review in 1993.
IEEE Transactions on Software Engineering, Nov. 1990, Mar. 1991, Dec. 1991, July 1992, Apr. 1993, and Aug. 1993.
Information Center Quarterly, Winter 1991.
Information Week, a CMP publication, July 1991, Aug. 1992, Jan. 1993, and May 1993.
INFOWORLD, Sept. 1992.
Introducing Ada 9X, Ada 9X Project Report, DOD, Office of the Undersecretary of Defense for Acquisition, 1993.
Jackson, M.: The Jackson Design Methodology, Infotec State of the Art Report, Structured Programming, 1978.
Jacobson, Ivar, et al.: *Object-Oriented Software Engineering,* Addison-Wesley, Reading, MA, 1992.
Johnson, A. L.: "Software Engineering Combines Management and Technical Skills," *SEI Bridge,* Aug./Sept. 1986.
Jorgensen, Paul C.: *Requirements Specification Overview,* SEI Curriculum Module SEI-CM-1-1.2 (preliminary), July 1987.
Journal of Object-Oriented Programming, a SIGS publication, June 1991.
Katzan, Harry: *Systems Design and Documentation,* Van Nostrand Reinhold, New York, 1976.
Khoshafian, Setrag, et al.: *Intelligent Offices: Object-Oriented, Multi-Media Information Management in Client/Server Architectures,* Wiley, New York, 1992.
Lee, Kenneth J., and Michael, S. Rissman: *An Object-Oriented Solution Example: A Flight Simulator Electrical System,* SEI Tech. Rep., 1989, Pittsburgh, PA.
Leveson, N. G.: "Software Safety: Why, What, and How," *ACM Computing Surveys,* June 1986.
Liskov, B., and J. Guttag: *Abstraction and Specification in Program Development,* M.I.T. Press, Cambridge, MA, 1986.
Liskov, B., and S. N. Zilles: "Programming with Abstract Data Types," *ACM SIGPLAN Notices,* 9(4): 50–60, Apr. 1974.
Love, T.: *Object Lessons,* SIGS Publications, 1993, New York, NY.
Lund, Simula System, 1970.
Marcotty, M., and H. F. Ledgard: *Programming Language Landscape, Syntax/Semantic/Implementation,* 2d ed., SRA, Chicago, 1986.
Martin, Charles F.: *User-Centered Requirements Analysis,* Prentice-Hall, Englewood Cliffs, NJ, 1987.
Martin, James, and James Odell: *Principles of Object-Oriented Analysis and Design,* Prentice-Hall, Englewood Cliffs, NJ, 1993.
Martin, James, and James Odell: *Object-Oriented Methods,* Prentice-Hall, Englewood Cliffs, NJ, 1994.
Mattison, R.: *The Object-Oriented Enterprise: Making Corporate Information Systems Work,* McGraw-Hill, New York, 1994.
McMenamin, S. M., and J. F. Palmer: *Essential Systems Analysis,* Yourdon Press, New York, 1984.
Meyer, Bertrand: *Object-Oriented Software Construction,* Prentice-Hall, Englewood Cliffs, NJ, 1988.
Mills, Everald E.: *Software Metrics,* SEI Curriculum Module SEI-CM-12-1.0, Oct. 1987.
Mills, H. D.: "Stepwise Refinement and Verification in Box-Structured Systems," *IEEE Computer,* 21(6): 23–36, June 1988.
Mills, H. D., M. Dyer, and R. C. Linger: "Cleanroom Software Engineering," *IEEE Software,* Sept. 1987.
Network World, Mar. 1993.

Nielsen, Kjell. *Object-Oriented Design with Ada,* Bantam Books, New York, 1992.

Objectivity, Inc. Objectivity/DB, Documentation I & II, 1991.

Object Magazine, a SIGS Publication, May 1991.

Palmer, J. F.: "Integrating the Structured Techniques with JAD: Leveled Systems Development," working paper presented at 12th Structured Methods Conference, Aug. 1987.

Parnas, D.: "On the Criteria to Be Used in Decomposing Systems into Modules," *Communications of the ACM,* 15, Dec. 1972.

Parnas, D. L., P. C. Clements, and D. M. Weiss: "The Modular Structure of Complex Systems," *IEEE Transactions on Software Engineering,* SE-11(3), Mar. 1985.

Partsch, H., and R. Steinbruggen: "Program Transaction Systems," *Computing Surveys,* 15(3): 199–236, Sept. 1983.

Pedersen, J. S.: *Software Development Using VDM Curriculum Module,* SEI-CM-16-1.0, Software Engineering Institute, Carnegie-Mellon University, PA, 1988, Pittsburgh, PA.

Peters, L. J.: *Software Design: Methods and Techniques,* Yourdon Press, New York, 1981.

Pohl, I.: *C++ for Pascal Programmers,* Benjamin/Cummings Publishing, Menlo Park, CA, 1991

Reingold, E. M., and W. J. Hansen: *Data Structure,* Little, Brown, Boston, 1983.

Rombach, H. Dieter: *Software Specification: A Framework,* SEI Curriculum Module SEI-CM-11-1.0, Oct. 1987.

Ross, D. T.: "Applications and Extensions of SADT," *IEEE Computer,* 18(4): 25–34, Apr. 1985.

Ross, D. T.: "Douglas Ross Talks about Structured Analysis," *IEEE Computer,* 18(7): 80–88, July 1985.

Royce, W. W.: "Managing the Development of Large Software Systems," *Proceedings 9th International Conference on Software Engineering,* IEEE Computer Society, 1987, pp. 328–338, New York, NY.

Rumbaugh, James, Michael Blaha, William Premerlani, Frederick Eddy, and William Lorensen: *Object-Oriented Modeling and Design,* Prentice-Hall, Englewood Cliffs, NJ, 1991.

Rush, G.: "A Fast Way to Define System Requirements," *Computerworld,* Oct. 7, 1985.

Sathi, A., T. Morton, and S. Roth: "Callisto: An Intelligent Project Management System." *AI Magazine,* 7(5): 34–52, 1986.

Scacchi, W.: *Model of Software Evolution: Life Cycle and Process,* SEI Curriculum Module SEI-CM-10-1.0, Oct. 1987.

Shlaer, Sally, and Stephen J. Mellor: *Object Oriented Systems Analysis, Modelling the World in Data,* Prentice-Hall, Englewood Cliffs, NJ, 1988.

Shlaer, Sally, and Stephen Mellor: *Object-Lifecycles: Modelling the World in States,* Prentice-Hall, Englewood Cliffs, NJ, 1992.

Sodhi, Jag: "Overview of Ada Features for Real-Time Systems," *Defense Science,* Nov. 1988.

Sodhi, Jag: "Evaluation of Teaching SERA," 7th Annual National Conference for Ada Technology, 1989.

Sodhi, Jag: *Computer Systems Techniques: Development, Implementation, and Software Maintenance,* TAB Books Inc., PA, 1990.

Sodhi, Jag: *Managing Ada Projects Using Software Engineering,* TAB Books Inc., PA, 1990.

Sodhi, Jag: *Software Engineering Methods, Management, and CASE Tools,* McGraw-Hill, New York, 1991.

Sodhi, Jag: *Software Requirements Analysis and Specification,* McGraw-Hill, New York, 1992.

Sodhi, Jag, and K. M. George: "Objects with Multiple Representations in Ada," 7th Annual National Conference for Ada Technology, 1989.

Software, a Sentry publication, Feb. 1991, Nov. 1990, Mar. 1991, Jan. 1992, May 1992, and Sept. 1992.

STARS Joint Services Team. Stars Software Environment (SEE) Operational Concept Document (OCD). Proposed Version 001.0, DOD, Oct. 1985.

The Starts Guide, NCC, Manchester M1 7ED.

Stevens, W. P., G. J. Myers, and L. L. Constantine: "Structured Design," *IBM Systems Journal,* 13(2): 115–139, May 1974.

Taft, Tucker: *Ada 9X Technical Report,* Intermetrics, Inc., 1993.

Taylor, D.: *Object-Oriented Information Systems,* Wiley, New York, 1992.

Technical Review 1992, Software Engineering Institute, Carnegie-Mellon University, PA.

Teichrow, D.: "PSL/PSA: A Computer Aided Technique for Structured Documentation and Analysis of Information Processing Systems," *IEEE Transaction Software Engineering,* SE-3(1): 41–48, Jan. 1977.

U.S. Department of Air Force, *ESD Implementation Guide for DOD-STD-2167A System Software Development Standard,* MA, Jan. 30, 1989.

U.S. Department of Defense, *Military Standard, Defense System Software Development,* DOD-STD-2167A, Washington.

Van Warren, L., and B. C. Beckman: *System for Retrieving Reusable Software,* NASA Technical Briefs, 1993.

VAX Ada Language Reference Manual.

Ward, T. Paul, and W. John Bracket: *Object-Oriented Requirements Definition and Software Design,* Boston University, Boston, 1991.

Ward, T. Paul, and Stephen J. Mellor: *Structured Development for Real-Time Systems,* vols. 1 to 3, Yourdon Press, Prentice-Hall, Englewood Cliffs, NJ, 1985.

Warnier, J. D., and Kenneth T. Orr: *Structured Systems Development,* Yourdon Press, New York, 1977.

Wasserman, A. I., P. A. Pircher, and R. J. Muller: "An Object-Oriented Structured Design Method for Code Generation," *SIGSOFT Software Engineering Notes,* 14(1): 32–55, Jan. 1989.

Wirfs-Brock, Rebecca, L. Wilkerson, and Lauren Wiener: *Designing Object-Oriented Software,* Prentice-Hall, Englewood Cliffs, NJ, 1990.

Wirth, N.: "Program Development by Stepwise Refinement," *Communications of the ACM,* 14(4): 221–227, April 1971.

Wood, William G., John P. Long, and David P. Wood: *Classifying Software Design Methods,* Tech. Rep., CMU/SEI-89-TR-25.

Yourdon, E. (ed.): *Classics in Software Engineering,* Yourdon Press, New York, 1979.

Yourdon, E.: *Modern Structured Analysis,* Prentice-Hall, Englewood Cliffs, NJ, 1990.

Yourdon, Edward, and Larry L. Constantine: *Structured Design,* Yourdon Press, New York, 1978.

Zave, P.: "An Operational Approach to Requirements Specification for Embedded Systems," *IEEE Transactions on Software Engineering,* 8(3): 250–269, May 1982.

Zheng, W., and V. Shanholtz: "Object-Oriented Programming Opens Gateway to Real-World Problem Solving," *GIS World,* Jan. 1993.

List of Vendors

Vendors	Products
Aion Corporation 101 University Avenue Palo Alto, CA 94301	ADS
AI Corp. 138 Technology Drive Waltham, MA 02254 617-891-6500	KBMS
American Management Systems 1777 North Kent Street Arlington, VA 22209 703-841-5507	Logiscope
Applied Business Technology Corp. 361 Broadway New York, NY 10013 212-219-8945	ABT Project Bridge, Workbench, Graphics, Metrics Manager
Ascent Logic Corporation 180 Rose Orchard Way Suite 200 San Jose, CA 95134 408-943-0630	RDD-100
Berard Software Engineering 301-417-9884	BOCS
Business Objects, Inc. 2500 Sand Hill Road Suite 240 Menlo Park, CA 94025 415-854-1500	BusinessObjects
CACI 3333 North Torrey Pines Court La Jolla, CA 92037 619-457-9681	MODSIM II

Vendors	Products
Cadre Technologies 222 Richmond St. Providence, RI 02903 401-351-5950	ObjectTeam, Teamwork/OOA, Teamwork/OOD, RqT
Chen & Associates 504-926-5765	ObjectModeler
Cisi-Ingenierie 2, rue Jules Vedrine 31400 Toulouse France (33) 6120 4324	HOOD
Dansk Datamatik Center Lundtoftevej 1 C DK-2800 Lyngby Denmark	VDM
Dynamics Research Corp 60 Frontage Road Andover, MA 01810 508-475-9090	AdaMAT
Evergreen CASE Tools 8522 154th Av NE Redmond, WA 98052	Easy CASE Plus
GEC-Marconi 12110 Sunset Hills Road Reston, VA 22090 703-648-1551	GECOMO PLUS
Goddard Space Flight Center Greenbelt, MD 20771 301-286-7631	GOOD
Grady Booch c/o Rational 835 S. Moore Street Lakewood, CO 80226 303-986-2405	OOD
i-Logix Inc. 22 Third Ave. Burlington, MA 01803 617-332-8678	STATEMENT
IBM Corporation P.O. Box 700 Suffern, NY 10901 914-578-3535	S-JAD AD/Cycle
Interactive Development Environments, Inc. 595 Market Street, 12th floor San Francisco, CA 94105 415-543-0900	STP

Vendors	Products
MAGEC AL Lee & Associates P.O. Box 260319 Plano, TX 75026 214-248-0823	MAGEC
MARK \/ Systems Limited 16400 Venture Blvd., Suite 303 Encino, CA 91436 510-658-9404	ObjectMaker ProcessMaker MethodMaker Ada Code Generation C++ Code Generation
Meridian/ Verdix Co. 10 Pasteur Street Irvine, CA 92718 714-727-0700	Ada Compiler C++ CASE Tools
Meta Systems, Ltd. 315 E. Eisenhower, Suite 200 Ann Arbor, MI 48108 313-663-6027	PSL/PSA
Michael Jackson Systems Ltd. 22 Little Portland Street London WIN 5AF United Kingdom (01) 499 6655	JSD
Objectivity Inc. 800 El Camino Real Menlo Park, CA 94025 415-688-8000	Objectivity/DB
Object Design One New England Executive Park Burlington, MA 01803	ObjectDesign, ObjectStore
Palladio Software Corp. Suite 360 16535 W. Bluemound Road Brookfield, WI 53005 414-789-5253	Palladio Software
Project Technology, Inc. 2560 Ninth Street, Suite 214 Berkeley, CA 94710 415-845-1484	OOA
Software Development Concepts 424 West End Avenue New York, NY 10024	WARD/MELLOR
Software Productivity Solutions 122 N. Fourth Avenue Indialantic, FL 32903 407-984-3370	Ali, Classic-Ada/ONTOS

Vendors	Products
Stepstone Corp. 75 Glenn Road Sandy Hook, CT 06482	Objective - C
Synthesis Computer Technologies 5199 E. Pacific Coast Hwy Long Beach, CA 90804 213-494-4069	case/ap
Teledyne Brown Engineering Cumming Research Park 300 Sparkman Dr. NW P.O. Box 070007 Huntsville, AL 35807 800-633-4675	RT TAGS
Transform Logic Corp. 8502 East Via de Venture Scottsdale, AZ 85258 800-872-8296	DesignAid II
Venue 1549 Industrial Road San Carlos, CA 94070 800-228-5352	Medley
Verilog Inc. 3010 LBJ Freeway, Suite 900 Dallas, TX 75234 214-241-6595	Verilog Object
Westinghouse Electric Corp. P.O. Box 17319 - MS A455 Baltimore, MD 21203 410-765-9966	ReuSE

Index

ABOUT THE AUTHORS

JAG SODHI is a well-known author, lecturer, and consultant. He has developed and conducted training in software engineering for government and industry organizations, and is the author of five best-selling books, including *Software Engineering: Methods, Management, and Case Tools* and *Software Requirements: Analysis and Specifications*, published by McGraw-Hill.

PRINCE SODHI is a consultant for the Born Information Services Group/Forte National Practice Group. He is an expert in several programming languages, including C++, and is completing a doctorate in scientific computing.